Mastering the Art of Depositions

Sawnie A. McEntire

Cover design by Tahiti Spears/ABA Design

The materials contained herein represent the opinions of the authors and/or the editors, and should not be construed to be the views or opinions of the law firms or companies with whom such persons are in partnership with, associated with, or employed by, nor of the American Bar or the Section of Solo, Small Firm and General Practice Division unless adopted pursuant to the bylaws of the Association.

Nothing contained in this book is to be considered as the rendering of legal advice for specific cases, and readers are responsible for obtaining such advice from their own legal counsel. This book is intended for educational and informational purposes only.

Printed in the United States of America.

20 19 18 17 16   5 4 3 2 1

ISBN: 978-1-63425-551-6
e-ISBN: 978-1-63425-552-3

Discounts are available for books ordered in bulk. Special consideration is given to state bars, CLE programs, and other bar-related organizations. Inquire at Book Publishing, ABA Publishing, American Bar Association, 321 N. Clark Street, Chicago, Illinois 60654-7598.

www.shopABA.org

ABOUT THE AUTHOR

Sawnie A. McEntire is a Shareholder and Director in the Law Firm of Parsons McEntire McCleary & Clark PLLC, a law firm with offices in Dallas, Texas and Houston, Texas. He has been practicing trial law for over 36 years and has substantial trial experience in both state and federal courts throughout the country. He has been involved in several hundred depositions. He is a frequent speaker and author. He specializes in products liability litigation and complex commercial tort litigation.

ACKNOWLEDGMENTS

The author wishes to thank several individuals who provided significant assistance in bringing this project to completion. Special thanks go to several attorneys in the Dallas, Texas office of the law firm of Parsons McEntire McCleary & Clark PLLC. They include Ryan Starbird, who provided substantial legal research regarding several topics, as well as ongoing editing advice; Sarah Sparling, who provided significant editing advice and direction; and Rob Rosen, who provided invaluable assistance in coordination, ongoing editing advice, and counsel. Additional thanks go to Margaret Ahlers, an attorney residing in Newport News, Virginia, and Todd Parrish, an attorney in Dallas, Texas for their significant counsel and excellent editing advice. Lastly, great thanks go to Gini Romero of Dallas, Texas, for her excellent word processing skills and patience.

CONTENTS

5 · *Overview of Video Depositions*   43

6 · *Preparing For And Deposing Adverse Experts*   55

7 *Preparing an Expert for Deposition* 89

11 *Deposing a Minor Child*   127

12 *Depositions of Organizations*   133

13 *Preparing Corporate Witnesses*   145

14 *Deposing the Corporate Representative* 155

15 *Special Witness Doctrines* 163

16 *Using Demonstrative Evidence in Deposition* 169

17   *Motions to Quash and for Protection*   177

18   *Making and Responding to Objections*   185

19   *Special Deposition Procedures*   193

INTRODUCTION

Many things go into a successful trial. A good jury and favorable facts are always important. However, credible witnesses, hard work, and good planning are also significant. Success is seldom a random event; rather, it is the earned result of preparation and good planning.

A cornerstone of any litigation plan is cost-efficient discovery, and a chief component of such discovery includes depositions. Depositions should be used to frame trial issues, develop favorable evidence, and neutralize unfavorable evidence. In many jurisdictions, depositions are used as direct evidence in a lawyer's case-in-chief. They are also a primary tool for impeaching and managing hostile witnesses on the witness stand. Cases are frequently won or lost based upon a pre-trial deposition record.

Some lawyers underutilize depositions by using them as mere discovery devices. Although meaningful discovery is always important, depositions can and should provide much more. Skilled trial lawyers use depositions to measure and weigh the credibility, strengths, and weaknesses of *all* witnesses—their witnesses, opposing witnesses, and independent witnesses alike. Good trial lawyers also use depositions to extract concessions from and create foundations to challenge experts. In addition, depositions provide a stage where the performance of opposing counsel is evaluated: How does the opposing lawyer handle the evidence, the witnesses, and the issues? In sum, there are many subtle (and not-so-subtle) tell-tales that are discerned from the deposition process which go far beyond a court reporter's transcript. Depositions are, quite simply, a proving ground for the issues, the witnesses, and the lawyers.

Every trial lawyer should have a good feel for his or her client's case before the first deposition is taken. This means that the lawyer must have a solid footing in the relevant law and an appreciation of the important fact issues. The lawyer should also develop a trial plan for how these issues will be resolved favorably for the client, and he or she should use every deposition to build toward that resolution. A house cannot be built without a blueprint, and a lawsuit cannot be prosecuted or defended without a discovery plan.

Every case has a story, and the witnesses and events make up the story line. Although there will be pitfalls and detours, the seasoned trial lawyer knows how to influence the direction of this story line and how the story evolves from the first day of a case until the end. Depositions are used to tell your client's side of the story and expose the weaknesses in the opposing story. Every witness—neutral, favorable, or adverse—offers something of potential value to help your case in some way. Successful trial advocates find ways to exploit this value; they use the deposition process to build storylines that reflect and advance their trial themes.

Depositions can have powerful, persuasive impacts on a jury. If lawyers fail to make this connection, they will be unprepared, their witnesses will be ill-prepared, and they will be following a path toward failure. Let there be no doubt that evidence lifted directly from depositions can sway a jury's decision just as if the witnesses were testifying live. Cases can be won or lost on the deposition record.

Depositions of party opponents are typically admissible in whole or in part in most jurisdictions. In many jurisdictions, depositions are deemed to be an exception to the hearsay rule or admissions of a party opponent. In some jurisdictions, depositions are admissible without predicates and are not considered hearsay, and they are admissible as if the witness were appearing at trial. What this means is that the trial lawyer should assume that every deposition will be used at trial in some way or another. The idea of a pure "discovery" deposition is an oxymoron. No such thing really exists. Every deposition should be treated as a "trial" deposition.

Experienced advocates enter the deposition room as if the jury is present. It is this awareness that informs the lawyer's questions, how those questions are asked, and what questions are *not* asked. It also drives the lawyer to prepare for every deposition with a sense of drama for jury consumption. This same awareness also drives the lawyer presenting witnesses at deposition to thoroughly prepare those witnesses, rather than feeding them to the lions. By approaching depositions with this heightened awareness, a trial lawyer increases the ability to positively impact the case, the settlement process and, if no settlement is achieved, the presentation of evidence at trial.

There are a variety of different deposition strategies for different types of witnesses. Lay witnesses are approached differently from expert witnesses. Corporate representatives are treated differently from percipient fact witnesses. A witness who resides within the subpoena power of the courthouse is treated differently from a witness who resides in another state. Different witness considerations dictate different strategies on how the deposition is approached, and different techniques as to how the deposition is conducted.

This book provides practical advice for both beginning lawyers and seasoned trial attorneys on how to take and use depositions for maximum advantage. This book also explores differing techniques for lawyers on both sides of the bar. It will specifically consider techniques that can be used when deposing hostile or adverse witnesses, expert witnesses, and lay witnesses. Lastly, this book presents best practices for preparing and presenting client representatives and testifying experts for deposition, as well as the effective use of objections during depositions.

The goal of every trial lawyer is to make every deposition come alive, making it interesting and compelling for the jury. *Mastering the Art of Depositions* uses a hands-on approach with real-life examples that explain how to achieve successful results.

The Bar is blessed with talented trial lawyers on both sides, and there are many examples of how imaginative lawyers apply their craft to create powerful, persuasive evidence. They do this through controlling the deposition environment, using effective demonstratives to highlight evidence or trial themes, and utilizing powerful examination techniques to create lasting impressions. This book provides a unique approach that practitioners can use to handle depositions successfully, no matter what type of case they are involved in or whom they represent.

Depositions Are Proving Grounds

A basic goal of discovery is to avoid surprise and ambush at trial. Nevertheless, there is much more that can be accomplished in a discovery plan. The pre-trial stages of a case are a proving ground where the factual bases and equities of a party's position are revealed and road-tested. As a key component of such a plan, deposition discovery is used to explore (and expose) the strengths and weaknesses of the witnesses and, equally important, opposing counsel. Knowledge is power; thus, knowledge about the opposition's case, its witnesses, and the skills of opposing counsel are important variables when evaluating any case.

All lawyers know that the claims in a lawsuit are first lodged in the initial lawsuit papers. The defenses are then lodged in the answer or responsive pleadings. Basic written discovery is then exchanged to ferret out the parties' respective positions, and documents are typically produced and exchanged. After this initial written discovery is completed, the lawyers, armed with basic information, begin taking depositions.

Depositions provide defense lawyers with a chance to undercut the allegations against their clients; they are where the plaintiff's lawyers advance their liability and damage claims. Thus, there are significant burdens placed on all lawyers to prepare their witnesses, as well as preparing themselves. All lawyers should appreciate that they must first understand their cases before this can be done. Clearly, a lawyer who does not understand the basic factual or legal issues in the case cannot prepare, much less perform, effectively in that case.

A lawyer's skills are on stage during a deposition. Is the lawyer prepared? Does he or she exhibit an understanding of the issues? Is the lawyer organized? Does he or she accurately appreciate the strengths and weakness of the client's case *and* the opposing party's case? There should be no doubt that an opposing lawyer's lack of preparation is an important factor in how cases are evaluated. A lawyer's conduct in deposition can reveal an ignorance or mastery of the important issues.

Indeed, if a lawyer is perceived poorly, the case is negatively impacted and settlement scenarios are adversely influenced. If the lawyer is respected and perceived as a threat, however, the settlement scenarios are positively enhanced.

Depositions are also a proving ground for fact witnesses, who come in all shapes, sizes, demeanors, and degrees of likability. The jury always weighs whether a witness is "likable," "jury friendly," or believable. Trial lawyers evaluate witnesses for these same characteristics, striving to predict whether the jury will embrace or reject a witness's testimony. Even if a witness is telling the truth and has important testimony to offer, the testimony may be disregarded if the witness is not likeable, lacks confidence, or appears untrustworthy. Thus, whether a witness appeals to or alienates jurors is an important factor in determining who a lawyer calls or does not call as a witness at trial. Performance in depositions will shed light on and inform these strategic decisions.

Witnesses also are evaluated for their sympathetic or empathetic appeal. Although courts typically instruct jurors not to consider bias or sympathy in reaching their verdicts, human nature is such that it is difficult for jurors to separate themselves fully from their likes, dislikes, and emotions. Jurors are naturally impacted by sadness, loss, and drama. Every lawyer should consider whether key witnesses will appeal to or alienate jurors, as well as whether the witnesses are sympathetic or aloof.

Trial Themes

An enduring adage is that a lawyer's first act in every new case should be to prepare a jury charge. Of course, every jury charge evolves as the case develops; however, by taking this first step, the lawyer is forced to create a disciplined legal framework for a storyline. Clearly, a lawyer cannot advance a client's case unless that lawyer has mastered the law and identified the factual goals of the case.

Once the lawyer understands the "law" of the case, the lawyer should then begin to prepare a list of factual themes for ultimate use at trial. This practice is akin to a road map for where the lawyer wants (and legally needs) to go. These trial themes, which should be rooted in the law, help the lawyer frame questions for every deposition and prepare his or her client for deposition. Trial themes should reflect what is important.

A typical case does not have numerous trial themes, and a simple case may have only a few. Indeed, a lawyer's objective is to simplify even complex cases to simple, readily understood concepts. These concepts should guide the witnesses and the lawyers throughout the deposition process, and these concepts should be adjusted as the case proceeds.

Basic trial themes may be shared with party witnesses to help the witnesses see how they can help advance the case. By acquiring a simple understanding of the case, witnesses gain a perspective that will help them when the going gets tough during cross-examination. They understand where they need to go and, through practice, can incorporate these trial themes into their answers during depositions. It also helps them place their testimony into the context of the bigger picture. If the witness effectively advocates these themes even in the face of an aggressive examination, then these themes will resonate with a jury even more.

Pathos, Logos, and Ethos

The three cornerstones of effective advocacy are *pathos, logos,* and *ethos*. These words are Greek in origin and were first developed as advocacy concepts by Aristotle. Every advocate should know and understand these terms, and every discovery plan should be developed with these cornerstones in mind. Strategically planned depositions should be used to cultivate these basic elements of advocacy to advance the case.

Pathos, which literally means "suffering" or "experience," represents the emotional or dramatic impact presented by the facts and the witnesses. The goal of every successful trial lawyer is to capture the jury's attention with dramatic facts and testimony. The trial lawyer should endeavor to develop a deposition record that tells a story that is both moving and forceful.

Logos represents the logic of the lawyer's reasoning or argument. The storyline presented by the lawyer should be internally consistent, reasonable, and coherent. It must make common sense. Also, this storyline should be supported by the facts developed during discovery; accordingly, the deposition record is used to accomplish this end.

Ethos is the third and equally important cornerstone. It represents the credibility of the witnesses and, therefore, the storyline. Every successful trial lawyer seeks to present a case that is believable and trustworthy. This is accomplished through the lawyer's tone and style. It is also accomplished through the demeanor of important witnesses and the credibility of their testimony.

Every discovery plan should include depositions as a key component, and every deposition should be approached with the goal of advancing trial themes. The trial themes should reflect drama (*pathos*), reasonable and understandable consistency and common sense (*logos*), and trustworthiness (*ethos*). This is the menu for success.

First Steps

Trial themes are typically prepared after initial witness interviews are completed and initial written discovery is exchanged. Documents should be obtained from the client and from opposing parties, and a timeline (or chronology) should be prepared that reflects all key events as supported by these documents and witness interviews. A chronology is an important tool in understanding how a series of interrelated events are factually connected. The relationship between events (and documents) helps tell a story and provides the logic (*logos*) to the argument. A chronology also provides an index to key documents that should be used to support the trial themes and used with the witnesses.

Once basic document discovery is completed, important documents should be gathered and arranged in chronological order. Preparing and using an electronic spreadsheet is an excellent way of organizing documents, and it allows sorting by a variety of categories. Documents can be sorted by date, topic, author, or recipient. This type of coding can guide the trial lawyer as to which documents are important for which witnesses. The universe of relevant documents is then readily available on a witness-by-witness basis.

Here are two basic examples of how a document database is effectively used to facilitate deposition preparations:

- If the attorney is presenting the witness, the database can be used to sort documents by the witness's name (either as author or as recipient). All relevant documents can be identified and assembled, then used with the witness during preparations for the deposition.

- If the attorney is presenting a corporate representative, the documents can be sorted by topic category. The key is to properly code the documents in the electronic spreadsheet by meaningful, relevant topics.

The sorting codes are important. Too many sorting codes may render the exercise less efficient because there is too much dilution. Too few codes may result in the inability to rapidly retrieve evidence. Accordingly, the trial lawyer (and the lawyer's team) should identify the key issues in the case as a way of defining what codes matter and what codes do not. Every coding system, however, should employ some method of identifying important documents and "hot documents." These are the documents that may be used on a recurring basis with many witnesses. Here are some specific examples tailored to specific types of cases:

- In a medical malpractice case, documents can be sorted by:
  ☐ Admission records
  ☐ Discharge records
  ☐ Billing records
  ☐ Diagnosis
  ☐ Prognosis
  ☐ Nurses' notes
  ☐ Medication
  ☐ Hot documents

- In a breach of contract case, documents can be sorted by:
  - ☐ Draft agreements
  - ☐ Negotiations
  - ☐ Final agreements
  - ☐ Amendments
  - ☐ Course of dealing
  - ☐ Breach
  - ☐ Repudiation
  - ☐ Damages
  - ☐ Hot documents

- In a product liability case, documents can be sorted by:
  - ☐ Design
  - ☐ Failure analysis
  - ☐ Safer alternative design
  - ☐ Quality control standards
  - ☐ Testing
  - ☐ Prototype
  - ☐ Human factors
  - ☐ Warnings
  - ☐ Manufacturing
  - ☐ Other incidents
  - ☐ Statistics
  - ☐ Hot documents

- In a negligence case, documents can be sorted by:
  - ☐ Standard of care
  - ☐ Incident report
  - ☐ Accident investigation
  - ☐ Company policies
  - ☐ Injury
  - ☐ Hot documents

These are just a few examples. Some documents may have several codes because of topical overlap or due to their unique importance. However, the goal remains the same: to provide the attorney with ready access to any document by quick reference code.

As a practical matter, depositions should not be initiated until after document chronologies and trial themes are prepared. This is particularly important in complex cases involving many witnesses, voluminous documents, and other moving parts. If the trial themes are the blueprints for a trial, the chronologies of key events are the bricks and the documents are the mortar that holds the plan together. If the case is document-intensive, there must be some mechanism for quick retrieval and access.

Next Steps

Once document chronologies are prepared, documents are coded and organized, and initial trial themes are developed, the trial lawyer should begin to select which witnesses will be deposed and which witness will *not* be deposed. This exercise will result in an evolving list because many witnesses are identified during the course of discovery. However, the plan must always start somewhere.

The key witnesses will certainly include the parties and the parties' representatives. The list also will include third-party witnesses who can add to the lawyer's trial themes or detract from the opposing party's case. All witnesses should be evaluated as to trustworthiness, jury "likeability," and strength. Again, all witnesses do not need to be (and should not be) deposed—only those witnesses who the lawyer believes can advance the case. These witnesses are the foundation of the deposition list, and this list will ultimately be the foundation of a trial witness list.

2

Evidentiary and Procedural Considerations

The best practice is to assume that *every* deposition is a trial deposition, and that all or portions of every deposition will be shown to the jury at some point during the trial. To not approach depositions with this awareness may lead to strategic blunders or, worse, disaster. No lawyer walks into a courtroom unprepared, and no lawyer should walk into a deposition room unprepared. By approaching depositions with this heightened awareness, the lawyer will make fewer mistakes and will bring a more disciplined approach to his or her trial practice.

Rules of evidence address the admissibility of depositions as substantive evidence, and these rules should be consulted in each jurisdiction where the case is pending. However, the use of depositions as evidence is routine, and experienced lawyers are artful in finding ways to open the doors for favorable deposition testimony regardless of the jurisdiction. All lawyers should assume that what happens in the deposition room will find its way into the jury room.

Admissibility in Different Jurisdictions

Depositions taken in a case are deemed to fall outside the hearsay rule in some jurisdictions. In such instances, depositions are admissible as substantive evidence regardless of witness availability. No predicate for admissibility is required in such jurisdictions. Depositions are permitted into evidence subject only to evidentiary objections to specific questions and answers. In other words, a deposition is treated like the examination of a live witness in the courtroom. The implications of this practice are significant for practitioners on both sides of the table. The deposition is, by definition, a trial deposition.

Many jurisdictions permit the admission of depositions as stand-alone evidence, but only if the deposition is that of a party or if the witness is unavailable. Examples of these permitted uses are found in Rule 32 of the Federal Rules of Civil Procedure, which provides a detailed matrix of how and when depositions may be used in the courtroom.[1] Several states have similar rules or track Fed. R. Civ. P. 32, including California, Michigan, Florida, New York, and Missouri.

Under Rule 32, depositions are generally admissible against another party if that party was present and the deposition satisfies the various conditions set forth under Rule 32(a)(2)–(8). One of these requirements deals with witness unavailability. A witness is "unavailable" under the Federal Rules (thus permitting use of deposition testimony at trial) when circumstances show that the witness is either deceased; located outside the subpoena range of the court[2]; unable to attend the trial due to age, illness, infirmity, or imprisonment; or other exceptional circumstances exist.

Although depositions may be treated as hearsay in many jurisdictions, they are typically permitted into evidence (in whole or in part) if certain predicates are satisfied.[3] Here are some examples of hearsay exceptions:

- **Prior Inconsistent Statements.** This use requires that the witness is on the stand when the impeaching deposition testimony is used, and a proper predicate for impeachment is established. Laying the proper foundation for a prior inconsistent statement generally requires the witness be afforded an opportunity to explain or deny the statement, and the opposing party must have the opportunity to question the witness regarding the statement.[4]

- **Admission of a Party Opponent.** This use is not dependent upon the witness being on the stand; instead the deposition can be offered as substantive testimony in many jurisdictions if the deposition is of a party opponent or of a party's authorized agent or representative.[5]

- **Declaration Against Interest.** This use is permissible when a witness is unavailable to testify, and this unavailability was not procured or wrongfully

---

[1] Fed. R. Civ. P. 32 (addressing, among other things, the use of depositions for purposes of impeachment, the use of depositions of a party, and the use of depositions when the witness is unavailable).

[2] Fed. R. Civ. P. 32(4)(B) ("that the witness is more than 100 miles from the place of hearing or trial or is outside the United States, unless it appears that the witness's absenec was procured by the party offering the deposition"); Fed. R. Civ. P. 32(4)(D) ("that the party offering the deposition could not procure the witness's attendance by subpoena").

[3] Depending upon the jurisdiction, those predicates may be based upon the applicable rules of procedure or the rules of evidence. *See Nationwide Life Ins. Co. v. Richards*, 541 F.3d 903, 914-15 (9th Cir. 2008) (noting that because certain deposition testimony was properly admitted under Rule 32(a)(4)(B), "it need not also meet the requirements for admissibility set forth in Rule 804(b)(1).").

[4] *See* Fed. R. Evid. 801(d)(1)(A); see also Fed. R. Civ. P. 32(a)(2) ("Any party may use a deposition to contradict or impeach the testimony given by the deponent as a witness, or for any other purpose allowed by the Federal Rules of Evidence.").

[5] Fed. R. Evid. 801(d)(2)(A)-(E); Fed. R. Civ. P. 32 (a)(3) ("An adverse party may use for any purpose the deposition of a party or anyone who, when deposed, was the party's officer, director, managing agent, or designee under Rule 30(b)(6) or 31(a)(4).").

caused by the statement's proponent. The statement is not hearsay if the declaration made was "so contrary to the declarant's proprietary or pecuniary interest" that a reasonable person in the declarant's position would have made the statement only if he or she believed it to be true.[6]

- **Refreshed Recollection.** This use is permitted when a witness is on the stand and counsel uses a writing to refresh the recollection of the witness. The adverse party is then entitled to introduce any portion of the writing that relates to the witness's testimony.[7]

Depositions Used by Experts

Depositions are frequently submitted to testifying experts who may review and typically rely upon such testimony to form their opinions if deemed "reliable." In most, if not all jurisdictions, experts may rely upon hearsay as a basis for their opinions. In this context, an expert can typically discuss the deposition testimony and why the deposition testimony is important to the expert's opinions, even though the actual transcript may not be accepted into evidence. There is really no difference between a deposition and a witness statement in this instance, but the deposition may be viewed as more reliable because it reflects testimony taken under oath and subject to the rigors of cross-examination.

Depositions in Other Cases

Federal Rule of Civil Procedure 32 specifically contemplates that depositions can be used against a party if "the party was present or represented at the taking of the deposition or had reasonable notice of it."[8] Rule 32(a)(8) specifically provides that depositions from earlier cases between the same parties and involving the same subject matter will be treated as if taken in the subsequent action. However, depositions involving just one of the parties are separately admissible if the party against whom it is offered was present and had a similar interest in the cross-examination of the witness in the earlier proceeding. This practice is typically seen in mass tort litigation, pattern litigation, or related litigation involving products, such as consumer products, automobiles, or pharmaceuticals. In such cases, there may be common allegations of product defect or marketing defect (failures to warn).

---

[6] *See* Fed. R. Evid. 804(b)(3)(A).

[7] *See* Fed. R. Evid. 612.

[8] Fed. R. Civ. P. 32(a)(1)(A).

The deposition testimony from prior cases also may be offered as substantive evidence to show notice of a defect or proof of the defect itself. In sum, a lawyer representing a defendant in one case should be aware that the deposition may be used before other juries in other cases. This awareness reinforces the need that witnesses be prepared thoroughly in the first instance. The following scenarios highlight the use of depositions in pattern litigation or related cases.[9]

A corporate representative of a foreign automotive manufacturer was cross-noticed in seven different cases pending in Kansas, Texas, and California. Each case involved allegations of a product design defect. There were four plaintiff law firms involved, and each firm insisted upon the right to examine the witness. There also were multiple defense firms involved. One lawyer was selected to represent the witness at deposition to assert objections on behalf of the entire defense group. By agreement, these objections could be supplemented if there were unique objections arising under the evidentiary rules of the different states. The gravity of the situation was clear. The deposition would be used as trial testimony in seven different cases.

In product liability cases, a plaintiff may seek to introduce deposition evidence of other incidents involving personal injury or death if these other incidents are substantially or reasonably similar. Again, the stated goal is to prove notice of either defect or actual defect. The potential for prejudice is clearly tremendous because the jury will be advised of other injuries or even deaths. Here is an example:

In an automobile accident case, a plaintiff's expert was provided police reports and other hearsay information concerning over 100 other accidents involving the same model of automobile. Some of these accidents resulted in litigation where depositions were taken. The plaintiff's lawyers then sought to introduce the depositions of witnesses or injured plaintiffs from dozens of cases, claiming that those cases involved substantially similar or reasonably similar events. This request caused a mini-trial that lasted several days to determine which events were similar or dissimilar. In the end, only three other accidents were permitted into evidence, but the court allowed the deposition testimony of injured consumers from those three cases. The potential effect on any jury is predictably significant.

Again, this example underscores the importance of every deposition. The lesson is clear: what happens in a deposition room may find its way into a variety of courtrooms (and jury rooms) around the country.

---

[9] It is not uncommon in certain tort cases involving similar products or issues to receive document requests seeking production of prior depositions of company witnesses.

In jurisdictions that permit wide latitude in the use of depositions as substantive evidence, excerpts from depositions may be permitted in opening statements. Both plaintiff's counsel and defense counsel may seek to use depositions in this manner and open their respective cases with high drama. Even though opening statements are not technically evidence, the jury will see such excerpts for what they are. The use of actual testimony to introduce key facts can have profound, lasting effects on the jury.

Rules Governing How Depositions Are Conducted

The practice of trial law has changed substantially over the years, and many jurisdictions have implemented rules designed to limit discovery and reduce discovery expense. The stated goal is to prevent discovery abuse and wasteful expense.

Rules regulating the number of depositions taken in a case and the duration of those depositions are now in effect in many jurisdictions. The details of these rules will differ from jurisdiction to jurisdiction, so the procedures for the jurisdiction where the case is pending should always be consulted. However, a common feature underlying these rules is that depositions are shorter in duration and fewer in number. The parties may modify these rules by agreement in most jurisdictions; some jurisdictions, however, may require leave of court.

Limitations on the number of depositions in a case are typically expressed by a specific number of depositions that can be taken by each "side" to a case. An example is found in the Federal Rules that impose an initial limitation of 10 depositions per side.[10] There are several jurisdictions that track the Federal Rules and have adopted this limitation.[11]

In other jurisdictions, a limitation may be expressed in terms of an allotment of total hours available to each side to conduct all depositions. For instance, each side may be provided a total of 50 hours to conduct all depositions in a case. Thus, lawyers representing co-parties on the same side of a case may be forced to allocate time between them; as a group, they must make strategic decisions as to which witnesses will be deposed and which witnesses will not be deposed. For the purposes of these types of rules, the term *side* distinguishes between plaintiffs, defendants, and third-party defendants, but not between aligned co-parties.[12] Of course, what constitutes an aligned party may be a point of significant disagreement.

---

[10] *See* Fed. R. Civ. P. 30(a)(2)(A)(i).

[11] For example, Wyoming, Washington, D.C., Hawaii, and Montana.

[12] *See* Fed. R. Civ. P. 30(2)(A)(i); *see also Thykkuttathil v. Keese*, 294 F.R.D. 597, 599 (W.D. Wash. 2013) (distinguishing between per party and per side limits and stating "[t]his Court has been unable to identify a single instance in which a court has deviated from interpreting Fed. R. Civ. P. 30 to impose a presumptive ten-per-side limit on the number of allowed depositions").

Cases involving smaller amounts in controversy typically require less discovery and, therefore, less expense.[13] A case involving $50,000 is logically different than a case involving millions of dollars, and such cases should be handled differently to control expense. Thus, some jurisdictions have enacted discovery regimes that limit the number of or total time for depositions depending upon the amount in controversy.[14] The goal is to achieve some degree of proportionality between discovery burdens and the complexity and size of the case.

In at least one jurisdiction, there are three different tiers within which a case may be classified for purposes of determining the amount of allowable discovery.[15] Tier 1 is for small cases. Tier 2 is for more standard cases with strict limits on discovery. Tier 3 is for complex cases that require a scheduling order, and classification as a Tier 3 case will be granted upon the motion of any party. The court can lift those limitations completely, but it can still impose deadlines within which the discovery must be completed.

Limitations on the duration of depositions may vary from state to state; they are intended to prevent abusive or inefficient examinations where a witness is subjected to endless questions late into the night or for successive days. Unnecessary expense and witness harassment are abuses that such rules are intended to address, and many jurisdictions seek to strike a balance between what may constitute abuse and what should be required for reasonable discovery. Again, an example of this type of limitation is found in the Federal Rules, which allow up to 7 hours of examination.[16] In a multi-party case, this allotment can be allocated by agreement if there are multiple parties on one side of the case. Some states impose even more stringent time limits.[17]

Seven hours is more than sufficient time to take a typical deposition. In fact, most depositions of most fact witnesses can be completed in substantially less time if the lawyer is prepared and the lawyer's deposition goals are clearly defined. However, time allotments become more complicated if there are multiple parties on one side. What constitutes a side becomes problematic if there are cross-actions or divergent interests among co-parties. Co-parties may constitute a side in name only. Thus, counsel should be prepared to seek modifications of these limits with a showing of good cause. No lawyer wants to split deposition time with another lawyer whose interests may be substantially at odds with the client's interests.

---

[13] The newest amendments to Fed. R. Civ. P. 26 went into effect in December 2015. They contemplate further restrictions on the scope and extent of discovery based upon the nature and magnitude of the case.

[14] California, Texas, and Utah are examples of several states where depositions may be limited based upon the amount in controversy.

[15] *See, e.g.,* Tex. R. Civ. P. 190.1–190.6.

[16] Fed. R. Civ. P. 30(d)(1).

[17] *See, e.g.,* Tex. R. Civ. P. 199.5(c) (imposing a six hour limitation per side, stating "[n]o side may examine or cross-examine an individual witness for more than six hours.").

Time allotments may also become patently unworkable depending upon the nature and complexity of the case. The following illustration underscores this problem:

> A private oil and gas exploration company sued an oil services company, alleging that its practices damaged over 120 oil wells in two different production fields in two different states. The case effectively presented 120 distinct transactions involving different producing reservoirs and 120 different damage models. Each well was drilled to different depths, no well was precisely the same, and the work orders for each well differed in some respect. Clearly, lawyers defending the case could not reasonably be expected to start and complete the deposition of the plaintiff's damage expert in just 7 hours. That would provide less than 3 minutes to examine the witness on each well.

Thus, if the issues are complex or if the nature of the controversy dictates that more time is required, then steps should be taken to address such discovery issues at the beginning of the case. This is actually contemplated under the Federal Rules in the pre-trial conference requirements. Fed. R. Civ. P. 26(f) requires that the parties participate in a conference to address the form, substance, and any limitations on discovery. Rule 26(f)(3)(E) specifically directs the parties meet and confer to discuss "what changes should be made on the limitations on discovery imposed under these rules or by local rule, and what other limitations should be imposed."

Thus, the Federal Rules contemplate that all lawsuits are not the same, and the parties may confront different discovery challenges that require modification of the discovery tools in a particular case. Under Rule 26, the parties are expected to confer in the development of a discovery plan that reflects the unique discovery needs of a case and whether the types of permissible discovery should be enlarged or reduced.[18] These modifications, if agreed upon by the parties, are typically approved by the court.

---

[18] Fed. R. Civ. P. 26(f)(2)–(3).

3

Preliminary Strategic Considerations

This chapter addresses basic strategic considerations that should be addressed before depositions begin. Some of these issues are complex and require substantive evaluation and decision making. Others are more simple and based on common sense.

Identifying Discovery Needs

One of the first strategic issues that a lawyer must consider is the amount and types of discovery that will be required to develop the case, and the identity of the key witnesses who will need to be deposed. Of course, this evaluation will be ongoing as the case evolves, but the task should begin during the early stages of the case.

Federal Rule of Civil Procedure 26 specifically contemplates that counsel will meet to discuss the discovery needs of the case, and counsel may specifically seek to modify the limits of discovery that are otherwise imposed by the Federal Rules. Many state court jurisdictions also provide for scheduling orders or docket control orders that contemplate either the timing of discovery, the sequencing of discovery, or both. The objective served by these procedures is to force the lawyers to identify their discovery needs during the preliminary stages of a case. Most procedures recognize that scheduling issues, sequencing issues, and the breadth of discovery may change or be modified as the case matures.

Deciding to Take or Not to Take a Deposition

Many lawyers, particularly less experienced lawyers, often feel compelled to look for witnesses under every rock. There may be an urge to depose all possible witnesses for fear that something may be missed in discovery. Doing so, however, can be a mistake for a variety of reasons.

Sometimes, witnesses boomerang and backfire. Every lawyer has been taught the golden rule of cross-examination: *Do not ask questions if you do not know the answers*. Scheduling and taking depositions is no different. Why schedule the deposition of a witness who may offer negative testimony? Why schedule the deposition of a witness whose testimony is unknown and which may be a waste of time and money or, worse, may generate harmful testimony?

The bottom line is that not every witness should be deposed. If a witness resides within the subpoena power of the court, and can be compelled to appear at trial, a witness interview and a witness statement may be sufficient. The witness can be compelled to appear at trial, and the witness statement provides the lawyer with the ability to control the witness on the stand. Furthermore, the other side may not interview this witness, and the opportunity to call such a witness under these circumstances may provide strategic benefits.

On the other hand, if the witness's testimony is important, and the witness's "likeability" or substantive performance before a jury is uncertain, then a deposition may be preferred over live testimony. The other side also may be reluctant to call the witness to trial because of similar uncertainties.[1] The deposition is thus a way to test the witness's credibility and likeability. If the witness fails these tests, then the deposition can be used in lieu of live testimony in jurisdictions where depositions are admissible even though the witness is "available." This approach may be less risky, and the trial lawyer is in a better position to control negative fallout from unfavorable testimony.

The question becomes more difficult, however, if the witness is expected to have important testimony and resides outside the jurisdiction, or if the parties know that the witness will be unavailable at trial. These types of depositions are clearly trial depositions and should be approached carefully. That means pulling out all of the bells and whistles to fully prepare. Unless expense is an issue, it is good practice to have such depositions videotaped to visually capture the *pathos* and *ethos* of the testimony for the jury. The witness's trustworthiness is in play, and the logic and credibility of the witness's testimony are also in play. A video can help reinforce this testimony. Indeed, the use of videotape to record these types of depositions is the norm, not the exception.

---

[1] The deposition can be used at trial in those jurisdictions where witness availability is not a condition to admissibility.

Video Depositions

A detailed discussion of video depositions is presented in Chapter 5. However, every trial lawyer should know that video depositions are an exceptional way to bring drama and emotion to the deposition process. This is true whether the witness is located out of the state or within the subpoena power of the trial court. To be clear, video depositions allow the lawyers to bring *pathos* and *ethos* developed in the deposition room into the courtroom; they provide a visual record of the drama and emotion of the witness's testimony, as well as an opportunity for the jury to evaluate the credibility and trustworthiness of the witness.

The trial lawyer seeking the deposition of an important witness should always consider the advantages and disadvantages of scheduling a video record of the deposition. The trial lawyer will not want video of testimony that is clearly harmful. However, if impeachment opportunities exist, then a video reflecting the witness's lack of credibility may become important, if not critical. Thus, if an adverse witness's deposition is scheduled by the opposing side and is not scheduled for a video recording, the lawyer should consider if the deposition should be cross-noticed for a video record. Ordinarily, no harmful testimony should be placed on video if that decision is within the lawyer's control. The decision matrix changes, however, if the witness can be substantially impeached and the witness's credibility is at issue.

Clearly, one purpose of a video deposition is to have a visual record of the witness's demeanor. The video record can be used subsequently to evaluate witness performance when planning cross-examinations or preparing the witness list. Videotaped depositions also can be used at mediations to maximize a party's position during settlement discussions. Excerpts from a video deposition can be used to convey powerful points to opposing parties and opposing counsel, and they are useful to a mediator to facilitate settlement. Lastly, videotaped recordings can be utilized by jury consultants and focus groups in larger cases to test the strength of various legal and factual positions, and to further validate a witness's veracity and likability. Focus groups can watch the videos and provide real-time feedback on how the witness performed and whether the testimony is credible and trustworthy.

Cross-Noticing Depositions

Another strategic consideration involves whether specific depositions should be cross-noticed. Sometimes other counsel may issue a deposition notice of a third-party witness. Then, on the eve of the deposition, the deposition notice is withdrawn and canceled. If this occurs late in the discovery period, there may be insufficient time to regroup and issue a new notice to reschedule the deposition. This cancellation may have occurred innocently, the party who canceled the deposition may have settled, or the cancellation could be the result of gamesmanship. In any event, relying upon an original subpoena and deposition notice may be misplaced and an opportunity to secure the testimony of an important witness can be lost.

Accordingly, a prudent strategy dictates that depositions of important third-party witnesses whose testimony is expected to be favorable should be cross-noticed in the event of any attempt by another party to cancel the deposition at the last moment. That way, the deposition is assured to go forward, and the opportunity to secure the testimony is protected.

Cross-Noticing Depositions in Multiple Cases

There will be instances where a witness's testimony may be relevant in multiple cases pending at the same time. This occurs where there are related cases involving similar issues and one or more of the same parties. This also may occur if there is parallel litigation involving an identity of the parties. The witness could be either a client witness or a third-party witness. In any event, the witness may be exposed to multiple depositions in several cases concerning common events or transactions.

Multiple depositions create special risks. The witness's testimony in one case can educate lawyers in subsequent cases, and these lawyers then have time to engineer ways to impeach the witness. Multiple depositions also may impose a severe strain on the witness and cause needless expense. Preparing for two or more depositions is both time consuming and taxing on everyone, but particularly the witness.

Thus, in such instances, counsel should consider cross-noticing the witness's deposition in all related cases. This achieves economies in preparing the witness and reduces the risk of inconsistencies in testimony. Of course, this decision must be balanced with other considerations. By cross-noticing the deposition in multiple cases, the admissibility of the witness's testimony in all such cases is substantially increased. This could be disadvantageous if the witness is a third-party witness offering unknown or unfavorable testimony. Thus, the trial lawyer must always weigh the benefits of securing the testimony against the risks of developing unfavorable testimony in two or more cases.

Timing of Depositions

A critical consideration is when to start the deposition process. Taking depositions too early may result in superficial examinations. However, taking important depositions too late in the case also has drawbacks: the lawyer sacrifices the opportunity to frame key fact issues at an early stage and then build momentum with other witnesses and experts.

There is a related timing issue that involves the order of witnesses. Plaintiffs frequently seek to depose the defendant or the defendant's representatives before presenting the plaintiff for deposition. The converse is also true, and sometimes there is a race to see who issues the deposition notices first. If possible, counsel should attempt to reach an agreement regarding the order of discovery to obtain structure, balance, and certainty.

Important depositions should be deferred until meaningful written discovery has been completed. This is particularly true in complex cases involving significant documents. Meaningful document discovery is always important to develop appropriate timelines and chronologies. This helps tie the case together and tell a story that can be elaborated upon and advanced in depositions. Taking a deposition in a complex case without the benefit of document discovery may be a waste of time or, worse, result in missed opportunities. Erroneous testimony also could result if witnesses do not have the benefit of seeing all relevant documents, and this erroneous testimony could haunt the case indefinitely.

Documents are needed to prepare witnesses and to examine witnesses. Federal Rule of Civil Procedure 26 contemplates many of these timing issues, and specifically directs the parties to abate discovery until all parties have participated in the so-called Rule 26 conference.[2] It is at this conference that the lawyers are expected to discuss the types of required discovery and whether the limitations or time limits on individual depositions should be modified. The parties are also expected to discuss any other unique discovery needs that may be anticipated in the case. One such issue involves whether a bifurcated deposition process should be followed.

Many trial lawyers prefer (and some jurisdictions require) that the parties complete all fact discovery, including fact witness depositions, before designating and deposing expert witnesses. Presumably, the goal is to make sure that the deposition record is not a moving target, and that all experts have the same fixed deposition record to consider before their expert opinions are finalized. In practice, however, experts in most jurisdictions can amend or supplement their reports if new facts (and deposition testimony) come to their attention. Indeed, it is not unusual for trial lawyers to identify additional discovery needs after receiving an expert's report. Usually, this situation arises because of a need to rebut some aspect of an expert's opinion. Here are some examples:

- In a wrongful death case, a medical expert may testify that the decedent experienced prolonged conscious pain and suffering before death. Accordingly,

---

[2] Recent changes to the Federal Rules dictate that certain discovery may be "delivered" prior to the Rule 26 conference; however, "the request is considered to have been served at the first Rule 26(f) conference." *See* Fed. R. Civ. P. 26(d)(2).

the need to depose fact witnesses at the accident scene may be necessary to undercut the expert's opinion.

- In a disability case, a life care planner may hold the opinion that a disabled plaintiff requires 24-hour nursing care. However, if the degree of the plaintiff's disability is at issue, the defense lawyers may be forced to cultivate additional fact testimony rebutting this need.

4

Preparing Fact Witnesses for Deposition

This chapter explores various techniques used to prepare fact witnesses for deposition. Many of these considerations apply equally whether the witness is an individual or a corporate representative. However, there are special considerations that apply only to corporate witness depositions; and, these more unique issues are addressed in Chapters 12–14.

Witnesses and The Attorney-Client Privilege

There are different approaches for how witnesses should be prepared depending upon the existence of the attorney-client privilege. If there is an attorney-client relationship, and the substance of witness preparations is protected from discovery, then a lawyer enjoys substantial freedom in what can be said to the witness during witness meetings. Such discussions can be cloaked with privilege and should be exempt from discovery. Clearly, however, if no privileged relationship exists, or if there is doubt as to its existence, then the lawyer should exercise greater caution in his dealings with the witness. This is because any statements made or documents shown to the witness may be discoverable.

The existence of an attorney-client privilege, and whether the privilege applies to a specific witness, is not always an easy determination. In fact, the question becomes murky in cases involving corporate clients, as well as current or former employees of such clients. The resolution of the privilege issue will likely depend upon the procedures and laws of the specific jurisdiction where the case is pending.

Former employees who were not part of the decision-making structure of a corporate client may not be "client representatives" for purposes of the privilege. The same may hold true for current employees. Different jurisdictions address this issue through the application of different legal and procedural standards with varying results. Some jurisdictions may apply what has been known as the so-called control group test; other jurisdictions may apply the so-called subject matter test; and some jurisdictions apply a hybrid or both. Thus, it is important to make a preliminary decision as to whether the witness qualifies as a client or a client representative for the purpose of protecting discussions from disclosure. This is a first order of business.

Some clients may go to great lengths to address the privilege issue by "offering" legal services to their former employees to cloak pre-deposition meetings with an attorney-client privilege. In one notable case, an oil field service company, caught in the middle of an energy recession, was required to terminate dozens of workers in the oil patch. A trial lawyer defending the company was authorized to "offer" legal services to dozens of former workers to facilitate deposition preparations in a pending case. However, the workers paid nothing for these legal services; they were never invoiced for legal services; and they never had any expectation that they would pay for such services.

This is a potentially dangerous practice. There are also ethical issues that should be addressed well before offering to provide counsel under these or similar circumstances. First and foremost, there may be a conflict of interest. If the witness discloses facts contrary to the company's best interests, then the trial lawyer may confront an actual conflict of interest. Similarly, the witness may share something with the lawyer that the witness does not want shared with the former employer. Again, a conflict of interest may arise. Another problem with this practice involves the ethical consideration of a lawyer "soliciting" clients, rather than clients soliciting lawyers for legal services.

Another real-life example involved high-stakes litigation and whether communications between counsel and a key witness were privileged. The issue turned on what constituted a "client representative" for purposes of asserting the attorney-client privilege:

A special purpose entity (SPE) was created to hold title to a valuable asset. Ultimate ownership of the SPE was vested in a series of offshore entities ultimately controlled by a foreign trust. The beneficiary of that trust—a high net worth individual—insisted on playing an active role in the litigation and had ongoing communications with counsel. In fact, this individual was actually involved in directing the litigation. Ultimately, after several years of litigation, the court ruled that this individual—the beneficiary—was not a "client representative," and that the attorney-client privilege could not be asserted to shield communications between that individual and trial counsel. An appellate challenge to the court's ruling was unsuccessful, and the end result was that the SPE was compelled to produce hundreds of communications between the law firm and the trust beneficiary which had taken place over a period of several years.

The lesson here is clear. Caution should be exercised if there is any doubt about the existence of the privilege. If an attorney-client relationship does not exist, then the lawyer should exercise more caution in dealing with the witness because these dealings may be discoverable. No lawyer wants to create a harmful record, much less an argument that he or she tried to coach the witness or, worse, attempted to manipulate testimony. The lawyer should avoid any statements to an independent witness that can be misconstrued or distorted. A lawyer's credibility is always essential.

Meetings With Independent Witnesses

If a decision is made to meet with an independent witness before a deposition, then certain precautions should be taken. If the witness has already provided a favorable witness statement, then the interviewing lawyer already has a means of controlling witness behavior. However, if no witness statement has been provided and the lawyer is unaware of what the witness may say, the interviewing lawyer may wish to bring an observer to monitor the discussions.

The purpose of an "observer" is to assure the ability of a third party to confirm what did or did not happen during the course of the interview. This is important if the witness becomes antagonistic. The witness may seek to distort the lawyer's statements, or the witness may falsely or unfairly characterize what was discussed or how the lawyer behaved. No lawyer wants to hear criticism from the witness stand or in the deposition room.

The observer could be an investigator, another lawyer, a court reporter, or a legal assistant. The observer effectively becomes an insurance policy. The observer can take notes of the meeting and be prepared to summarize the contents of substantive discussions. The bottom line is that due care should be exercised when talking with third-party witnesses. Affirmative statements that could be misconstrued should be avoided, and any potentially offensive conduct should be avoided. If a meeting occurs, a third-party observer is recommended. A more detailed discussion of meetings with independent witnesses is set forth in Chapter 10.

Showing Documents to The Witness

A second order of business is what documents can (or should) be shown to a client (or a client's representative) during witness preparations without risking subsequent disclosure. What is shown to the witness may be discoverable under various discovery doctrines, and the lawyer should take precautions to protect particularly sensitive or "undiscoverable" documents. These documents would certainly include attorney work product, attorney notes, and sensitive documents that have not been produced in discovery.

Document-intensive cases typically require substantial document review by fact witnesses, with the lawyer acting as a tour guide of what documents should or should not be reviewed. However, if documents are used during the preparation session to refresh the witness's memory, then the identity of such documents is likely discoverable. The determination of the discoverability of such documents is, again, not always easy. Thus, an important order of business is to first determine which documents may or may not be discoverable if shown to the witness. Again, this issue should be resolved on a jurisdictional basis, where the case is pending.

Another issue to consider is *document overload*. This is frequently a real problem, and the lawyer should be sensitive to the fact that a witness can be overwhelmed when too many documents are discussed or presented during a preparation session. A witness should not be expected to review dozens, much less hundreds, of documents and asked to absorb the contents of those documents. This would be a numbing exercise for anyone. Witness burnout is a common issue and should be avoided.

As a general rule, depositions are not memory tests, and lawyers should be sensitive to exposing a witness to excessive documentation or extraneous facts. The witness may become confused and lose focus of key trial themes. In depositions, the witness also may confuse facts that the witness *actually knows* based upon personal knowledge and knowledge gained from documents authored by others. This confusion can then create significant problems for the witness during deposition. A witness is best prepared if the witness is instructed to limit his or her answers to only what is known, and the witness should not extend beyond this easily defined boundary. This is a general standard for preparing almost all witnesses, and this standard has withstood the test of time. Of course, there is an important exception when dealing with a corporate witness where the witness is required to be well versed in corporate knowledge.[1]

On the other hand, the witness should be exposed to important documents to understand the storyline of the case. This is certainly true for all documents that the witness authored or received during the ordinary course of business. The lawyer should also identify particularly helpful or "hot" documents, and then make sure the witness is prepared on these documents. It should be assumed that the witness will be examined with "hot" documents—that is, those documents that are prejudicial or detrimental to the witness or the client's case. By preparing the witness with such documents before the deposition, the witness will not be caught off-guard.

---

[1] This topic—preparing corporate witnesses—is discussed in more detail in Chapters 12–14.

Another technique for preparing witnesses is the creation of a key document binder for the witness's use and review. The most important documents can be included in this binder, and they can be arranged either chronologically or by topic to facilitate review. The witness can consult this binder throughout the preparation meetings; alternatively, the witness can actually take the binder and use it as "homework." This will help advance the witness's understanding of the case, and it will also ease the witness's concerns about mastery over many documents that may be relevant to the case.

If a key document binder is used, the sponsoring attorney should be aware that it is probably discoverable. Thus, due care should be taken concerning the contents of the binder. Key documents reflecting a transaction are certainly appropriate. Other documents such as key discovery responses and pleadings are not controversial and can also be included. A well-vetted chronology, which has been reviewed and verified, also can be included. The goal is to not create evidence for the other side, but to provide the witness with ready access to important information to help him or her during the deposition.

Making The Witness Comfortable

An important goal when presenting a witness for deposition is to make the witness feel comfortable. Depositions are intense experiences for any witness, especially for those who have limited or no prior experience. Every witness is different, and they come to the legal process from a variety of backgrounds. Some are highly educated; some are less educated; some are natural-born advocates; and some are challenged regardless of preparation. Some witnesses are veterans of the process, and some are beginners. The bottom line is that the sponsoring lawyer should spend time with each witness to make sure the witness is adequately prepared and comfortable with the process. Every witness will appreciate this effort and will perform better as a result.

All too often, a witness will disclose that he or she met with his or her lawyer for the first time at dinner or at a breakfast meeting immediately before the deposition. Clearly, the lawyer devoted minimal, if not superficial, efforts to preparing the witness, and the witness likely received little instruction on how to act in the deposition. Even veteran witnesses will appreciate the lawyer's effort to get them prepared, and all witnesses can learn something from a substantive session with the lawyer. A meaningful meeting goes a long way in giving the witness self-confidence and a positive attitude, and this positive attitude frequently translates into improved performance.

There are several ways to make a witness feel more comfortable with giving a deposition. Some techniques reflect nothing more than good common sense, but others require time and practice. The basic goal is to give the witness a sense of control over the process, and not just throw the witness into a den of hungry lawyers. Again, most witnesses will respond favorably to such techniques. Here are some simple suggestions:

- If accessible, show the witness the deposition room to provide a physical orientation of where the deposition will occur.

- Show the witness key documents or "hot" documents that you expect will be used at the deposition so the witness becomes familiar with these documents and will not be surprised.

- Explain to the witness what will happen in the deposition, who will ask questions, and what the lawyers' roles will be.

- Explain the purpose of various objections, as well as what the witness should do if an objection is made.

- Reassure the witness that the case will not be won or lost on the witness's testimony alone; too much pressure on any witness is detrimental and counterproductive.

- Teach the witness basic techniques for responding to different types of questions and how to spot questions that are difficult or ambiguous.

- If known, advise the witness concerning the personalities of the other lawyers so the witness is not caught off-guard by aggressive or confrontational behavior.

- Encourage the witness to take breaks when necessary to alleviate fatigue or stress.

- Provide the witness with a short course on deposition etiquette, attire, and posture.

- If applicable, explain how and why a video record is made, and instruct the witness on the best way to sit and respond to questions in the presence of the video camera.

- Show the witness how to assert control over the tempo of the deposition, and how to avoid being rushed into answering questions.

An overly anxious witness will not perform well. The presenting lawyer should reassure the witness that he or she is not alone and that the witness has rights. If the witness is a client or client representative, make the witness feel like he or she is part of a team. The presenting lawyer should assure the witness that the opposing lawyer will not be allowed to use abusive techniques, and that the witness and the record will be protected.

The Deposition Room

The deposition room is not a *Star Chamber*, but the newcomer witness does not know this fact. Again, every lawyer responsible for witness preparations should try to provide the witness a preview of the physical geography of the room, and how the cast of characters will be seated. That cast includes the witness, the examining lawyers, the court reporter, and the videographer. The lawyer should also show the witness where each player will be seated in relationship to every other. If accessible, the witness should be given an opportunity to see the actual deposition room. If not accessible, a reasonable proxy should be described so the witness can visualize the surroundings.

If possible, the witness should sit down at the deposition table and get a feel for how he or she will be seated in juxtaposition to other participants and, if applicable, the video camera. This orientation helps alleviate anxieties that come with the unknown. This is particularly helpful for beginning witnesses. Although veterans likely know the drill, beginners and relatively inexperienced witnesses will appreciate this knowledge.

Technique Versus Content

One of the biggest mistakes that a lawyer can make is to force-feed numerous facts to a witness during deposition preparations. A witness is not a sponge. The temptation to teach too many facts is always risky. This is particularly true in large, factually complex cases that involve many moving parts and numerous documents. Again, it is not advisable for the typical witness to see all relevant documents. Rather, the witness should be shown only those documents that the witness authored or received, or other "hot" documents that the lawyer knows will be used during the examination.

Showing a witness too many documents may cause oversaturation. There is always a point of diminishing returns because a witness cannot efficiently memorize dozens of facts, much less the contents of dozens of documents, as part of the preparations. Few witnesses can pass such memory tests, and memory tests become more difficult when the witness is exposed to the stresses of cross-examination. A typical witness will stumble under these circumstances, and no witness should be expected to have a mastery of every relevant fact; it would be a mistake to force a witness to do so.

Thus, in lieu of force-feeding endless documents to the witness, the better practice is to teach the witness good "witness technique." This is done by teaching the witness how to spot bad questions, difficult questions, objectionable questions, and still provide answers that are positive and consistent with the client's case. Once good technique is understood, then the handling of documents becomes a less onerous task for the witness.

Primary, Secondary, and Tertiary Facts

One helpful strategy is to "rank" facts by relative importance for each witness. Few witnesses need to know everything about a case; in many cases, witnesses will have limited factual roles. Again, an exception to this rule is a corporate representative designated to testify on behalf of a corporate client on a variety of topics. More extensive preparations are required for such witnesses because of their responsibilities to prepare for deposition as a corporate representative, and different techniques will apply.[2]

There are basically three categories of facts: primary facts, secondary facts, and tertiary facts. Primary facts consist of facts that the witness *already* knows based upon personal firsthand knowledge. The witness already "knows" these facts because the witness was directly involved in or personally observed the events or transactions at issue.

Secondary facts are facts that may be readily or easily inferred by the witness because of the witness's experience or training. The witness "knows" these facts because they may be reasonably inferred from what the witness already knows from personal observation or experience. Examples of inferred facts include the following:

- The company is *honorable and trustworthy*: The witness knows this because he or she spent years working for the company.

- The employee in question *would never intentionally* hurt anyone: The witness knows this because he or she has worked with this employee for many years.

- The passenger was wearing a seatbelt: The witness knows this because this is the passenger's standard habit.

- The driver was not drinking: The witness knows this because he knows the driver is very cautious and never drinks while driving as a matter of practice.

---

[2] Preparing a designated corporate representative for deposition is discussed in Chapters 12–14, *infra*.

Inferred facts are known to a witness because of the witness's experiences and relationships. Such facts are based upon the witness's historical observations and may not constitute speculation.

Tertiary facts are facts that the witness does not know and probably does not need to know. To burden the witness with this type of information could cause brain overload. Again, the witness should not be forced to memorize dozens of facts outside of the witness's ordinary realm of knowledge.

Personal Knowledge and Speculation

Corporate representatives are required to prepare for deposition by making a reasonable inquiry into the facts to make sure they are prepared to address pre-selected topic categories. Their due diligence duty is dictated by procedural rules; as such, the testimony topics may include factual areas where the witness has no personal knowledge. With this exception, fact witnesses should be instructed to testify only on the basis of personal knowledge and never to guess or speculate in their answers. Speculation is always risky and creates problems for the witness, the testimony, and the lawyers.

Witnesses should typically stick with what they know. This instruction is made easy by focusing on how we, as human beings, gain and acquire knowledge. Simply put, personal knowledge is derived from our five basic physical senses and reasonable inferences from those senses:

- What did the witness hear?

- What did the witness see or read?

- What did the witness taste?

- What did the witness smell?

- What did the witness feel from tactile touch?

- What did the witness reasonably infer from what the witness saw, heard, felt, etc.?

If a witness does not "know" facts within this framework, then the witness *does not have* personal knowledge. If the witness goes beyond this framework, the witness begins to speculate and guess, leading to objectionable testimony. Thus, the lawyer should instruct the witness to stay within this solid framework and not to stray from what is "known." The witness should be given the comfort that he or she can simply say "I was not involved, so I do not know" or "I never saw that document, so I do not want to guess." This is a best practice, and it avoids the hazards of speculation.

Responding to Different Types of Questions

A witness should become familiar with the differences between open-ended questions and leading questions. The witness also should be instructed to expect leading questions that are tough, aggressive, and challenging. Using examples of leading questions is an excellent teaching tool, exposing the witness to the tone, pace, and barbed nature of an aggressive examination. This can help get the witness ready, both psychologically and substantively.

Depositions are conducted using different conversational rules from those in typical social settings. What is said and how something is said in everyday, informal conversation should not be how a witness should conduct himself or herself during deposition. The witness must understand this basic truth. Every witness should learn to be more guarded in deposition and more careful in word selection to avoid misinterpretation or distortion by the other side. Every witness also should be taught to be careful to ensure that questions are clear and unambiguous. This is a difficult task for any person who does not have substantial experience in listening to the subtleties in questions, particularly under the spotlight of an opposing lawyer.

It is difficult to train a person to do something that is unfamiliar and inconsistent with daily habits and experiences. There is a natural tendency for people to volunteer testimony by falling back into informal conversational patterns because that is comfortable and familiar. However, a deposition is anything but informal, and the witness should be reminded of this on a consistent basis.

There are many ways to identify leading questions which will become readily apparent to the witness after brief instruction. The witness should also become familiar with open-ended (or direct) questions that seek narrative or descriptive responses. The clear signal words for such questions are "How," "What," "When," "Where," "What," or "Who." A witness also may be asked to "describe" or "explain" certain events. When responding to these types of questions, the witness should be mindful not to volunteer information that does not specifically address the pending question. The answers should be short, concise, and to the point. If the witness goes beyond a disciplined answer, then the response may inspire new questions on new topics that the examining lawyer never contemplated.

As a general rule, a witness should limit answers to "Yes," "No," "I do not know," or "I do not recall at this time." These are typical instructions that have been used with witnesses for many years. However, a witness also should understand that these brief answers may not always do justice to the witness's testimony or fairly describe the facts. A witness, particularly a client, is an advocate for the case, and he or she should be encouraged to supplement his or her answers to make sure that any "Yes" or "No" response is not taken out of context. As a party to the case, a client witness has a responsibility to advance his or her case and may need to elaborate certain responses to make a point. This is particularly important when inflammatory or highly aggressive questions are asked. Again, a beginner witness may encounter difficulties in perfecting this technique. Practice always helps, and a practice or mock examination can drive these lessons home. Practice helps the witness understand how to react to tough questions that may be encountered.

Identifying Loaded Questions

The witness should be taught to listen to each question carefully and make sure that the question is *fully* understood—that is, *all* of the words used in *every* question—before answering. Emphasis should be placed on the notion that *all* words are important. The witness must exercise patience and listen to each word in each sentence. This is good practice for many reasons.

A refresher course in the basic rules of grammar may be helpful. Sentences include different types of words with different purposes—nouns, pronouns, verbs, prepositions, adjectives, and adverbs. Each word type has a distinct grammatical function. Adjectives and adverbs give everyday language power and punch. Special nouns and verbs can be used to communicate enhanced qualities or powerful messages. The key is to look for drama in the words used by the examining lawyer. If possible, and if time permits, the witness should practice exercises in spotting "punchy" or "loaded" words.

Creative lawyers use drama words in their questions. Again, this is where the *ethos* and *pathos* or emotional impact of a question is invoked. Most good lawyers have an inventory of preplanned "attack" words, and they use these words to communicate powerful images to the jury. The witness should be aware that descriptive words may literally alter the character of a question, the inferences created by the question, and any answer they may provide. Some examples are listed below:

Noun	Adjective	Loaded Phrase
event	"deadly"	deadly event
accident	"foreseeable"	foreseeable accident
accident	"tragic"	tragic accident
danger	"known"	known danger
risk	"foreseeable"	foreseeable risk
risk	"unnecessary"	unnecessary risk
incident	"unfortunate"	unfortunate incident

incident	"avoidable"	avoidable accident
injury	"terrible"	terrible injury
death	"needless"	needless death
act	"intentional"	intentional act
transaction	"dishonest"	dishonest transaction
transaction	"fraudulent"	fraudulent transaction
conduct	"careless"	careless conduct
conduct	"harmful"	harmful conduct
conduct	"secretive"	secretive conduct

Like adjectives, adverbs are word enhancers. They are used to convey augmented "action" or add a heightened zest to verbs. Here are a few examples that frequently find their way into aggressive questions. They can be quickly recognized as the "Y" words:

Very

Especially

Hardly

Poorly

Maliciously

Dangerously

Recklessly

Fraudulently

Consciously

Carelessly

Largely

Knowingly

Purposefully

Intentionally

Reasonably

Unreasonably

Necessarily

Probably

Possibly

Likely

Every witness should be counseled to listen to each sentence, spot the drama words, spot the "Y" words, and make sure that his or her answer is accurate. A mere "yes" or "no" to loaded questions using drama words may result in the witness's adoption of the lawyer's dramatic characterizations and the *pathos* and *ethos* of the opposing case, and this is precisely what opposing counsel intends. Thus, every witness must understand that such characterizations are loaded to benefit one side and meant to harm the witness and the other party. The witness should acquire a heightened sensitivity to this word play and, frankly, gamesmanship.

When responding to loaded questions, every witness should be counseled that he or she can disagree with unfair descriptions or inferences built into the question. Again, by answering "yes" or "no" to these questions, the witness adopts the lawyer's words. Alternatively, a fair response can be prefaced with a statement that the witness disagrees with the lawyer's characterizations, and then proceed with a specific answer. This diffuses the bullet in the loaded question. The witness also may rephrase the question in the response, making it clear that the witness is eliminating the unfair words or phrases, and then provide a specific answer. By qualifying responses in this manner, the sting of the question is removed. Again, every witness is different in terms of his or her capability of handling aggressive lawyers and difficult questions. Practice is always helpful and will enhance the witness's comfort level in the most challenging deposition.

Restating the Question

Another effective technique is to have the witness restate the question as part of the answer. This serves at least three purposes.

First, by restating the question, the witness is forced to listen to each word in each question carefully, thereby making sure the entire question and all of the various words (adjectives, adverbs, etc.) are properly considered. This allows the witness an opportunity to make sure that the question is fully understood.

Second, by utilizing this technique, the witness can rarely be criticized for being nonresponsive. While restating the question, the witness can repudiate the entire question or a portion of the question by disagreeing with specific words or inferences created by the question. Moreover, by restating the question as part of the answer, the witness reduces the risk of any objection that he or she is not cooperative and responsive. The jury will likely perceive the witness as cooperative.

Third, this practice allows the witness to better manage the pace of the deposition by providing more time to fashion an appropriate response. This is particularly helpful when confronted with difficult questions. The whole question-and-answer process is slowed down significantly.

Identifying Compound Questions

Conjunctions are important words. The use of conjunctions in a question, such as "and," "either," "or," "neither," or "nor," suggests that there is more than one subject in the question, and that there are really two or more questions linked by a conjunctive word or phrase. These are known as "compound" questions, and they often present challenges to the witness and the lawyer. Although compound questions are sometimes harmless, this is not always the case. Did the witness answer "yes" to the first part of the question or did the witness answer "yes" to the second part of the question? The witness should be taught to spot this type of question and request the examining lawyer to break the question down into distinct parts before an answer is provided. The witness can also ask the court reporter to restate the question. This allows the witness an additional opportunity to make sure all of the moving parts are defined. It is good practice to do this even when the subject matter is benign, because it forces the witness to practice technique that improves performance when the going gets tougher.

Identifying Questions That Are Not Questions

Many loaded questions are not questions at all, but declarative statements that pretend to be questions. In reality, the examining lawyer is seeking from the witness a confirmation of the lawyer's words, and not the witness's testimony. One way to spot these types of questions are telltale phrases that are frequently used. The witness should be alerted to spot particular phrases as red flags. Such phrases betray the fact that the lawyer is not interested in narrative testimony but is seeking confirmation of the lawyer's spin on the facts. These "facts" are frequently inflammatory or beneficial to just one side of the case. Here are some examples:

Signal Phrases

Isn't it reasonable that … [declarative statement]

Isn't it fair to say that … [declarative statement]

Isn't it correct to say that … [declarative statement]

Isn't it possible that … [declarative statement])

Isn't it probable that … [declarative statement]

Isn't it likely that … [declarative statement]

Would you agree with me that … [declarative statement]

Would it be fair to say that … [declarative statement]

Would it be reasonable to conclude that … [declarative statement]

Do you not agree that… [declarative statement]

Sometimes the question is flipped. Sometimes the phrase comes at the beginning of a declarative sentence, and sometimes afterwards. Under either scenario, such questions seek to corner the witness into a "yes" or "no" answer using the lawyer's words, not the witness's words. The witness should be familiar with this technique and exercise caution when answering. Again, the witness should be instructed to explain his or her answer fully, if necessary, and not feel restricted to just providing a mere "yes" or "no."

Every witness needs to know that he or she cannot be forced to answer questions without an opportunity to explain. The witness also needs to be encouraged to at least request the right to explain an answer or, if he or she disagrees with the inferences created by the question, to say so plainly. This encouragement will have a positive effect on the witness's self-confidence during the deposition, and this added comfort will translate into improved performance.

The "Possibility" Questions

The use of so-called "possibility" questions frequently surfaces in depositions, and these questions are usually veiled attempts to have witnesses speculate. Human nature is such that most witnesses want to be agreeable with others in social settings when they engage in informal conversation. Trial lawyers know this, and they may try to lure the witness into agreeing with notions that all things are possible. However, before walking into the deposition room, every witness should understand that this is not the case.

Quite simply, some things are not possible. In the pale of human experience, we know that the sun will rise tomorrow, and that this is a reasonable certainty. Although not scientifically guaranteed, we have virtual assurance that a new dawn will rise tomorrow, the next day, and every day thereafter. It is not possible that the sun will not rise.

Likewise, certain events may not be possible within the realm of a witness's personal experiences. Because of the witness's lifetime of learning and acquired habits, it may not be possible that he or she did certain things on a specific date contrary to established habits, even though he or she may not have a recollection of what happened on a specific date.

Lawyers frequently try to take advantage of a witness's lack of specific memory to usher in "possibilities." But, even in the absence of a distinct memory of a specific event on a specific date, the witness does have a lifetime of memories that may be relied upon. The following example illustrates this point:

> Whether the plaintiff was wearing a seatbelt when he crashed and rolled over in the vehicle was a significant issue. However, the plaintiff, who was seriously injured, had no memory of the event, having been rendered unconscious. The defense lawyer taking the deposition tried to take advantage of the plaintiff's failed memory and posed a question in the following manner: "Isn't it possible that you were not wearing your seatbelt?" Having no specific recollection of the events, the witness could be lulled into conceding this possibility. But, in fact, the witness knows that his standard habit is to always wear a seatbelt. Thus, the witness can be properly instructed on how to handle this question. A reasonable (and honest) answer to the question could be that "No, I do not believe it is possible given my custom and habit to always wear a seatbelt."

By explaining his answer, the witness remains responsive to the question. Some things are just not possible. A witness has personal knowledge of his customs, habits, and personal practices. The witness should invoke this knowledge even though he or she has no specific recollection of a particular event.

Another example involves "inferred knowledge." Although a witness should not speculate as to what is in someone else's mind, a witness can reasonably and reliably infer facts from surrounding circumstances and personal knowledge of those circumstances. Here is an example of inferred knowledge:

> A witness might be asked: "Would you agree that it is possible that John Doe reasonably relied upon the financial misstatements in the summary proforma?" The witness can legitimately answer: "No. That is not reasonably possible because John Doe had a team of auditors and outside financial experts who investigated the finances of the company for several days prior to the investment that John Doe made."

Again, some things are not possible because they defy common sense due to the surrounding circumstances. A witness may reasonably infer facts dictated by common sense, logic, and the witness's personal experiences in life.

Summary Questions

Many lawyers use a technique of summarizing a witness's testimony, then asking the witness to confirm the accuracy of that summary. The examining lawyer is effectively asking the witness to commit under oath that the lawyer's summary accurately reflects the totality of facts with nothing more to be added or supplemented by the witness. All witnesses should listen for these types of questions and recognize that the lawyer is trying to "box in" the witness and eliminate further flexibility that the witness may need. Sometimes, the lawyer places a self-serving spin on this summary. So, once the witness makes sure there is no improper spin, he or she can legitimately condition any answer by indicating that the summary is based upon the witness's *current* recollection, and the witness reserves the right to supplement the list as needed. This caveat allows the witness to supplement the testimony at a later date, if necessary.

Sound Bites From Documents

Witnesses should be thoroughly counseled concerning techniques for handling questions involving exhibits. An examining lawyer may take a multipage letter or document, then focus the witness's attention on a solitary sentence or phrase. The obvious risk is that the lawyer is taking the sentence or phrase out of context, whereas the entire document needs to be reviewed to place the pending question into context. All witnesses should be encouraged to read as much of the document as reasonably necessary to understand how the spotlighted sentence fits into the larger context. The witness also should be encouraged to resist any demand that just one sentence or a single phrase be considered without reference to the remainder of the document. The goal should always be truth, and truth can be lost through manipulation of words and taking concepts out of fair context. Putting things back into fair and reasonable context serves the objective of truth.

An additional benefit of looking at the complete document involves time management. If the witness properly invokes the right to look at the whole document before answering a question, the witness can utilize this additional time to better articulate an answer to the pending question. The witness should never feel rushed into answering any question at any time. Reviewing the complete document provides justification for taking more time to formulate an appropriate and truthful answer.

Freedom to Pause

Witnesses are not prisoners shackled to a chair in a *Star Chamber*. They have rights, and they should be reminded of these rights. Witnesses should be encouraged to take breaks when fatigued or when they need relief from the intensity of the examination. A witness who desires to talk to his or her lawyer has the right to do so. However, the witness should be encouraged not to overuse this privilege because it may be perceived as abusive. Most witnesses will be comforted to know, however, that this important right exists.

Interestingly, there are some jurisdictions, particularly in Europe, that prohibit lawyers from talking to witnesses once a deposition begins. Substantive communications between the lawyer and the witness off the record are not allowed during breaks. This restriction has been enforced in cases pending in the United States, but where the witness resides in Europe and was represented by counsel in Europe. In one instance, no one was allowed to have a substantive discussion with the witness off the record after the deposition began.

Most jurisdictions (and also lawyers) frown upon breaks if a question is pending. The idea is that the witness should not be allowed to receive assistance after a question is posed but not yet answered. Taking a break while a question is pending also does not look good to the jury. An exception, however, exists if the witness believes the question encroaches upon privileged communications. In such instances, the witness should be encouraged to make clear he or she needs legal advice to determine if the pending question can be answered. The presenting lawyer should insist on this right.

Clearly, a witness may not fully understand the scope of the attorney-client privilege and what communications are protected. The "pause" button should be pushed when this confusion occurs to make sure the privilege is protected. This same consideration applies to trade secrets or other highly confidential or proprietary information. The witness may have legitimate concerns that a specific question calls for the disclosure of highly sensitive information, and the witness should consult with legal counsel on this point before responding.

Understanding The Question

An important lesson for every witness is that he or she is not required to answer vague questions. A deposition is not a test of whether the witness can interpret a lawyer's meaning or decipher poorly crafted or unintelligible questions. The witness is not required to answer questions that he or she does not understand, and the witness is not required to guess at the meaning of a question or be forced to speculate. If the witness understands this important right, the witness will be more at ease with the examination.

Ambiguity is the enemy of accuracy and ambiguity is frequently the enemy of truth. Therefore, the witness should be taught to listen to each question and make sure that a complete understanding is reached *in his or her mind* before proceeding with any answer. To do this, the witness should be taught to listen to *each* word in *each* question. If there is any doubt as to the intended meaning, then the witness should request that the question be restated. In theory, this request may be repeated as often as needed until the witness feels comfortable with proceeding with an answer. When in doubt, the witness can (and should) ask the court reporter to repeat the question to ascertain whether the question is fatally vague or answerable. A case in point illustrates this practice:

> A street-smart but inexperienced witness was asked to identify his address. In response, he indicated he did not understand the question. He was asked the question again, and he again responded he did not understand. When probed, the witness stated he was confused about whether the lawyer was seeking his "residence," "business," or "mailing" address.

Although this example is extreme, if not silly, it illustrates the point that language can be inherently ambiguous. Words may have different meanings to different people and may change depending upon context. Here, the word "address" could mean one of several locations, and the witness had a right to specificity. Indeed, every witness has this right and should request the examining lawyer ask questions that the witness personally understands. The witness is the only person in the deposition room who can say with certainty whether the questions make sense or not.

Obviously, witnesses should act reasonably. If questions are readily understandable, then the witness should make a good faith attempt to answer. If the witness consistently demands that questions be restated or rephrased, such demands will appear evasive and the witness may lose credibility with counsel, the judge, and the jury. Therefore, all witnesses should be counseled to exercise their rights when needed, but to do so while striking a balance. Reasonableness is always the litmus test.

Making Mistakes

All witnesses—veterans and beginners alike—will make mistakes during the course of a lengthy deposition. This is inevitable because a deposition is, by definition, an antagonistic environment with lawyers—some of whom are very skilled, pushing and cajoling witnesses with word play. Thus, mistakes will be made, and some mistakes may be "unforced errors" due to fatigue or distraction.

Thus, a presenting lawyer should make sure the witness does not get swallowed up by a mistake and lose focus or concentration for the next questions. If the witness is preoccupied with an earlier misstatement, the witness's performance level will drop rapidly, which will compound the error. Professional athletes are reminded not to get caught up in slips or errors. To do so will jeopardize performance overall. Witnesses are no different, and they should be reminded it is okay to make mistakes; and even if an error is made, the mistake can likely be resolved through later examination.

Witnesses should not feel that the weight of the world is on their shoulders. If they feel the case rises or falls on their testimony, they will likely stumble under the stress. Most mistakes can be fixed, and the witness needs to understand this.

If permitted by the applicable rules, the presenting lawyer should discuss any significant mistake with the witness during a break and advise the witness on how to correct the error if and when an opportunity arises. These breaks are also opportunities to bolster the witness's positive attitude. The witness should not be overly criticized during a break, but should be encouraged and given confidence.

Examining lawyers, particularly less experienced lawyers, frequently ask questions that invite opportunities for correction. A well-prepared witness can take advantage of these opportunities if they arise. In some cases, it may be advisable for the witness to state simply on the record that an error was made and ask for an opportunity to clarify the prior response. It is rare the examining lawyer will refuse such a request.

Pace and Tempo

Many skilled lawyers seek to control the witness through the tempo by which questions are asked. Experienced trial lawyers know that tempo is important for a variety of reasons. The appearance of control is important psychologically. Quick questions prevent a witness from regaining composure during difficult questioning. Rapid-fire questions also keep the witness off-guard and may cause the witness to rush or stumble when answering. A quick change in tempo may have a similar effect. Significant voice inflections are frequently used to catch a witness off-guard. A sudden explosion of righteous indignation may startle a witness and cause the witness to lose composure or concentration.

Some lawyers alternate between a slow pace and a quickened pace to remain unpredictable. If the witness can predict the lawyer's tempo, then the witness gains comfort and control. However, if the tempo is changed, the witness becomes more uncomfortable. A jury that later listens to and views the video will be intrigued by the rhythm and counter-rhythm of the examination. They will also see any insecurity or discomfort exhibited by the witness. The examining lawyer will certainly seek to control the tempo because it communicates to the observer (the jury) that the lawyer is in control. This makes the examination more forceful and persuasive; it also creates the impression the lawyer is "winning" and the witness is "losing."

Thus, a witness should be taught to "expect the unexpected" and should understand that there are many ways he or she can exert control over the pace of the examination. The witness should be reminded that depositions are not timed tests; thus, the witness should take time to listen to each question and never feel rushed in responding. After all, the deposition is important to all parties.

The witness should not feel compelled to answer questions based upon a tempo set by the examining lawyer. If the witness wants to slow the pace, reduce the intensity, pause, and think about the answers, then the witness should do so. This is particularly true when looking at documents because a witness should never be rushed when undertaking a document review.

Here are some examples of witness techniques to better control the tempo of the deposition:

- If appropriate, the witness can ask to see specific documents relevant to a pending question.

- The witness may ask the court reporter to repeat a question.

- The witness may ask the examining lawyer to restate a question if there is any legitimate concern that the question is ambiguous, confusing, or not fully understood.

- The witness may ask for a break in the deposition if no question is pending.

- The witness can restate the question as part of the witness's answer; this allows the witness to focus on all of the words within the question, allowing a better understanding of the question, but it has the added benefit of slowing down the tempo of the deposition.

Testimony About Documents

There are special techniques witnesses should employ when reviewing documents in deposition. All witnesses should be encouraged to take time to read and understand all pertinent portions of a document and not feel rushed. The witness can simply tell the examining lawyer that he or she wants to read the *entire* document and make sure the *context* of the question is understood. Of course, the opposing lawyer may protest and object but, unless the witness is acting unreasonably, such protestations will not sit well with a court.

Again, the conduct of the participants in a deposition should be reasonable. This applies to the lawyers and the witnesses alike. It would be unreasonable for a witness to insist upon reviewing a 50-page document to answer one question concerning a specific paragraph on a specific page. It is doubtful the entirety of an extended document needs to be read to put such a question into appropriate context. Accordingly, a witness should be counseled to always review enough of a document to ensure proper context for a pending question, but he or she should not abuse this privilege needlessly. Because many depositions are subject to time limits, the presenting lawyer can always offer to "go off the record" if a lengthy document needs to be reviewed. The converse also is true. The examining lawyer can insist to "go off the record" to preserve time while the witness is reviewing a lengthy document.

Witnesses also should ask to see documents if needed to refresh their memory. If one document is presented to the witness, but the witness wishes to see another document for context, then there is nothing improper in making such a request.

By requesting an opportunity to see documents during the examination, the witness effectively shifts the burden to the examining lawyer. The tempo of the deposition is changed, and the witness begins to exert control over this tempo. The examining lawyer is then confronted with a dilemma. Either the document is shown to the witness as requested or the examining lawyer ignores or refuses the request. If the latter occurs, the witness should be instructed to "stay the course" and reurge the request to see the document before any further response. If the examining lawyer still refuses to comply, the lawyer becomes the "bad guy." The witness has a justification to later amend or modify any response to the question; alternatively, the witness can simply state that the question cannot be answered without looking at the requested documents.

5

Overview of Video Depositions

Capturing The Jury's Attention

Video depositions present great opportunities to advance your case—or lose it. Once a videographer's lights are lit, the witness is sworn, and the camera rolls, then the action begins. What follows has the potential to captivate, bore, or alienate the jury. Repackaged for the courtroom, a jury will watch a video deposition just like a television show or a movie. The courtroom lights will be dimmed, and the jury will watch the video monitors with expectation because the jury wants to see drama. Thus, the lawyer's job is akin to that of a movie director; like a director, the goal is to deliver a drama with an appealing storyline. Simply put, the goal is to capture and hold the jury's attention and do so with logic, emotion, and credibility. Again, these are the cornerstones of advocacy—*pathos, logos,* and *ethos.* Video depositions are always an excellent advocacy tool.

All jurors lose mental focus at some point—some more rapidly than others. This is a predictable reality that every trial lawyer should recognize. Successful Hollywood producers know this about their audience, and that is why they keep the plot of a film moving forward, building toward a crescendo. They are seeking to hold the audience's attention. Advertising agencies follow this strategy as well, where the goal is to deliver marketing messages in a short period of time. The marketing goal is to "grab" the audience quickly. All of this holds true for video depositions in a lawsuit.

The goal is to generate captivating sound bites that can be edited and spliced together to form a powerful package of testimony. Movies and television shows are edited this way; in fact, media presentations are nothing more than a string of sound bites (or scenes) connected to tell a story. They are edited to capture and retain the audience's attention. The editing and use of video depositions at trial is similar.

What is a sound bite? In essence, a sound bite is a group of thematically linked questions and answers that are particularly compelling, dramatic, or inflammatory. Developing sound bites is a typical technique used by the television press when conducting news interviews. A televised interview may actually last for several minutes or even longer, but the newscast only shows a few questions and answers calculated to communicate a specific message to the audience. The obvious risk of this technique, of course, is that sound bites can be lifted out of context to distort the intent or meaning of the person interviewed. In a deposition setting, this shifts the burden to the attorney presenting the witness to minimize negative sound bites that hurt the witness or the case.

There are numerous studies that show that a jury's attention span begins to wane in as little as 17–20 minutes.[1] There is further evidence that the first 4 minutes of a presentation are critical in determining whether a juror will remain focused for the balance of the presentation.[2] This puts a premium on capturing the jury's attention at the beginning of any presentation with dramatic appeal. Otherwise, the lawyer may quickly lose the jury's focus. Thus, the lawyer should cultivate deposition testimony with these objectives in mind, then edit that testimony in a manner calculated to keep the presentation exciting.

One of the worst things to do in trial is to play hours upon hours of video depositions with boring subject matter or unnecessary testimony. Likewise, presenting an extended deposition of one witness to the jury that lasts for hours is never a good idea. The jury will quit paying attention.

Some testimony may be technically relevant, but still boring. Regardless of relevance, continued repetition of the same or similar facts from the same witness will dull the presentation. The temptation to use all of a video deposition should be avoided whenever possible, and only key testimony should be used. This helps keep the presentation crisp and interesting.

To help guide the editing process, one rule of thumb is to keep deposition excerpts to an effective maximum of 20-minute snippets or less. Some lawyers and jury consultants recommend even less, with video clips no longer than 10 minutes. Thus, assuming that the deposition of a witness lasts up to 7 hours in many jurisdictions, the examining lawyer has ample opportunity to mine effective testimony "nuggets."

Because a jury actually sees the witness in a video deposition, the jury will make judgments concerning the witness's trustworthiness. The jury invariably evaluates witness performance not only on substantive levels, but also on visceral

---

[1] *See*, e.g., Amy Singer, *Using Psychology to Win in Court*, Trial Consultants, Inc., http://www.trialconsultants. com/Library/UsingPsychologytoWin.html (last visited June 14, 2016) (noting that "research indicates that jurors have roughly a 17-minute attention span; and that the first four minutes the attorney speaks will determine whether the jurors pay attention for the remaining 13 minutes.").

[2] *Id.*

or subjective levels. This is where the intangibles come into play, such as "likeabil-ity," "credibility," "evasiveness," "aloofness," or "nervousness." This is also where the *ethos* or "trustworthiness" of a witness is manifested or, as the case may be, destroyed by an effective cross-examination or poor witness demeanor.

An examining lawyer may purposefully try to make the witness feel uncom-fortable, thus appearing less likable and not trustworthy. The lawyer presenting the witness has the opposite goal. This is why simple factors such as lighting conditions, surrounding environment, clothing, posture, and eye contact are important. This is also why preparing the witness for an aggressive examination is always important. These all become particularly significant considerations in a video environment.

Effective preparations apply to both sides of the table. The examining lawyer must be prepared because he or she is essentially taking a trial deposition. Extended pauses between questions or fumbling with exhibits are highlighted in a video record. Sloppy examination styles will become apparent. Boring ques-tions will be evident and ultimately ignored. Confusing, compound questions will lose the jury. Thus, the examination strategy should be well planned, and the questions crisp and concise. Exhibits should be organized much like an examination in the open courtroom.

The converse is also true. The lawyer tendering the witness should devote suf-ficient time to prepare the witness for the emotional stress of sitting in the deposi-tion "hot seat" under the bright lights and harsh lens of a camera. After all, what is at stake is the creation of trial testimony that will either be helpful or harmful. No one should underestimate the power of an effective video deposition and the 20-minute sound bites that can echo and resonate with a jury.

Using Videos: Other Considerations

Trial lawyers should be strategic in how they use video depositions at trial. As a general guideline, depositions should not be used as evidence at the beginning or end of a trial. The goal in every trial is to develop immediate momentum, and live witnesses are typically more effective in generating this momentum. Lawyers also want to end their case with a bang by presenting a live witness who is charismatic or particularly sympathetic. They want a "closer." As such, deposition excerpts are generally utilized as substantive evidence in the middle of a party's case-in-chief. By structuring the order of proof in this manner, depo-sitions are strategically flanked by live testimony.

It is unwise to have hours of deposition testimony uninterrupted by live wit-nesses. Too many depositions in succession will numb the jury. Again, after sev-eral video exposures, the jury will become increasingly more resistant to or bored with the deposition process. It is therefore recommended that live testi-mony be used to break up multiple deposition presentations.

Depositions should be edited for maximum impact. Extended deposition excerpts should be avoided. Sound bites should be used to create maximum impact, drama, and emotion. Opposing counsel may seek to integrate deposition excerpts under the rule of optional completeness, and many courts may require that all parties' excerpts be integrated into one presentation. However, unless ordered by the court, the trial lawyer should resist any invitation to integrate video presentations with the excerpts of the opposing party. This is because integration dilutes the impact of the presentation, which should be avoided if possible. This is particularly so for plaintiffs who are starting their case.

Making Witnesses Feel Comfortable in Video Depositions

It is important to make witnesses feel as comfortable as possible before entering the deposition room. Speaking in front of a video camera is never easy for a typical witness, and this challenge is compounded by the stress of confronting an antagonistic lawyer in an unfamiliar environment. This is particularly true if the witness has limited or no prior deposition experience.[3]

It makes good sense to show the witness the deposition room beforehand, where he or she will be sitting, and where the camera will be located. Placing the witness in the hot seat will help the witness visualize the experience and reduce real-time anxiety when the deposition begins. Professional athletes are taught to visualize successful performances, and witnesses should be instructed in the same manner. An anxious witness will not perform at the same level as a self-confident witness. Knowledge about the deposition process is an important way to enhance this comfort.

A thorough witness preparation session promotes confidence and makes the witness feel more comfortable. Spending time with the witness gives the witness the comfort that the lawyer is on the witness's team. It also increases the witness's mastery of documents and facts. All of this increases the witness's comfort level in the face of stress.

Another way to enhance self-confidence is to increase the witness's understanding of the unknown. This can be done through a mock examination where the witness is exposed to an aggressive examination in a practice session. The goal here is to push the witness aggressively so the witness is no longer fearful of the unknown but actually experiences what may happen in the deposition room. It helps the witness toughen up mentally and be prepared for the unexpected.

---

[3] Various ways of making witnesses feel comfortable with the deposition process apply equally to depositions where no video record is created. These techniques are discussed in detail in Chapter 4, *supra*.

Mock Examinations

A mock examination challenges the witness with difficult questions and documents. The witness should be pressured aggressively to test newly acquired skills in spotting bad questions, loaded questions, and framing correct answers under stress. If possible, it is good practice to have another lawyer conduct the mock examination. Adding a new, previously unknown personality to the exercise enhances the learning experience. The new lawyer is an unknown quantity and will enhance the realism of the exercise.

A mock examination should be long enough to give the witness an appreciation of the pressure that can be imposed by an aggressive lawyer. The examining lawyer should use a variety of questioning techniques so the witness can practice spotting and responding to loaded questions, summary questions, duty questions, etc.[4] Variety in the types of questions gives the witness a real taste of what to expect.

Mock drills should be undertaken toward the end of a preparation session so the witness is first instructed on basic techniques and deposition etiquette. The preparation session should already have included a discussion of trial themes, key issues, types of questions to look out for, and techniques for responding to difficult questions. The mock examination is then used to test the witness and what the witness has learned, and to then identify where improvement is needed.

Any mock session should leave enough time at the end to discuss the results and to build the witness back up. No one wants to aggressively cross-examine the witness, have the witness do poorly, lose confidence, and then have no follow-up encouragement. The goal is to inspire confidence, not diminish that confidence. No lawyer wants a crestfallen witness walking into the deposition room.

Practice Videotapes

Another available tool is to videotape a mock examination so the witness can personally observe and gauge his or her performance. This is an excellent teaching tool. The witness can see specific examples of body language and demeanor and will more readily appreciate the process because a picture (or video) is worth a thousand words.

When used with a client or client representative, a video practice session is likely protected as attorney-work product or as a privileged attorney-client communication. However, it is recommended that the laws of each jurisdiction be

---

[4] These type of questions are discussed in Chapter 4, *infra*.

consulted to ensure these videos are not discoverable under some exception to privilege. The last thing any lawyer wants to encounter is a motion to compel discovery of a practice video. Therefore, the best practice is to make sure the use and creation of the practice video is exempt from discovery. The use of practice videos is not recommended with third-party witnesses or experts because they will be discoverable. The opposing lawyer may try to use such videos to embarrass the lawyer and witness in front of the jury.

Suitable Attire

Jurors come into the courtroom with preconceived expectations of how people should dress and act, and they expect witnesses and lawyers to conform to these expectations. Any departure from these preconceived notions may cause jurors to feel puzzled or even alienated. Thus, every witness should be advised to dress respectfully and consistently with his or her professional background.

There are studies on how to dress effectively for successful job interviews. The same holds true for a witness in a courtroom or deposition setting. The goal is always to make good first impressions because these impressions invariably last. The target audience is the jury. Unflattering attire is distracting and potentially alienating to a jury. Opposing counsel is also sizing up the witness and how the witness's favorable or unfavorable characteristics may impact the case.

As a general proposition, witnesses should dress conservatively and appropriately. A corporate executive should not appear for deposition in a t-shirt and blue jeans, and business executives should lose expensive-looking watches. Similarly, a female witness should not wear expensive-looking or gaudy jewelry. A businessman should typically wear a coat and a tie. Flamboyant clothing with exciting patterns or colors should be avoided because such clothing will be distracting. Conservative clothing is generally preferred.

Clothing color is important. There have been studies concerning what colors are most effective with a jury as used in visual aides. Certain guidelines can be inferred from these studies on the issue of clothing and its impact in the courtroom. For men, it appears that solid bright ties will capture a jury's attention. Red is a preferred color for commanding attention.[5] Blue is perceived as a soothing color and is associated with trust.[6] Earth tones (such as tans or browns) have been found to be appealing and well received.[7] Black and grays ("lawyer colors")

---

[5] Amy Singer, *Using Psychology to Win in Court*, Trial Consultants, Inc., http://www.trialconsultants.com/Library/UsingPsychologytoWin.html (last visited June 14, 2016).

[6] *Id.*

[7] Katherine James, *Costuming for the Courtroom*, Plaintiff Mag. (Feb. 2008), *available at* http://www.plaintiff-magazine.com/TOC%20Feb08%20page.html (follow "Costuming for the courtroom" hyperlink).

are not recommended for witnesses.[8] Again, the goal is to present a positive image to the jury, not a boorish image. Here are some simple, but illustrative recommendations of what not to do:

- A former CEO of a manufacturing company wore a noticeably expensive watch during his examination in a wrongful death case. The plaintiff's counsel went out of his way to repeatedly hand the witness documents in a manner that forced the witness to expose the watch on dozens of occasions; the jury had been preconditioned to stare at this expensive watch with any visible movements of the witness's hand.

- An eyewitness in a death case appeared for deposition wearing a t-shirt with a pack of cigarettes rolled in one of the sleeves. He was encouraged to smoke during the deposition, which he did frequently, causing a fog of smoke to curl around his face as he testified. The jury would spend more time watching the curling smoke than listening to the testimony which also degraded the witness's appearance. The plaintiffs' counsel ultimately dismissed certain claims to which the witness's testimony was relevant.

- A corporate witness appeared for deposition with a coat and tie, as encouraged by his lawyer, but he sported shorts and tennis shoes. Although the video camera did not focus below the table, the witness made a poor impression. He did not appear to be taking the deposition seriously, even though it was a significant case.

- A director of a nursing home appeared for deposition in a wrongful death case involving an elderly resident-patient. The witness was adorned with several gaudy rings. The plaintiff's lawyer had a field day. He alternately inflated the witness's ego, then cut the witness down to size. It had a dramatic effect in the video testimony, particularly with a video focus on the witness's jewelry.

Posture, Demeanor, and Seating Position

Every witness should be given guidance on good posture. Unfortunately, too many depositions are taken where the examining lawyer may try to make the witness appear uncomfortable. The witness, therefore, should be taught to maintain a consistent posture to avoid the appearance that he or she is uncomfortable or uncertain in responding to questions. The witness should never slouch in the witness chair, but should always sit upright. Most importantly, the witness

---

[8] *Id.*

should never lose his or her temper; he or she should always remain polite and calm, even if baited to behave otherwise.

There are different schools of thought about the direction a witness should face when answering questions. One school believes the witness should face the video camera; this suggestion is endorsed by those who believe that it makes the witness seem "strong" or in control. The effect, however, frequently appears contrived and artificial. Because the camera lens becomes the eye of the jury, the video camera provides the angle and perspective the jury will have to judge the witness's demeanor, body language, and substantive testimony. If the witness consistently looks straight into the camera with each answer, the jurors may be turned off and avert their eyes. The jury may see the witness as a "talking head," staring through the camera lens as if lecturing those in the jury box.

A recommended option is to have the witness face the examining attorney and make eye contact with that attorney. This posture is less aggressive to a watchful jury, and it is the same strategy used by television news reporters when conducting press interviews for the evening news. This style is more conversational, less intrusive, and more credible. The jury is not "pushed" away but pulled into the conversation. This posture also conveys a sense of confidence. The witness, far from appearing intimidated by opposing counsel, appears self-assured such that the witness is consistently making eye contact with the opposing counsel. The jury members see this fact, and it has a positive effect on their feelings about the witness. It is also more impressive to opposing counsel. A witness who constantly avoids eye contact with the examining lawyer will leave a bad impression. The witness appears weak, defensive, or unsure.

Witness Tics and Body Language

Body language provides signals to a jury (and opposing counsel) about who we are and how we feel at any given moment. Body language can telegraph confidence or insecurity; it can also telegraph deceit, fear, anger, and untrustworthiness. Every witness should be reminded of these facts and instructed with some simple lessons for the deposition room:

- Witnesses should be encouraged not to cross their arms. It sends a negative cue of defensiveness, unfriendliness, anger, or defiance.

- Witnesses should not fidget or make excessive movements before the video camera. Repeated hand or other body movements are distracting. The jury will focus less on the testimony and more on the sudden jerks or movements. Such fidgeting also may be interpreted as a lack of confidence or nervousness. Again, the witness should be encouraged to sit upright in the chair, with hands folded on the table or in his or her lap.

- The witness should be instructed to minimize head movement between questions and answers. Repeated head movement is distracting and can be misleading.

If the witness looks to his or her lawyer each time a question is asked, the witness appears uncertain or untrustworthy, as if seeking help or confirmation of the answers. Therefore, the witness should be counseled not to look back at the presenting counsel before an answer; the impact of looking toward the sponsoring lawyer is almost always negative.

Another bad habit is for the witness to look to his or her attorney after providing an answer. The jury may infer that the witness is unsure of the answer and is seeking ratification. Alternatively, the jury may infer that the witness is particularly pleased with the answer and appears "cocky" or not appropriately serious. Both inferences can be damaging to the witness's credibility and likability.

The Witness as Part of a Team

Every client witness should be encouraged to feel that he or she is a member of a team. The witness is in partnership with the presenting lawyer. Therefore, a good working relationship is important, and the witness must trust the lawyer. The witness must also believe the lawyer will protect his or her interests during the deposition; this includes protecting the witness from abusive questioning or other offensive conduct.

One way to reinforce this partnership is to let the witness know that the lawyer will be seated immediately adjacent to the witness during the deposition, which should give the witness added comfort. The witness should also be told that the lawyer will endeavor to control the timing of breaks and will not allow extensive examination without some pause in the action. At the deposition, the lawyer should insist on sitting immediately adjacent to the witness. The opposing counsel should never be seated next to the witness, but should be next to the court reporter who sits between the witness and examining counsel. Some physical separation is appropriate to prevent the examining lawyer from invading the witness's space.

Environmental Considerations

Basic environmental factors should be considered before every video deposition. This includes an inspection of the physical layout of the deposition room, as well as the seating positions of the witness and the lawyers. The lawyer should evaluate whether there are any lighting issues, visual distractions, or noise distractions that may impact the quality of the video. Some of these variables can be controlled, while others are beyond an attorney's control. However, there should be no doubt that simple environmental factors may favor one side or the other.

The backdrop of a deposition room is like a stage. A lawyer, like a director of a drama, should try to control the stage to enhance the finished product. Backgrounds convey subtle, and not so subtle, messages to the observer. That is why many professional videographers use neutral background screens. These screens are portable and are typically brought to the deposition by the videographer. However, there will be cases where these screens are not available, or where one lawyer seeks to control (or manipulate) the surroundings to his or her client's advantage and to the disadvantage of the opposing party. Here are some real-life examples:

- A video deposition in cramped quarters with few chairs, many lawyers, and lots of bulky video equipment may make the witness feel "caged" or claustrophobic.

- A video deposition in a lawyer's library with a backdrop of legal books may add an air of importance or seriousness to the deposition and may actually provide the witness with enhanced credibility; the witness may appear more intelligent, sophisticated, or trustworthy.

- A witness flanked by the American flag or other patriotic symbols may give the witness instant credibility and likeability; the opposing attorney should rightfully object to such contrivances and insist that the flag or other props be removed.

- A witness whose back is to a window will fight for the jury's attention if there are visible distractions from the outside. The jury's gaze will be drawn to movements outside the window behind the witness, and jurors will look past the witness. This type of setting also increases the risk of sound interference that may negatively impact the quality of the audio track.

- A witness who is facing a window may be distracted by outside activities, preventing the witness from fully concentrating on pending questions.

- A large, imposing piece of art behind a witness may cause a distraction to the jury; this is particularly true if the art incorporates loud colors that attract the observer's attention.

- A witness placed in direct sunlight may be forced to repeatedly blink. This makes the witness uncomfortable and will distract the jury; the sunlight also may cause color fade and washout in the background.

- A deposition of a dying or severely ill patient in a hospital setting will have a compelling effect; sympathy will resonate loudly in this setting.

- Witnesses are usually placed at the end of a conference table, and the video camera is typically focused on the upper torso and witness's head. The presenting lawyer should make sure there are no extraneous items on the table that may obstruct the view of the witness, such as coffee cups, soda cans, paper files, or other litter that could detract from the testimony.

- A dark, poorly lit room may cause shadows that detract attention away from the witness; appropriate and ample lighting should be insisted upon.

This is only a partial list. Professional videographers, like court reporters, should be neutral and unbiased. They should not take liberties at the behest of one lawyer over the other. Just like court reporters, their duty is to remain impartial. If videographers refuse to provide a neutral environment, then appropriate objections should be lodged. If significant prejudice is at risk, then the deposition should be adjourned and the court's direction obtained.

All parties to a lawsuit are entitled to a level playing field, and the deposition setting should not be tilted in favor of one party or the other. Thus, consistent with their professional obligations, videographers should take precautions to minimize visual and auditory distractions. This underscores the need for the lawyer to inspect the physical surroundings of the deposition before the deposition begins. This will provide an opportunity to make any needed changes or objections for what follows.

Other General Recommendations

Before deposition preparations end, the tendering lawyer should counsel the witness concerning other basic matters that can impact performance. First, the witness should be encouraged to get a good night's sleep and plenty of rest. Second, the witness should be encouraged not to consume excessive alcohol that could have residual effects on performance. Third, the witness should be advised to eat a healthy breakfast, avoiding sugar and sweets. Blood sugar levels change throughout the day, and no one wants a witness who crashes and burns because of significant changes in blood sugar. A high-energy meal is recommended. Fourth, the witness should be counseled concerning meals during the course of the deposition, most particularly lunch. A heavy meal is discouraged because it can adversely impact performance in the early afternoon. Lastly, the preparing lawyer should make sure there are no medications that the witness is required to take that might impact performance. In essence, the lawyer should underscore the importance of controlling all external variables that can potentially influence the witness's fatigue level and mental acuity.

6

Preparing For And Deposing Adverse Experts

Some expert witnesses are veterans in the courtroom, and they may be polished testifiers on the stand. Their savvy as trial witnesses poses special risks to the examining lawyer because their self-confidence and education may fill the average juror with awe. Thus, the trial court should exercise important gate-keeping functions to control what evidence the jury actually hears. Naïve jurors are vulnerable and may be lulled into accepting ill-founded opinions or they may give too much credibility to an expert who is not qualified. This potential scenario is why all trial lawyers should use the discovery processes, including depositions, to shed light on the weaknesses in an opposing expert's work product, the expert's opinions, the expert's potential bias, or deficiencies in the expert's qualifications. The goal is to illuminate weaknesses or flaws in the opposing expert's work product. Pre-trial depositions constitute an important tool for conducting this inquiry.

Although most states permit depositions of experts as a matter of procedural right, there are some exceptions. Some states prohibit expert depositions except upon leave of court or agreement of the parties; a few states limit expert discovery to written interrogatories. Many jurisdictions control the timing of expert discovery, with some courts sequencing discovery and requiring all fact discovery be completed before expert designations are allowed. However, expert depositions are typically allowed in at least 40 state jurisdictions. Moreover, as a practical matter, expert depositions go forward by agreement in almost all jurisdictions.

Pre-deposition research should be conducted before taking an expert's deposition. Important background information should be ascertained from an expert's published articles and abstracts, published case opinions that address the expert's credentials, and prior testimony in other cases. A variety of resources provide this type of information, ranging from professional associations to online computer services. Indeed, computer research is now an invaluable "go-to" resource that should be consulted as a matter of course. Using such information helps inform the lawyer's examination. Although most jurisdictions mandate disclosure of basic information about experts, independent research significantly enhances the examining lawyer's knowledge about these witnesses before the depositions begin.

Preparing a Game Plan

Specific goals for an expert's deposition should be identified as part of basic preparations, and a game plan is important. Although these goals will differ from case to case, there are common denominators underlying all cases. A deposition outline organized to address strategic goals is a valuable tool. A proposed, generic outline for deposing an expert is provided at the end of this chapter. It includes such basic topics as qualifications, motivation, bias, reliability of method, information considered by the witness, scope of the witness's opinions, and the basis for those opinions. A generic outline should be used as a foundation for an examination upon which case-specific questions can be layered.

"Boxing In" the Expert

Every deposition of an opposing expert should include questions that define the scope and extent of the witness's opinions, as well as the bases for those opinions. Although this practice may seem obvious to most lawyers, the objective is not always achieved. Seasoned experts may be skilled in the art of dodging questions. They know how to condition their answers, and they know how to build verbal loopholes into their testimony. They may be "masters of the caveat." Thus, a key strategy is to make sure the expert is "boxed in" so no different or new opinions are offered at trial. The examining lawyer should never leave the deposition without confidence that the universe of adverse opinions has been defined and that the opposing expert is constrained as to what opinions he or she can offer at trial.

Thus, every deposition should include a series of questions that confirm that all opinions have been identified and that the expert does not plan to do further work. If further work is anticipated, then this new work should be described in detail. Depending upon the nature and substance of any new work, a follow-up deposition may be required. An example of this type of examination is set forth in Chapter 7.

Saving Important Questions

An important goal is to create a foundation for the expert's cross-examination at trial. Most retained experts will appear at trial if they survive any relevant *Daubert* challenges. In any event, the examining lawyer should assume that the expert will be presented live. Accordingly, the trial lawyer should save key questions for cross-examination at trial and not give the expert or the other side a preview. The goal is to create a foundation for an effective cross-examination, not to forecast the examination before it occurs.

The most powerful questions at trial are questions that neither the expert nor opposing counsel anticipates. If all of the important questions are previewed during deposition, the expert and opposing counsel will take heed, try to repair the damage, and rehearse modified answers for the witness stand. Therefore, even if these critical questions are asked again during trial, much of the sting is taken from the question because the expert is likely prepared with a prompt response that diffuses the power of the question. The expert may attempt to confuse the record or recharacterize prior testimony.

The true art in taking an expert's deposition is to know what should be discovered in deposition and what should be left for trial. The deposition should not be used to showcase all of the strong points that can be used against the expert. That is like giving the enemy complete battle plans. The goal is to put the expert in a position where he or she has little flexibility to wiggle out of answers when confronted with difficult questions in the presence of the jury.

Laying The Foundation for an Expert Challenge

Yet another important objective is to lay the groundwork for limiting (or excluding) the expert's opinions because of flawed methodology or lack of qualifications. These are the so-called *Daubert* challenges, based upon the Supreme Court's decision in *Daubert v. Merrell Dow Pharmaceuticals, Inc.*[1] and a succession of cases that apply similar principles. Although some jurisdictions have not adopted *Daubert*, most state court jurisdictions apply some variation of the factors identified by the Supreme Court in *Daubert* or, alternatively, have developed special criteria that must be satisfied before expert opinions are admissible at trial.

As a general matter, expert opinions are admissible only if the opinions are offered by a qualified witness, the opinions are helpful to the jury, and the expert

---

[1] 509 U.S. 579 (1993).

uses a reliable method or reliable data.[2] An examining attorney should use these guiding principles as a framework for the deposition. This will include an examination as to:

1. Whether the expert is qualified.
2. Whether the expert opinion or method has been or can be tested.
3. Whether the opinions or methodology have been subjected to peer review or publication.
4. Whether there is a known rate of error in the expert's method.
5. Whether there has been compliance with applicable standards relating to methodology.
6. Whether the data upon which the expert relies is reliable.
7. Whether the expert's opinion has been limited or excluded in any prior case.

The level of general acceptance of an expert's opinion (and methodology) within the relevant scientific community should also be explored.[3] These principles, and how these guiding metrics are incorporated into a deposition outline, are discussed throughout this chapter.

Defining The Scope of an Expert's Work Product

Many jurisdictions require parties to exchange expert reports in advance of any depositions. In other jurisdictions, experts may be designated without reports, but summary descriptions are typically required that reasonably (and fairly) describe the expert's opinions and the basis for those opinions. These disclosures typically include a list of materials, data, and facts that the expert considered in forming his or her opinions. In some jurisdictions, no reports are necessary unless specially ordered by the court, and summaries of the expert's opinions or "disclosures," which are prepared by the lawyers, are used in lieu of formal reports.

In federal court, and in the many state jurisdictions that follow the Federal Rules, expert designations for retained experts are typically accompanied by a formal report *signed by the expert*. Importantly, the report should contain, among other things, a "complete statement of all opinions" and the bases for these opinions, including the "facts and data" considered by the expert.[4] At the time of an expert's disclosure, the designating party should identify any exhibits that the expert

---

[2] *See, e.g.,* Fed. R. Evid. 702, 703.

[3] *See, e.g., Daubert v. Merrell Dow Pharmaceuticals, Inc.,* 509 U.S. 579 (1993).

[4] *See* Fed. R. Civ. P. 26(a)(2)(B)(i), (ii).

intends to use, a list of the expert's publications for the last 10 years, and a list of the expert's trial and deposition testimony for the last 4 years.[5] Federal court designations also require identification of the expert's basis for compensation.[6]

Regardless of the jurisdiction, however, discovery processes in most jurisdictions typically provide the parties, and their counsel, with some meaningful detail concerning the scope of the expert's opinions and the foundation for those opinions. These disclosures provide an excellent starting point for preparing for the expert's deposition.

Document Requests or Duces Tecum

Under the Federal Rules, an expert must disclose "all facts and data" which the expert "considered."[7] In some state court jurisdictions, however, an expert may be required to disclose all materials reviewed by or provided to the expert. What is actually "considered" may be more limited than what was "provided to or reviewed by" the expert. Also, in some state court jurisdictions, where mandatory disclosures are not as broad as the federal practice, a good strategy is to use formal document requests or subpoenas *duces tecum* as part of the discovery process.

The rules of practice for each relevant jurisdiction should be consulted because jurisdictions likely differ concerning the scope of what documents and other expert information are properly discoverable. Each jurisdiction also may differ as to the proper procedure for obtaining this information. In jurisdictions allowing additional discovery from experts, a typical document request or subpoena *duces tecum* might include the following:

- The expert's *complete* file relating to the case.

- All written communications between the expert and opposing counsel.

- All draft reports (if discovery of draft reports is permitted).

- All billing records, invoices, and timesheets generated by the expert and any consultants working with the testifying expert.

- An updated and current CV.

- All published articles or treatises relevant to the issues (for as many years as permitted in the jurisdiction).

---

[5] *See* Fed. R. Civ. P. 26(a)(2)(B)(iii), (iv), and (v).
[6] *See* Fed. R. Civ. P. 26(a)(2)(B)(vi).
[7] *See* Fed. R. Civ. P. 26(a)(2)(B)(ii).

- A list that identifies the history of prior testimony (for as many years as permitted in the jurisdiction).

- All materials reviewed or considered by the expert in connection with the expert's involvement in the case.

- All exhibits used to support or that reflect the expert's opinions.

- All notes or other work product.

- All demonstrative evidence or models that may be used at trial.

Invoices and Billing Records

An expert's invoices and billing records are a valuable source of information about what an expert did or did not do in a particular case. Every deposition should devote some portion of the examination to questions about these records because they often yield important insights into the thoroughness of the underlying work product or deficiencies and gaps in that work product.

Billing records frequently provide descriptions of what an expert did and when the tasks were done. Recorded time charges may reveal when the expert first began substantive work on a file and how much time the expert (or his staff) devoted on any particular day or in connection with any particular task. These records also may reveal time entries that inspire more detailed, probing examination. Here are some items to look for:

- If billing records reflect significant time charges incurred late in the process, a reasonable argument may be fashioned that the expert's work was rushed.

- If billing records reflect significant time charges occurring *after* the expert had already been disclosed, a forceful argument arises that the expert's conclusions are biased and not trustworthy since the expert was identified *before* significant work began.

- If billing records reflect that the expert devoted minimal time reviewing specific evidence (such as important depositions, photographs, scene inspection, etc.), a reasonable inference may arise that the expert's review of important evidence was superficial or lacking.

- If billing records reflect that the expert's total investment of time was minimal and that the expert is relying upon the work of others, then the jury may infer that the expert is *not* an expert or that the underlying work product is questionable.

Correspondence Files

Correspondence between an expert and opposing counsel is frequently an important source of information. Such files may contain not only letters but also emails that tell a story about the expert and his or her involvement in the case. For example, communications between the expert and counsel may demonstrate when the expert received important evidence or, in some cases, that the expert never received such evidence. If significant evidence was not provided to the expert before the expert report was prepared and this fact can be documented through correspondence, the jury may form negative conclusions. If the expert received critical evidence on the eve of an expert report or disclosure deadline, such late timing suggests that the expert's work was rushed or the opinions were not based on a disciplined review of the evidence. In essence, correspondence files should be evaluated as a platform to cross-examine the expert concerning the timing and thoroughness of the underlying work product.

What may be missing from a correspondence file also can be used to build a cross-examination. Missing data is used to undercut the expert's opinions, particularly if the missing data is material. Here is an example:

> An expert was designated on the issue of design defect in an automotive case, but the expert's file did not contain the formal expert designation that had been used by the lawyer to formally disclose the witness's opinions. When presented with a copy of the designation, the witness conceded he had never seen the formal disclosure, he was unaware of its contents, and he had never discussed the disclosure with trial counsel. Importantly, the disclosure statement misstated that the expert had inspected the accident scene and had conducted dynamic testing at the scene prior to the disclosure date. The expert's invoices, however, reflected time charges for an inspection and testing several months later, and *after* the formal disclosure had been prepared and served. Thus, the disclosure statement was substantially inaccurate. The trial court excluded the expert's opinions concerning the late testing and scene inspections, and the appellate court affirmed.

Correspondence files between an expert and opposing counsel also should be reviewed to determine if the opposing lawyer is controlling the information flow by censoring information provided to the witness. If opposing counsel is controlling what information is provided to the expert, as opposed to the expert selecting what information is needed, the expert may lose credibility in the eyes of the jury. The lawyer's credibility may also be impacted because it looks like the lawyer is manipulating the case. Thus, a deposition should explore whether the lawyer, and not the expert, is controlling what the expert sees and considers. Evidence of selective dissemination of information is an excellent foundation for later cross-examination at trial. A jury will be interested in knowing whether the lawyer is orchestrating the expert's work and resulting opinions. Of course, if this is the case, the jury may infer that the expert's opinions are not objective, independent, or scientific.

The Expert's CV

Experts should always be questioned about their CVs or resumes. It is not uncommon for an expert witness, particularly newcomers to the "business" of litigation, to exaggerate their credentials. Experienced experts typically do not take such risks because they have learned their lessons on the witness stand. However, less experienced experts may "puff" when describing their involvement in professional organizations, academic institutions, or their educational achievements. Indeed, an expert's CV is frequently used by the expert as a marketing device to attract new business. Thus, the expert's CV may contain inflated statements, and these exaggerations may be subtle and not easily identified at first glance. The CV may gloss over or omit key facts that call into question whether the designated expert witness is qualified to testify. If possible, pre-deposition research should be conducted to determine whether an expert's CV contains such "puffery." All trial lawyers should know that inflated egos are easily crossed with embellished CVs, and these egos can deflate rapidly on the witness stand.

There are dozens of examples of how CVs are potentially misleading and exaggerated or gloss over important items. Here are a few examples:

- A witness with an engineering degree may not be licensed as an engineer.

- An accountant may have failed the CPA exam on multiple occasions.

- An article that an expert authored may not have been peer reviewed.

- An expert's CV may list a variety of professional associations that, at first glance, sound important and exclusive; when probed, however, the expert may concede that membership is not by invitation, but is open to anyone willing to pay an initiation fee.

An effective strategy is often to allow experts to "puff" about their credentials, unaware that the examining lawyer is already cognizant of these exaggerations. In fact, some examining lawyers encourage these exaggerations, lay a trap, and then spring the trap for the first time in the courtroom in the presence of the jury. The jury is shown that the expert "fibbed" or exaggerated his or her credentials, and the witness is then put on the defensive without having had a preview of the examination. This can have lingering effects on the jury's attitude about the witness. An example of this strategy follows:

> In a pharmaceutical liability case, the plaintiff was alleging a failure to warn of adverse reactions to a prescription medicine. One of the plaintiff's liability experts was a physician who claimed to be on the faculty of a teaching hospital in a major metropolitan area. He was an inexperienced witness and was neither prepared for nor expecting to be challenged concerning his credentials. Although his CV stated he had served as a visiting professor on the faculty of the hospital, he was examined in the courtroom with a real-time download from the hospital's web site reflecting the names of *all* tenured professors, assistant professors, and adjunct professors at the hospital. Unfortunately for him, his name was not on the list. As it turned out, he had been a "guest" lecturer on a single occasion several years before the lawsuit. His CV had exaggerated this tenuous, one-time connection, and he was left explaining this to the jury. The witness was put on the immediate defensive by this examination.

Education and Licensing

An expert's CV typically reflects his or her educational background, and the CV should serve as the starting point for a thorough examination of this background. An expert should be questioned on undergraduate and postgraduate studies, as well as any professional licensing exams that may be required within the witness's relevant industry or scientific discipline. The examination also should consider what specific licenses the expert has obtained (or has not obtained), and whether the expert failed any required licensing examinations. The examination also should identify any continuing education that the witness pursued, and whether minimum standards within his or her industry have been satisfied.

In one case, a consulting engineer failed introductory engineering courses during his 4-year undergraduate education. Experts who identify themselves as engineers may not be licensed as mandated under state law. In a similar vein, it is not uncommon to find that a CPA may have failed the CPA exam (or parts of it) on numerous occasions, or an attorney expert in a legal malpractice case may have failed the bar exam. Although such evidence may not rise to a knockout punch under *Daubert*, this type of evidence is obviously useful during cross-examination. The examining lawyer should use the pre-trial process, including depositions, to probe what may be lurking behind glossy language in a CV.

The "Professional" Witness

A deposition should typically include questions regarding the expert's history in the field of litigation or forensic consulting. This type of examination should focus on whether the expert devotes a significant amount of professional time to litigation or nonlitigation pursuits. An expert who devotes 100% of his or her professional career to litigation may be viewed negatively by a jury; such a witness may be viewed as a "professional witness" or "hired gun." Thus, the deposition should include questions concerning the percentage of time devoted to litigation matters, how much of the expert's annual income is derived from such matters, and how many "new" cases the expert gets each year. If the expert's annual income is substantially derived from serving as a "testifier," then the witness's income is dependent upon lawyers. The jury may react to this financial dependency and infer that the witness is "bought and paid for."

A similar inquiry involves the percentage of time the expert has devoted to working for plaintiffs, on the one hand, and working for defendants, on the other. If a witness's litigation involvements are substantially skewed to one side, a predisposition or bias may be legitimately inferred. Certainly, the most dangerous experts are those who are balanced in their consulting relationships and who testify for both defendants and plaintiffs. They appear more open-minded and not "result oriented." Witnesses who testify only for plaintiffs, or only for defendants, may be viewed by juries less favorably.

Another line of examination includes whether the expert is involved in other cases concerning similar events, products, or issues. Substantial or repeated involvement in similar cases suggests that the expert's financial interests are vested and the expert is financially interested in a specific outcome. More "wins" means more consulting jobs, which means more money. The jury will be interested in knowing whether the expert is making a living by going into the courtroom with a substantially similar agenda each time. A fair inference is that such an expert has a direct financial incentive in winning, and this fact should not be lost on the jury. An example of this type of examination, which developed during deposition discovery and later used at trial, follows:

> An engineering firm had been engaged by several different manufacturers within the same industry over many years. Over objection at trial, plaintiff's counsel was allowed to examine the testifying expert (who worked at the engineering firm) concerning the extent of his prior involvements, and the fact that the expert (and his firm) had been compensated many millions of dollars by the industry at large. The argued inference was that the witness was biased and financially motivated. The sheer magnitude of past compensation was used to diminish the witness's credibility. The plaintiff's lawyer repeatedly (and effectively) referred to the expert as the "$6 Million Dollar Man."

This type of strategy should be considered by all counsel. Expert consultants become financially entrenched on both sides of the bar. They may be seen as "professional" witnesses with their livelihood dependent upon lawsuits. Every trial lawyer should pursue the development of the theme that the consultant is nothing more than a "hired gun," "bought and paid for," and predisposed with vested interests in the outcome.

Prior Testimony History

Under the Federal Rules, an expert's history of providing prior testimony must be disclosed for the immediate prior 4-year period.[8] Many state jurisdictions impose similar requirements. Thus, in many jurisdictions, a list of the expert's prior depositions and trial testimony will accompany the expert report or formal witness disclosure. The trial lawyer then has the opportunity to do "homework" by researching this list before the deposition. Actual transcripts of the expert's prior testimony can be identified and obtained, and these transcripts should be reviewed in preparation and as a guide for the upcoming deposition. This history is relevant and potentially probative for a variety of reasons:

- The testimony may be relevant to the expert's involvement in the immediate case and may shed light on the expert's opinions and inconsistencies in those opinions. It also may reveal significant admissions or concessions on relevant topics.

- Prior testimony may show successful examination techniques used by other lawyers with the same witness, and provide a preview of how the witness handles different types of questions.

- Prior testimony may provide insights into how an expert responds to questions, whether the expert is straightforward or evasive, and whether the expert tries to condition or qualify answers. These prior depositions also may reveal bad deposition "habits," and the examining lawyer can strategically modify the tenor and substance of the examination accordingly.

- Prior testimony also may disclose "baggage" with which a veteran expert must live. The witness may have slipped and erred in prior testimony, and substantive concessions or inconsistent opinions may have been given under oath providing an immediate, and potentially powerful, basis for impeachment.

---

[8] *See* Fed. R. Civ. P. 26(a)(2)(B)(v).

In one case, an expert had given more than 10 prior depositions on similar product design issues. A review of his prior testimony revealed consistent testimony in nine of these depositions, but a critical inconsistency in one instance. The expert had no explanation for this discrepancy except to say that it must have been a court reporter's error. However, the deadline for correcting such errors in the earlier case had long since passed and no errata sheet or correction had been provided. Thus, the error was glaring and part of a permanent record. Fortunately, this "slip" was caught before the witness was designated by the disclosing party. Otherwise, it could have been damaging. Thus, every effort should be made to obtain all relevant transcripts.

Do Not Repeat Questions Already Asked

If an adverse expert has been deposed in prior cases on similar issues, it is frequently wise *not to repeat* questions already asked and answered. This is particularly true if the witness's prior answers are favorable. If the witness is expected to appear live at trial, then such questions should not be repeated because the expert may be primed to qualify or explain prior answers. At trial, the prior testimony should be used for impeachment purposes when the expert takes the stand. The witness will be forced to explain the prior, inconsistent answer for the first time in the jury's presence. Because the witness had no preview of the question, the witness may be caught off-guard since he had no time to "rehearse" an explanation.

Not repeating prior questions is also an efficient time management tool, which is often important because many jurisdictions impose time limits on the length of depositions. Indeed, some jurisdictions may impose even more stringent time limits for expert witnesses. If significant background information has already been developed in prior depositions, a good practice is not to re-ask such questions. The examining lawyer should not waste time asking basic questions to which answers have already been provided under oath. Some examples of information that should not be "rediscovered," if appropriately developed in prior depositions, include age, address, prior job experiences, and basic information concerning prior education, etc. Much of this information is not controversial, and there is no need to reinvent the wheel.

The "No True Expert" Expert

A veteran expert may have been involved in dozens of cases involving a variety of products or issues. As such, a jury may fairly question whether one person is truly qualified to testify to a vast array of dissimilar topics, products, or issues. Thus, the more depositions given by the expert, and the greater the degree of substantive variation in the products, issues, or topics, the more likely the expert can be characterized as overreaching or a "hired gun." An entire line of questions can be developed with the objective that the vast array of prior opinions cast doubt on the witness's trustworthiness; the "expert" claims he or she has expertise in too many disciplines and is a master of none, a "No True Expert" expert. A few examples follow:

> In an automotive products case, an expert produced a list that reflected prior testimony against all of the major automotive manufacturers involving different makes and models of trucks and passenger cars. The expert had a history of prior testimony on almost every aspect of vehicle design for almost every type of vehicle on the road, and had actually opined that almost every vehicle was defective in at least some regard. Thus, the witness's "testimony list" became a powerful exhibit during cross-examination. The examining lawyer aggressively questioned the witness with the theme that the expert had never looked at a vehicle without finding at least one defect. Because the expert's "purposeful" mission was to find defects, his *bona fides* could not be trusted.

In yet another case, an expert claimed to be an engineering expert but was not a licensed engineer. He had testified in dozens of different types of cases involving a vast array of unrelated products, creating a foundation for later cross-examination:

> The witness previously testified concerning defects in dishwashers, brakes, engines, electrical systems, transmissions, brakes, vacuum cleaners, power cords, kitchen blenders, crash helmets, and a variety of other unrelated products. He was easily portrayed as a "self-declared expert of much, but a true expert concerning little." The examining lawyer had a field day examining the witness pursuing this simple but effective theme, demonstrating that any opinion could be bought "if the price was right."

Legal Industry Research

There are many organizations or associations that provide networking opportunities for counsel on both sides of the bar. Many of these associations and industry groups provide resources for background information on experts and forensic consultants.

The AMERICAN ASSOCIATION FOR JUSTICE (AAJ), formerly the ASSOCIATION OF TRIAL LAWYERS OF AMERICA (ATLA) is one such group providing its members (primarily plaintiffs' attorneys) with a library of background information on many experts. Deposition transcripts may be available for particular experts. The DEFENSE RESEARCH INSTITUTE (DRI) is an example of an organization for defense, insurance, and corporate counsel that facilitates the exchange of similar information.

Professional groups should be consulted routinely as part of a lawyer's basic preparations to examine an expert. The examining lawyer should try to identify, and actually network with, lawyers who previously cross-examined the same witness. First-hand accounts from past depositions are valuable and frequently yield insights into how the expert should be deposed, the personality of the expert, and the witness's weaknesses and strengths. This preliminary "homework" may show whether the witness is combative or responsive, evasive or direct, or identify other unique habits the witness may have. The examining lawyer can modify the strategic approach to the deposition accordingly.

Online Information Services

There are numerous online companies engaged in the business of providing background information on experts for both sides of a case. A quick online search of "expert information services" will generate numerous hits. Many of these companies possess a library of information on all types of consultants, and many serve as clearinghouses for expert services. Experts are categorized by discipline, industry, or by name. Many of these services also promote their ability to research and identify prior *Daubert* challenges, prior deposition testimony, trial testimony, and relevant articles on adverse expert witnesses. This information is available on short notice.

Computer Research of Published Opinions

Computer research may identify published cases where an expert's name is discussed, and these published opinions may include holdings that address prior expert challenges. Obviously, there is no better pre-deposition preparation than to be armed with the knowledge that an opposing expert was previously limited in the scope of opinions that could be offered or completely excluded from testifying in a prior case because of deficiencies in either the witness's qualifications or methodology. This knowledge is a powerful silver bullet. Certainly, the court should consider such evidence when exercising its gatekeeping function, and an entire deposition can be structured around successful *Daubert* decisions in earlier cases that excluded or limited the expert's opinions. If any of these prior cases involved substantially similar issues or facts, the examining lawyer is poised to hit a home run.

Articles and Publications

Most jurisdictions require disclosure of an expert's relevant publication history, which usually accompanies the expert report or formal expert disclosure. By way of example, Fed. R. Civ. P. 26(a)(2)(B) requires that retained experts set forth their publication history for the last 10 years. Once disclosed, the examining lawyer can review this database to identify and then retrieve articles or publications with potential relevance to the issues in the pending case. Again, the expert's prior publications may include statements inconsistent with the expert's opinions in the immediate case. This is powerful evidence for any cross-examination.

Also important is the expert's failure to publish on topics relevant to the case. A lack of peer review reflects directly on an expert's lack of qualifications and, perhaps, the admissibility of the expert's opinions. Indeed, a failure to publish is one of many criteria that a court should consider as part of any *Daubert* challenge. A lack of peer review of the expert's method is also a basic element of a *Daubert* challenge.

Some experts are cunning and may seek out publishing opportunities in selected second-tier journals to enhance their credentials. They look for opportunities to publish with the calculated goal of satisfying one of the *Daubert* criteria. The examining lawyer should carefully scrutinize the nature and quality of each of the publications sponsoring the expert's work. Some of these publications may not be well respected, and some may not include a rigorous peer review process. Indeed, some may not exercise any editorial scrutiny at all. Likewise, some articles are nothing more than industry presentations at professional legal seminars where either plaintiffs' lawyers or defense lawyers congregate. Presentations to such groups may be nothing more than glorified marketing promotions. Some online services actually offer publishing opportunities. The lesson here is that *mere publication* may be nothing more than *mere marketing*, and a detailed examination may be needed to confirm whether this is the case.

Another area of inquiry is whether an expert has submitted proposed articles to a peer-reviewed journal or other publication, and the papers were rejected. Every expert deposition should contain some questions to ferret out this possibility. If the expert's work has been rejected, then the examining lawyer has an additional opportunity to hit a home run. One hint is whether the expert's CV includes any old "abstracts" of articles. The failure to identify an actual publication may reveal that the article was ultimately rejected. The examining lawyer should make this inquiry.

If an expert has published an article or presented a paper on topics relevant to the case, computer research for other articles on the same topics or issues should be conducted. This research may reveal articles written by others that evaluate (or even criticize) the witness's work product or provide insights into the strengths and weakness of the expert's methodology. This type of information can guide an effective cross-examination, and it can lead to the identification of new consultants who can be recruited for the client's case.

Thus, key examination points relating to articles and publications are summarized as follows:

- Has the expert failed to publish on the opinions or methodology at issue in the case?

- Has the expert published on topics relevant to the case; if so, was a peer review process involved?

- If the expert has been published, are the publications well respected in the industry or are they merely marketing efforts disguised as academic publications?

- Has the expert made presentations or published on relevant topics to professional legal associations or groups? If so, when, what, and where?

- Have the expert's papers or articles been rejected by peer-reviewed journals? If so, what, when, and why?

- Has the expert published articles and publications that express opinions or utilize methodologies at odds with those presented in the current case?

Testing an Expert's Sincerity: "Practicing What Is Preached"

Another area for examination involves an expert's failure to act proactively in a manner consistent with the expert's opinions. In essence, the examining lawyer should ask *whether the expert practices what the expert preaches*. This area of examination is particularly useful in consumer products cases or other cases dealing with safety issues. Here is an example:

A design safety expert claimed that a particular type of vehicle—a sport utility vehicle (SUV)—was inherently dangerous because of handling and stability issues. The expert opined that SUVs were generally too narrow and tall, which created stability and handling problems. During deposition, however, it was discovered that the witness's wife and teenage son drove

SUVs. A jury may have a difficult time rationalizing how an expert can criticize the safety features of a product but still allow family members to use the allegedly "unsafe" product.

Another example involves experts who fail to act proactively in contributing to the safety of their industry even though they criticize the industry on safety issues. Here is another example of information that was developed during deposition and later used at trial:

An expert repeatedly testified in cases involving automotive crashworthiness. However, it was discovered that when personally invited to respond to and participate in rulemaking initiatives by the National Highway Traffic Safety Administration (NHTSA) on crashworthiness devices, the expert failed to respond. The jury could perceive such "inaction" negatively, given the aggressive criticisms the witness was making.

Thus, although every case is different, an examining lawyer should explore whether the expert's opinions lack sincerity and, likewise, should specifically explore:

- Whether the expert (or members of his family) use products that the expert criticizes.

- Whether the expert has failed to take opportunities to publish work reflecting his or her opinions, especially if invited to do so.

- Whether the expert has acted consistently or inconsistently with the opinions expressed in the case.

The Initial Engagement

The deposition of an opposing expert should also address basic information concerning the expert's initial engagement. This type of examination typically includes a determination of: (a) when the expert was first contacted; (b) who retained the expert; (c) the expert's understanding of how the lawyer (or other person) knew to contact the expert; (d) what information was provided to the expert upon the initial engagement; (e) what was discussed at the time of the initial engagement concerning the case; (f) what was discussed in terms of the expert's scope of work and anticipated testimony; (g) whether the expert previously consulted (or is currently consulting) with opposing counsel (or members of the same firm) in other cases; and (h) whether there is a history between opposing counsel (or counsel's firm), the opposing party and the expert.

This background examination is important because it may reveal the witness's relationship with the opposing lawyer, the opposing law firm, or the opposing party. Alternatively, it may reveal that the expert was contacted because the expert uses a brokerage service or advertises and markets litigation services. Clearly, if an expert has an established, recurring relationship with either the opposing counsel or party, it suggests bias and an economic incentive to provide what the other side wants to hear. If the expert was contacted because of advertising or through a clearinghouse, the expert may appear as a "hired gun" or "professional witness" who is less interested in scientific objectivity than making money.

The timing of an expert's initial engagement is also relevant because it may reveal that the expert was given insufficient time to investigate the case and important facts underlying the expert's opinions. If an expert consultant is retained just days or even a few weeks before the expert is formally disclosed or before a report is finalized, then this attenuated involvement suggests that the expert's work product was hurried and superficial. The jury can rightfully infer that the witness was hired on the eve of a disclosure deadline and had little opportunity to evaluate the case with objectivity or thoroughness.

Ghost Writers and Draft Reports

Many state jurisdictions allow discovery of draft reports and communications between counsel and the expert relating to the drafting process. However, the Federal Rules were amended in 2010 to limit disclosure of materials considered by the expert to "facts and data considered by the witness" in forming the expert opinions. These rules expressly exempt draft reports and certain other types of communications with counsel from the discovery process.[9] The authors of these amendments apparently recognized the challenge of developing expert testimony in complex or technical cases where the lawyer is not provided flexibility in working with the expert. There was an apparent recognition that trial lawyers had been employing creative, albeit expensive, ways to communicate with experts prior to these amendments. The Civil Rules Advisory Committee noted that the fear of discovery under the prior rules inhibited "robust communications between attorney and expert trial witness, jeopardizing the quality of the expert's opinion."[10]

---

[9] *See* Fed. R. Civ. P. 26(b)(4)(C), which clarifies that "regardless of the form of the communications," Rules 26(b)(3)(A) and (B) protect communications between attorneys and experts with the exception of (1) communications relating to compensation, (2) the facts or data received from the attorney that the expert considered in forming the opinion, and (3) any assumptions the attorney provided to the expert that the expert used in forming the opinion.

[10] Report of the Civil Rules Advisory Committee, at 3 (May 8, 2009), *available at* http://www.uscourts.gov/rules-policies/archives/committee-reports/advisory-committee-rules-civil-procedure-may-2009.

Nevertheless, if permitted in the jurisdiction where the case is pending, an examination should include whether the expert generated draft reports, and whether draft reports were shared with or modified by opposing counsel. In jurisdictions allowing such discovery, every effort should be made to obtain all written communications between the testifying expert and opposing counsel, which would include correspondence or emails transmitting or exchanging draft reports. These drafts may reflect a lawyer's heavy hand in structuring or editing the report. If ghost writing occurred or if there is a legitimate inference that it did occur, then counsel can effectively question the witness's "independence." The expert should certainly be questioned to determine whether any opinions were changed or modified after discussions with the opposing lawyer. This may have been done to hide opinions inconsistent with the opposing party's theory of the case. An example follows:

> An expert was asked at deposition whether he had transmitted any hard copies of draft reports to opposing counsel, and he smugly replied "no." When asked whether the expert had generated any draft reports, he again replied "no." He also testified that his drafting work was done on a computer with "volatile" memory, which meant there was no record of prior drafts because all edits morphed into a final written product, and all prior drafts were "overwritten." With probing, however, it was discovered that opposing counsel had sat with the expert at the computer for several hours and had personally inputted changes using the computer keyboard. The objectivity of the expert was now subject to challenge.

Modern technology provides several ways that adverse experts can work with opposing counsel to prepare reports without leaving a paper trail, and some lawyers go to great lengths to avoid any paper trail. Experts frequently travel with draft reports on flash drives or portable laptop computers. They can travel, modify, and edit the report regardless of location. Thus, experts may incur the expense of traveling to the lawyer's office and working on their reports with opposing counsel without any written communications between them. However, their billing records may actually reflect this travel time.

Similarly, several computer interface programs are available that currently allow experts and counsel to review reports and other work product remotely, but simultaneously, even though they may be hundreds or thousands of miles apart. Draft reports and demonstrative exhibits can now be shared through computer meeting or sharing programs. Some programs even allow lawyers to take control of the document, and they can actually edit the document in real time without downloading it. Thus, the deposition should include questions regarding whether this type of real-time editing occurred, or whether the opposing lawyer had an opportunity to review and modify the draft report and opinions of the expert in the lawyer's office, in the expert's office, or on the computer.

Pre-Deposition Investigation of Scientific Method

Preliminary research should be conducted before the expert's deposition to investigate the integrity of the expert's scientific or technical method. This is accomplished through online research, a review of articles or publications that discuss the specific method and any competing methods, and through consultations with industry organizations. Many industries have professional organizations that report evolving methodologies and technologies. Here is an example of the benefits of doing "homework":

> A literature search of a particular accident simulation program revealed a published survey that had reviewed the program and several other competing programs. The authors of the survey were contacted, and this led to the discovery that the opposing expert had been involved in a dispute concerning patent rights relating to "his" program. Apparently, the program had been developed while the expert had been tenured at a well-known university. When he attempted to purchase the patent rights from the university, a dispute arose over the value of the software. During negotiations, the expert corresponded with the university claiming that the program had *minimal* value because of programming quirks. Incredibly, this was the same computer program utilized in the courtroom to support the expert's opinions. Of course, this correspondence became a valuable exhibit in a subsequent *Daubert* challenge.

In yet another case, a literature search identified articles that had critiqued an expert's methodology. These articles also became exhibits at a *Daubert* hearing. The author of the articles was contacted, and he became a testifying expert in response to the opposing expert.

The converse also holds true. The absence of literature addressing the expert's method or opinions may be evidence that the expert's method has not been vetted in the relevant industry or *is not generally accepted*. If the expert has not submitted the method to peer review scrutiny, then the absence of such scrutiny is evidence that the method has not gained acceptability within the relevant industry or discipline.

Areas of Nonexpertise

Every deposition should explore areas where an expert is *not qualified* to offer opinions. There are several benefits flowing from this strategy.

First, in doing so, the examining lawyer can effectively limit the scope of the expert's testimony at trial. No lawyer wants new opinions injected into the case for the first time at trial.

Second, the tempo of an examination that demonstrates that the witness is *not an expert on multiple topics* can be highly effective. An examination that includes a litany of areas where the witness has no expertise can be replayed in the presence of the jury. It fosters the impression that the lawyer controls the witness because the lawyer appears to be managing the witness in cross-examination, and this suggests that the lawyer is "winning." It also forces the expert to concede that he or she is not an expert in areas that may be substantively relevant to the case, and these concessions may sow seeds of doubt in the jury's mind concerning the value of the expert's opinions. Several examples follow:

- An accident reconstruction expert in an automotive accident case may have no formal medical training and, therefore, must concede that he or she is not qualified to offer opinions concerning occupant kinematics, the biomechanics of injury, or injury causation.

- A statistician may have no expertise in accident reconstruction and, therefore, must concede that he or she is not qualified to discuss the differences in specific accidents that comprise the database utilized for the statistical analysis.

- A medical expert may not be qualified to offer opinions concerning medical subspecialties and, as a result, is not qualified to provide a differential diagnosis.

- An attorney expert in a legal malpractice case may have to concede to an absence of expertise in a subspecialty of law that may be at issue.

- An architect may be forced to concede that he or she has no expertise in designing buildings in humid or temperate climates and, therefore, is not qualified to discuss the growth or presence of mold in a "mold" case.

Lack of Experience

A similar examination strategy involves questions that focus on the absence of practical experience. Even if the expert is qualified to offer specific opinions in a given subject area, the expert may have no practical, real-world experience. This is a standard cross-examination technique at trial, and the fodder for this cross-examination is developed during the expert's deposition. The examining lawyer should consider deposing the expert to confirm whether the expert has specific, real-world experience. Here are some examples:

- In an automotive design defect case, an examining attorney may wish to establish that the plaintiff's design expert has never been involved in the design of an automobile or any component part in an automobile.

- In a business case involving economic damages and corporate business valuations, an examining attorney may wish to establish that the expert has never managed or operated a business, or that the expert is not a licensed CPA or certified business valuation expert.

- In a medical liability case, an examining attorney may wish to establish that although the testifying expert teaches at a medical school and has published articles, the expert has no real-world clinical experience treating real patients.

- In an architectural malpractice case involving a building that experienced water intrusion and subsequent mold, the examining attorney may wish to establish that the testifying expert has no practical experience in designing buildings or structures in wet or humid climates where mold is a risk.

These are just a few examples. Again, every case is different, and the questions should be tailored accordingly. There should be no doubt, however, that a carefully crafted examination can reveal distinct areas where an adverse expert can be forced into concessions as to an absence of real-world experience, and these concessions, once made, may become important when the jury weighs the witness's testimony.

Materials Reviewed and Considered

Every deposition should include questions to identify the significant materials reviewed or considered by an adverse expert. The converse is also true. Every examination should include a discussion of what materials, data, or evidence the expert *did not* consider.

Most jurisdictions require automatic disclosure of the facts, data, or materials relied upon as part of the expert report or in connection with the expert disclosure. Thus, in most jurisdictions, the examining lawyer should have a preview of what the expert relied upon *before* the deposition begins. These materials (or a list of these materials) should be reviewed to determine what may be missing because such omissions can be significant and may provide a basis for a powerful cross-examination.

The strength or weakness of an expert's opinion (and its admissibility) is directly impacted by the underlying foundation upon which it relies. The expert's opinion may be questionable, if not inadmissible, based upon a failure to consider all material facts, documents, and data. Evidence missing from an expert's file goes to the heart of this reliability issue. Thus, missing evidence, and a failure to consider such evidence, can strengthen any expert challenge. The ability to demonstrate that an adverse expert failed to consider important facts also can be used to diminish the expert's credibility in the eyes of the jury.

Every witness is different, and the questions in cross-examination should be tailored to the specific issues in each case. Here are a few examples of successful cross-examination points that focus on a deficiency in the facts that the expert evaluated before forming opinions:

- In an automotive products liability case, an accident reconstruction expert was effectively cross-examined by showing that he did not visit the accident scene before the witness disclosure was prepared and filed.

- In an economic damages case involving lost profits from the sale of real estate, an adverse expert was effectively cross-examined by showing that he failed to consider the impact of the global recession in 2008 and the ensuing downturn in the real estate markets across the nation.

- In an automotive products liability case, a plaintiff's defect expert was effectively cross-examined by showing that he did not consider the requirements of the Federal Motor Vehicle Safety Standards (FMVSS) or whether the design of the automobile (or its component parts) satisfied government safety criteria.

- In a medical liability case, an adverse expert was effectively cross-examined by showing that she did not undertake a differential diagnosis to eliminate other health or disease conditions that could explain the patient's condition.

Mirror, Mirror on The Wall

Another technique used by some lawyers is to take advantage of an expert's inflated ego or quirks in personality. This is similar to questions relating to an expert's "puffery" in a CV. The concept is to identify the expert's personality traits and, if appropriate, incorporate that personality into an examination strategy.

Because of their significant academic achievements, some academics may have a superiority complex. They may feel untouchable because of their academic credentials, and this "haughtiness" may be alienating. Juries, just like everyone else, typically find egotism and arrogance offensive. Such witnesses ultimately come across as condescending or rude.

One technique used by some trial lawyers is to encourage arrogance or haughtiness. The expert is led to believe that he or she is dominating the intellectual discussion at the deposition. The lawyer can play "dumb." Well-prepared lawyers, however, have typically researched and gained a substantive understanding of the expert's discipline. It may be advantageous not to display this knowledge at the deposition, but to hold critical questions until trial. The expert has no preview of the lawyer's true grasp of the facts and the expert's method until it is too late.

Grudges and Bias

The expert may have particular grudges or a bias against a particular party or an industry, and this potential should be explored. There may be something unique in the expert's background that is motivating the expert to become involved in certain types of cases. This could be a work-related experience or a personal experience, such as an injury to or death of a family member that may impact an expert's objectivity. The expert also may have been fired from a job position that is motivating criticism of a particular company or industry.

If an expert has been terminated by an industry employer, and is unable to gain new employment within that industry, the expert may become an anti-industry witness marketing his or her services to lawyers suing companies within that industry. Accordingly, the expert's background in the industry should be explored, and the expert should be questioned on the reasons for the departure from former employment. This is a fruitful area for questioning and could lead to significant impeachment evidence.

Testing

Some experts may manipulate product testing to achieve desired results or, alternatively, may experiment with testing protocols and procedures until the desired results are obtained. They then use their "final" testing as a basis for their opinions.

If an expert is relying upon any type of laboratory or dynamic testing, questions should be asked to determine whether the test procedures were "rehearsed" or "practiced" before performing the final test to support the expert's opinions. Here are some examples of what to look for:

- An expert may rely upon the result of a dynamic test procedure, and the expert may produce a videotape of the testing to support the legitimacy of the procedure and the testing protocol. It is important to determine whether there were any dress rehearsals before the video camera was turned on. If so, the videoed test may be a rehearsed result.

- If an expert is suspected of rehearsing tests before final testing, questions should be posed to determine whether the expert conducted the test with different results and whether any documentation of those results exists.

- The expert should be examined to determine whether any test procedures have been modified and, if so, when, how, and why. The witness should be forced to explain any significant alterations to testing procedures, and should be questioned whether there is any documentation, photograph, or video evidence of the testing protocols before modification.

Controlling "Artful Dodgers"

Trial lawyers routinely encounter experts who are no strangers to the courtroom. Many have testified in dozens or more depositions and trials, and they have acquired significant witness skills. These veterans have learned tricks for how to handle lawyers and the lawyers' questions, and they have learned how to dance around challenging questions by qualifying answers and imposing conditions on their responses. They have become "masters of the caveat."

Experienced witnesses are difficult to handle for even the most experienced trial lawyers. Thus, the more knowledge the lawyer has about the opposing expert witness, the better. This knowledge is not limited to only hard data; it also includes information about how the witness handles questions and whether the expert is combative or unresponsive. Reading transcripts of prior testimony and networking with other lawyers who previously deposed the same witness can be significant sources of information. More knowledge about the witness typically translates into more witness control.

A key goal in every expert deposition is to gain control over the proceedings. Another goal is to eliminate any risk that the expert will inject surprise opinions or new work product at trial. Thus, the examining lawyer wants to define the universe of adverse opinions so the opposing expert has no flexibility to add new or modified opinions at a later date. Some examples of how to accomplish this follow:

- Review the expert's report and cull out the opinions, list them one by one on the deposition record, and have the witness confirm that the list fairly summarizes all of the witness's opinions in the case; if the expert seeks to condition or qualify the answer to this simple question, the lawyer should require the witness to describe each reason why the answer is qualified.

- An expert might claim that he or she will offer opinions at trial to the extent requested by counsel, and those questions are not precisely known. If this occurs, have the expert commit that the expert *is currently* unaware of any other opinions that the witness might offer at the current time other than those that have been identified during deposition.

Here are some specific examples of how this examination might flow:

Q: Your report states that you have the following opinions, which are:

_____.

A: That is correct.

Q: Is that all the opinions you have in the case?

A: I may have other opinions based upon future work.

Q: Have you planned any future work as you sit here today?

A: It all depends upon what the lawyer asks me to do.

Q: Has the lawyer asked you to do any further work as you sit here today?

A: No.

Q: Okay. Accordingly, as we sit here today, the only opinions you have at this time are the opinions reflected in your report, is that correct?

A: Yes.

Strategic Impeachment

Well-timed impeachment helps tame an opposing expert because no witness wants to be impeached. Letting the witness know that the examining lawyer is capable and ready to impeach the expert's testimony will tend to make the witness more guarded. The expert may be less inclined to stretch or exaggerate positions if there is a sense the examining lawyer is prepared to undercut the testimony. In effect, the lawyer instills fear by selective use of impeachment evidence. It has a chilling effect that makes the witness more cooperative.

Of course, this strategy assumes the trial lawyer is ready, willing, and able to impeach the witness. That is why pre-deposition "homework" is important, and the examining lawyer should thoroughly research the expert's prior testimony before the deposition.

One approach is to selectively impeach the witness (if possible) on collateral points before key opinions are discussed. Once the expert knows the lawyer has done "homework," the witness will be more likely to concede some points. There will be less pushback and fight.

Unless required to do so, the trial lawyer should reserve major impeachment questions for trial. For that reason, it is often a better practice not to preview key or critical impeachment evidence. Instead, critical impeachment evidence is best used by springing it on the witness for the first time at trial.

Using Consultants

Depending upon expense issues, trial counsel should consider using consultants to both prepare for and attend the deposition of an opposing expert. This is an efficient way to get a handle on complex issues or technical methodologies used by the opposing expert. Consultants can recommend examination strategies to better demonstrate weaknesses in the opposing expert's work product. They also can provide specific questions to enhance potential *Daubert* challenges. They can also identify topics for which more information is needed to complete their own expert reports or analysis.

An opposing expert may be less combative if a consultant (his or her intellectual peer) is in the deposition room. The presence of an opposing consultant may have a deterrent effect on the witness because the witness knows that any bluffs can be called. The relevant rules for each jurisdiction on whether the consultant can attend should be consulted. Some jurisdictions may limit the number of attendees at a deposition, so this factor should be considered as well.

There is also some risk that a consultant's presence at deposition may waive the consultant's privilege, so the relevant rules should be considered on this issue as well. If permitted, and the risks of waiver are remote, there is no doubt that real-time feedback from a consultant is invaluable. A consultant can help steer the examination on technical issues and provide specific guidance on follow-up questions in light of the answers being given. The following example illustrates this point:

> One of the parties retained an accident reconstruction expert in an automotive crash case who utilized a computer program that purportedly simulated an accident based upon driver inputs, environmental conditions, and vehicle characteristics. The software program was technically complex and had been evaluated by an outside consultant. The simulation was intricate in nature and accounted for multiple dynamic and fixed variables, including environmental conditions (such as slope, soil type, surface friction), driver inputs (such as vehicle speed, vehicle braking, steering input) and vehicle characteristics (such as tire pressure, wheel camber, shock absorber stiffness, and suspension), vehicle weight, vehicle height, track width, occupant

positions, vehicle length, steering responsiveness, and location of the vehicle center of gravity (loaded with occupants). After using the simulation to review the data input and output files that had been produced in discovery, the consultant discovered that certain variables could be modified. Modifying some of these variables slightly resulted in substantially different outcomes, some of which were inconsistent with the factual evidence in the case. By demonstrating these subtle variations in deposition, the opposing expert was exposed to a potential *Daubert* challenge.

Thus, consultants can provide the key to understanding the weakness in an expert's method. In some cases, as in the illustration cited above, the consultant is worth his weight in gold.

Impeachment Using Variable Assumptions

Many experts are skilled at spotting broad questions, and they may refuse to answer such questions unless *all* assumptions are defined on the record. They fear answering sweeping questions because their answers may have unintended consequences.

If experts refuse to answer a broad question, they should be asked to identify each variable they claim is missing that, if assumed, would allow them to fully answer. Through this process, the examining lawyer effectively isolates the variables that the expert considers critical. The lawyer should not be required to "guess" about the missing assumptions. The expert should be required to detail what information is needed to fully answer the hypothetical question. In this manner, the expert is "boxed in" on all of the moving parts of the issue.

If one of the assumptions identified by the expert later proves to be incorrect, or if the expert fails to define all relevant variables, then the expert's opinion is vulnerable. Here is a simple example of how this examination can unfold:

Q: Please describe your opinion concerning the weather.

A: I cannot answer that question because I don't understand the location that may be at issue.

Q: Alright. Please describe the weather immediately outside this building.

A: I still cannot answer that question because you haven't identified a precise time.

Q: Please describe the weather immediately outside this building at the current time.

A: Okay. Now since you have defined the missing pieces to the question and because I am now looking out the window, it appears that it is sunny with only a few clouds.

Q: Is that your opinion at this time?

A: Yes. That is my opinion.

Q: You are not aware of any other facts that would alter your opinion—is that correct?

A: That is correct.

The expert is now committed to an answer that leaves him exposed. The examining lawyer forced the expert to commit to an unequivocal opinion based upon clearly defined assumptions, and the expert lost flexibility as a result.

In this example, the witness is exposed to a later cross-examination because he failed to consider all relevant data; that is, he did not look out of all windows facing all four directions—north, south, east, and west. The examining lawyer can later impeach the witness by showing that there were storm clouds gathering on the opposite side of the building. In essence, the lawyer pushed the witness to define assumptions the witness considered important and, in the process, the expert committed to an answer without consideration of all relevant data. The lawyer was aware of the missing data, but was holding this data for use at trial.

Here is another example that demonstrates a technique which requires the expert to reconsider an opinion if factual assumptions change:

Q: Do you have an opinion concerning how the accident occurred?

A: Yes.

Q: What is that opinion?

A: The truck ran the red light at a high rate of speed and ran into the car crossing the intersection.

Q: What is the basis for your opinions?

A: The police report, the measured skid marks on the roadway, and the extent of damage on both the car and the truck.

Q: Are you relying upon any eyewitnesses?

A: No. I am not aware of any eyewitnesses.

Q: As a general proposition, would you agree that it would be reasonable to consider the testimony of an eyewitness who saw the accident if such a witness existed?

A: Yes.

Q: Would you also generally agree that the evidence of an eyewitness would be relevant to your opinion?

A: Yes.

Q: Would you agree that you would be required to reconsider your opinion if an eyewitness testified that the red light was not working on the date of the accident?

A: Yes.

The bottom line is the lawyer should create a framework in which the expert commits to opinions, and is then later forced to concede that missing data or incorrect data may impact those opinions. This technique underscores the importance of identifying all data, facts, and assumptions that the expert did not consider in reaching his or her opinion(s). The deposition is then used to lay a trap, and the trap is sprung at trial. If the witness pushes back, he or she does so with the risk that the jury may doubt the witness's credibility.

Preparing a Deposition Outline

Every lawyer should prepare an outline to identify the strategic goals for the deposition of the opposing expert, and this outline should be used as a roadmap or checklist to ensure that key examination points are addressed. Because many jurisdictions limit the time duration of depositions generally and some jurisdictions may impose even more stringent time limits on an expert's deposition, the use of a well-prepared outline ensures good time management and provides a checklist to make sure all key areas are covered before the deposition concludes.

Although the details of an outline logically differ from case to case, there should be no doubt that creating an outline is an excellent way for any lawyer to prepare for deposition. It forces the examining lawyer to work through the issues and identify specific examination goals. It provides a disciplined approach to the examination, which ensures that key issues are addressed. At a minimum, the outline should seek to identify and isolate the expert's key opinions to avoid later surprise. The outline also should explore the bases for these opinions and test the reliability of these opinions under relevant *Daubert* principles. Indeed, an entire deposition can be organized around the principles set forth in Federal Rules of Evidence 702 and 703, and the case law interpreting those rules.

Generic Outline

There are common issues that lawyers typically face when deposing any expert in any case. Provided below is a generic outline that contains common features that should be considered for every expert deposition. Most of these topics, which can be organized in a variety of ways, have been discussed throughout this chapter.

General

- Where permitted, review the expert's document production and verify that the expert's *entire file* has been produced, including draft reports (if permitted), communications with counsel, emails, handwritten notes, billing files, all data reviewed or considered by the expert, and all exhibits that the expert intends to use to explain or support his or her opinions at trial.

- Determine if the expert advertises litigation consulting services and, if so, to what groups, and identify the publications where these advertisements are placed.

- Probe the witness's prior testimony history and determine which testimony bears relevance to the case at hand.

Qualifications

- Explore the expert's personal and employment background using an updated CV or resume to confirm or challenge the expert's credentials relevant to the witness's involvement in the case.

- Explore the expert's educational background and look for deficiencies or exaggerations.

- Explore the expert's professional background and whether that background has any bearing on the subject matter of the case. Also explore the absence of any professional background or experience that may be relevant to the subject matter of the case.

- Establish and confirm all of the areas where the witness is *not* an expert relating to the subject matter of the case.

Motivation and Bias

- Explore the expert's prior history as a litigation consultant and as a testifying expert witness, whether the witness consults more for the plaintiff's side or the defense side of the bar, and how the expert's litigation business breaks down on a percentage basis.

- Explore the income received by the expert generally, as well as in the specific case in which the deposition is taken; determine if the expert's annual income is primarily generated in connection with litigation; establish what percentage of that income is devoted to litigation endeavors compared to nonlitigation endeavors; and lay a foundation to argue that the expert is "bought and paid for."

- Explore the expert's prior and current involvements with the opposing party, opposing counsel, or opposing counsel's firm; seek to determine whether the expert is financially entangled with opposing counsel, the opposing counsel's firm, or the opposing party.

- Determine whether the expert has a grudge against a party in the case or against a particular industry, and if the expert was fired, laid off, or lost his job.

Reliability of Method

- Determine whether the expert has published peer-reviewed articles on the subject matter of the opinions at issue, whether there is any other peer-reviewed literature that addresses the opinions of the expert or supports the expert's methodology, or whether the expert's work product has been rejected or called into question by a peer-reviewed publication.

- Explore prior challenges and whether the expert's testimony has ever been excluded or limited in prior cases; obtain sufficient information about these prior cases so the lawyers in those prior cases can be contacted for additional information.

- Identify all important evidence, facts, or materials the expert did not consider; review the list of materials the expert relied upon and confirm whether important evidence is *not* in the expert's files.

- Confirm whether opposing counsel controlled the information made available to the expert, or whether the expert controlled what information was gathered and considered.

- Determine whether the expert's methodology is generally accepted within the relevant industry and, if so, force the expert to provide a description of that support. Be prepared to cross-examine the expert on any published literature that indicates that the expert's method is or is not reliable.

Thoroughness of Analysis

- Review all time charges and invoices issued by the expert as of the date of the deposition, the total hours worked by the expert on the case, when those hours were worked, any descriptions of the work undertaken, the rates charged, and any outstanding receivables on the case.

- Review all written communications between the expert and opposing counsel, including letters and emails, to confirm when the witness was first retained and when important evidence was given to the expert.

- In cases involving testing, confirm whether the expert conducted "trial runs" or other tests before the final test was conducted and determine if these "trial runs" were videotaped or the results were reduced to writing.

Impeachment

- Identify all cases in which the expert previously testified that involved similar fact issues; identify the jurisdiction, the parties, and opposing counsel (if known) in those cases; identify who retained the expert in the cases and who may have deposed the expert in those cases.

- Identify all articles and publications the expert has authored and identify any inconsistent statements in the articles that can be used in the case at issue.

Case-Specific Topics

- Explore whether the expert is relying upon the work product of other con-sultants and, if so, which consultants and what material these consultants generated.

- Identify *all* opinions of the expert and confirm there are *no other* opinions.

- Identify *all* specific bases for all opinions of the expert.

- Confirm that the expert does not intend to conduct further work in the case.

- Identify the universe of exhibits that the expert intends to use to explain his or her opinions to the jury.

7

Preparing an Expert for Deposition

Expert witnesses should be prepared for deposition like other witnesses with one caveat: communications with a testifying expert are discoverable in most jurisdictions. In other jurisdictions, including federal court, some communications (but not all) may be discoverable.[1] Thus, the tendering lawyer should become familiar with the applicable rules governing expert discovery and exercise discretion in what is said to or shown to the expert in pre-deposition meetings. The substance of these communications will likely be requested by opposing counsel. Indeed, it is standard practice for expert witnesses to be examined concerning communications with the sponsoring lawyer.

Even though some experts are not strangers to the courtroom or the deposition room, and may require less preparation time, they still derive significant benefits from basic pre-deposition preparations. Meetings with the expert should be used to provide reminders about the deposition process and standard examination techniques. A pre-deposition meeting also allows the examining lawyer an opportunity to preview the testimony of the expert, spot issues or weaknesses in the work product, and smooth over rough edges. It is also an important opportunity to prepare the expert for *Daubert*-like questions.

Many expert consultants are relative beginners in the world of litigation, and they will need more intense preparations before their depositions. Basic strategies concerning how to behave in a deposition, the types of questions reasonably anticipated, and various tips for identifying "trick" questions, should be reviewed with such witnesses. Beginner experts also may be anxious and apprehensive about the deposition process, just like lay witnesses. The tendering lawyer should therefore try to put them at ease. All basic techniques for

---

[1] *See* Fed. R. Civ. P. 26(b)(4).

preparing fact witnesses should be addressed with the less experienced expert witness as a matter of course. Again, however, the tendering lawyer should control how this discussion is handled since the details of these discussions may be discoverable.

Reviewing the File

An expert's file should be reviewed by the sponsoring lawyer prior to production to the opposing side. The goal should be to produce only those documents requested or otherwise required to be produced in the relevant jurisdiction. Materials not required to be produced should not be produced unless they are clearly helpful to the expert. There are several reasons for withholding this information.

Producing extraneous material that is not discoverable may lead to a series of unnecessary examination questions and expose the expert to unintended results, such as unforeseen impeachment. Therefore, *less may be best* when producing the expert's work product and files. By way of another example, under the amended Federal Rules, draft expert reports are no longer discoverable. Therefore, in federal court proceedings and state jurisdictions that follow the Federal Rules with similar disclosure limitations, draft reports should be removed from the file. Draft reports can become a distraction or, even worse, a basis for cross-examination if there are significant differences in the drafts and the final report. Clearly, such differences provide fodder to a skilled examining lawyer who can create bias against the expert if there are such differences.

Other extraneous materials should also be removed from the file. In the absence of an agreement between the parties or specific rules mandating disclosure, billing invoices and time records should be removed. Here is a list of some specific items that the sponsoring lawyer should consider removing, depending upon the rules of the relevant jurisdiction, court orders, or agreements between the parties:

- Draft reports

- Transmittal correspondence with counsel

- Billing records and time records

- Invoices

- Materials *not* relied upon in connection with the expert's opinion

Compliance with Discovery Obligations

It is always important to make sure the expert fully complies with all disclosure requirements in the relevant jurisdiction. In some jurisdictions, this means that *all* documents that the expert has "reviewed" or "considered" must be produced, because discoverability may not be limited to materials "relied upon by the witness." Many states use broad disclosure requirements to avoid arbitrary, self-serving classifications of what materials were "considered" but not "relied upon."

Many jurisdictions also allow discovery of correspondence files and billing files. Thus, the disclosure requirements of each jurisdiction should be consulted. As a general practice, however, the lawyer tendering the expert should conduct a fair review of the file to ensure that the procedural rules are fully satisfied. It is always ill-advised, if not unethical, to knowingly withhold discoverable material from an expert's file. No lawyer should ever do this. The expert also does not need to run this risk. If the expert's testimony is limited or excluded because of discovery abuse, this fact will live with the expert for many years to come.

Key Assumptions and Opinions

The tendering lawyer should review the expert's key assumptions and opinions before the deposition. In many jurisdictions, including all federal jurisdictions, expert reports are required unless otherwise ordered by the court. Thus, a properly prepared expert report should serve as an immediate reference source in support of the witness's testimony during the deposition. This report should be reviewed with the expert before the deposition to make sure there are no lurking issues. The expert can always fall back and rely upon this report during the deposition. The tendering lawyer should review the report with the expert in detail to make sure the assumptions have not changed and all key facts were appropriately considered.

In jurisdictions where expert reports are not required, it is equally important to review the expert's key assumptions and opinions before the deposition. This allows the tendering lawyer an opportunity to make sure the witness is properly prepared to opine on all key issues for which the expert was engaged. It also allows the tendering lawyer to gauge the expert's strengths and weaknesses. The template for this review is the formal expert disclosure prepared by the lawyer, and this disclosure should be used as a guide to make sure there are no lingering issues before the deposition. The expert should review this disclosure personally and should be entirely comfortable with its contents. The expert can also take notes that, although discoverable, can be used as an aid during deposition.

Key Documents

The tendering lawyer should make sure the testifying expert has considered all key documents and discovery. The goal is to make sure the expert had a meaningful opportunity to evaluate all key facts in the case. Thus, all depositions, discovery responses, pleadings, and underlying documents should have been provided to the expert during the course of the case. The delivery of this evidence to the expert should be closely monitored from the date of initial engagement until the date of the deposition to make sure there are no last-minute data dumps or, even worse, a failure to provide important evidence. A log should be maintained to verify materials sent to the expert and this log should be updated as new materials are provided. The tendering lawyer should use this log during the preparation session as an opportunity to verify that the expert has had access to all important evidence. Any gaps should be identified before the deposition begins.

A disciplined approach regarding document logs is invaluable if there is a *Daubert-like* challenge. The objective here is to make sure the expert has considered all relevant data. If relevant data is missing from the expert's file, this fact may be used against the witness on cross-examination or, even more likely, as a basis for a *Daubert* challenge. The opposing counsel should be expected to challenge the reliability of the expert's work if important factual evidence is missing.

Overextension

Many lawyers use experts as storytellers at trial to open or close their case-in-chief. As such, there may be a tendency to overuse an expert to address multiple areas and, in some cases, there may be overreaching. The sponsoring lawyer should be sensitive to the risk of overextending the expert.

If the witness's ability to opine in some areas is weaker than others, then at least some consideration should be given to jettisoning weaker opinions. This is particularly true if the weaker opinions are not critical to the case. Otherwise, the expert's vulnerability in these weaker areas may taint the expert's credibility in the stronger areas. Of course, such determinations should be made early during the process of developing an expert's work product. Some opinions can be dropped or at least de-emphasized.

Some experts are eager to please. This is particularly true for younger consultants just starting their careers. This eagerness may translate into a willingness to overextend with opinions that ultimately cannot be supported.

Experienced trial lawyers should not encourage an expert to "go out on limbs," because doing so may be injurious to both the expert and the case. Experts should stay within their areas of expertise, and they should only advance opinions they can reasonably and reliably support. No lawyer wants his or her expert struck, and no expert wants to be struck.

Timing Issues

Many examining lawyers will seek to create the impression that the expert's work was hurried or incomplete. The obvious reason is to create negative inferences regarding the reliability or credibility of the opinions. Therefore, it is important to provide the expert with all critical evidence as it is developed and not wait until the last minute before expert disclosure deadlines. Otherwise, the opinions are vulnerable. The sponsoring lawyer should use the preparation meeting to identify any problems in this area and suggest appropriate solutions.

Other Depositions

The tendering lawyer should assume the expert witness will be questioned concerning prior depositions or trial testimony in other cases. Ordinarily, the tendering lawyer should be aware of this prior testimony before the consultant is retained, much less designated as a witness. If problematic testimony exists, then these issues should be evaluated and weighed as part of the initial decision to engage the expert. No lawyer wants to hear or learn of inconsistent testimony on the eve of or during an expert's deposition.

In any event, if the tendering lawyer anticipates the use of prior testimony at deposition, then any potentially controversial testimony should be discussed in advance and appropriate responses identified. The expert, and the tendering lawyer, should enter the deposition room fully prepared for all types of questions concerning the expert's prior litigation involvements. The witness should be prepared on these topics to avoid surprise.

Review Daubert Factors

The expert should be made familiar with the requirements of *Daubert* (or other similar authority in the jurisdiction where the case is pending), then tested for compliance with the relevant standards. The following criteria should be reviewed to confirm that the expert is ready for deposition:

- Whether the expert's opinion has been peer reviewed

- Whether the method used by the expert has been peer reviewed

- Whether the expert has submitted any articles to periodicals or publications concerning the method and the opinion, and whether they were rejected or accepted

- The rate of error, if any, created by the method

- Whether the opinion and method are derived from purely subjective criteria

- Whether the method is generally accepted within the relevant scientific community or technical discipline

The standards for expert admissibility will vary according to jurisdiction. Again, some states do not follow *Daubert*, and may have relaxed standards, especially when nonscientific testimony is provided. Many jurisdictions allow expert opinions that do not comply with each of the *Daubert* factors, particularly if the opinion is based upon experience and training rather than upon a specific technical method. Thus, although rigid satisfaction of all *Daubert* criteria may not be required, the expert's opinions should still be reasonably based on some foundation, and the opinions must be helpful to the jury. The requirements of Federal Rules of Evidence 702 and 703 should be reviewed with this in mind, and the witness should be "prepped" with *Daubert*-type questions that the tendering lawyer expects are consistent with the law of the relevant jurisdiction.

CHAPTER

Asking Powerful Questions

This chapter explores winning techniques for deposing adverse (or hostile) fact witnesses and opposing experts. The techniques discussed include how to ask different types of questions, the substantive content of questions, and the timing of when to ask certain questions. Technique is always important, and a lawyer's examination style can vary to maximize effect. The goal is to walk out of the deposition room with fodder for cross-examination in the courtroom.

Keep It Simple

The best questions are simple. An examining lawyer should avoid complicated, compound questions because simple questions are more easily followed by the court and the jury. The aim is to achieve impact and clarity. Compound questions are often confusing, and the jury may get lost in the questions and not fully appreciate important answers.

If possible, the examining lawyer should avoid highly technical terms. Alternatively, technical terms should be defined by using commonly understood words. The jury can more easily track simple questions using common words rather than long sentences with complex structures. Simple questions also give an examination more "punch." Again, the goal is to avoid confusion and boredom by presenting captivating and dramatic testimony.

Easily understood adjectives and adverbs artfully inserted into questions provide dramatic effect. The use of action verbs in a series of questions is also an effective technique. Once again, the objective is to capture both the *ethos and pathos* of the witness and the testimony, using the witness to help the client's position in the case. This can be done by using questions that contain words conveying action, as well as colorful adjectives and adverbs.

It is seldom that a single question and a single answer will win or lose a case. However, questions should be used as building blocks upon which success is achieved. By peppering questions with dramatic or "punchy" words, the jury's attention span is extended; the jury will be more interested in the examination and will listen for longer periods of time. If questions are long and complicated, the jury's focus will diminish quickly. Similarly, if the questions are boring or disjointed, the jury's focus will stray. Thus, a time-tested principle comes into play—keep it *simple, simple, simple.*

The examining lawyer will necessarily tailor questions to the specific type of case at issue. Thus, the words used in the examination logically change depending upon the legal and factual issues involved—whether it is a business tort case, a personal injury case, a contract case, or a negligence case. Deposition questions for each type of case involve different *buzz words* because there will be different types of testimony sought. Creative and case-specific planning is thus required.

The lawyer asking questions should think about his or her case, the key trial themes necessary to win the case (which should have been previously developed), and then select significant "drama" words that promote the trial themes. The questions should incorporate words and phrases the jury will likely consider in the jury charge. By doing this, the lawyer can develop a script that may be presented to the jury during final argument. If all goes as planned, the lawyer will have specific answers to specific questions that translate immediately into answers in the jury charge.

Here are some examples of complex questions that are simplified and, in doing so, become more powerful:

Document Retention Issues

Complex and boring: What are the details of your company's document retention policy?

Simple and interesting: What are your rules to prevent improper document destruction?

Premises Liability

Complex and boring: Does your company have a system for minimizing the risks of accidents on the work premises?

Simple and interesting: What rules do you follow to makes sure workers are safe?

Design Processes

Complex and boring: What design protocols does your company follow to better ensure your product prototypes are designed safely for consumer use?

Simple and interesting: What rules do you follow to make sure your products don't kill people?

Drug Liability Litigation

Complex and boring: Does your company have written policies for moni-
toring the incidence of adverse reactions associated
with pharmaceutical products?

Simple and interesting: What does your company do to find out whether
people are hurt or dying because of bad reactions
to your drugs?

Breach of Contract

Complex and boring: Do you agree that the merger clause in the contract
provides that the contract supersedes all prior
understandings and prohibits amendments to the
contract unless agreed to in writing?

Simple and interesting: Isn't it true that the contract reflects your entire
agreement?

Fraud

Complex and boring: Do you agree that it is important not to misrepresent material facts?

Simple and interesting: Do you agree people shouldn't lie?

Here are some additional examples of questions made more interesting and more
powerful by selective use of adjectives and adverbs:

Negligence Case

- Do you agree that it is a **best practice** to [insert phrase that describes activity at
issue]?

- Do you agree that it is a **reasonable practice** to [insert phrase that describes
activity at issue]?

- Do you agree that everyone should **exercise reasonable care to** [insert phrase
that describes activity at issue]?

Fraud/Negligent Misrepresentation Case

- Isn't it **reasonable** to expect that a **sophisticated** businessman will investigate
an investment before investing money?

- Do you agree people should **not misrepresent** facts known to be false?

- Do you agree parties in negotiations should **exercise reasonable care not** to lie?

- Do you agree that the financial statements of a company should **never mislead** the public?

Premises Liability

- Isn't it correct that all companies should be expected to provide **reasonably safe** workplaces?

- Do you agree that a business owner should take **reasonable steps** to warn customers of **known dangers** on the premises?

Product Liability

- Do you agree that companies have a **duty** to design their products safely to avoid **killing innocent** people?

- Do you agree that people who use consumer products should take **reasonable steps** to make sure they understand how to use the product?

The "No Lose" Questions

A variation on the "simple question" technique is the use of questions that trigger helpful answers regardless of how the witness responds. These are typically broad, leading questions that call for a "yes" or "no" answer, but either response is helpful to the examiner's case. These are the so-called "No Lose" questions because any response is a "No-Win" answer for the witness.

"No Lose" questions are typically crafted using common sense that a witness must fairly concede. The questions call for responses predicated upon moral, ethical, or universal imperatives. If the witness resists the question, the witness will likely lose credibility. Because such questions reflect common sense and fairness, any attempt to argue with the question or the examiner will be poorly perceived. Fighting or resisting common sense is alienating. Thus, the goal of the question is to place the witness in a position where the question's basic premise must be conceded. The question is framed in a way that the witness has little or no option in how the response is framed. Here are some examples:

Products Liability Case

- **The plaintiff can be asked:** "Do you agree it is important to read warnings before you use equipment?" The witness, an injured plaintiff, cannot credibly answer "no." But, by answering "yes," the witness provides a foundation for an effective cross-examination.

Negligence Case

- **The defendant can be asked:** "Do you agree it is important to follow written safety policies provided by the company?" If the witness answers "no," then the witness loses credibility. If the witness answers "yes," and assuming the company's policy manuals address the conduct at issue, then the plaintiff's case is significantly advanced.

Auto Accident Case

- **The witness can be asked:** "Do you agree it is important to follow the speed limit?" or "Is it important to wear safety belts?" or "Is it important to follow roadway warning signs?" If the witness answers "yes," then a foundation has been laid to show that the witness was negligent if, in fact, the witness ignored those safety rules.

Fraud Case

- **A plaintiff can be asked:** "Do you agree it is important to conduct due diligence before you make a significant investment?" If the witness, a sophisticated businessman, says "no," then credibility is lost.

Breach of Contract Case

- **A defendant can be asked:** "Do you agree it is important to keep a promise?" If the witness answers "yes," then a general concession has been obtained. The witness cannot say "no" to such a question, and any attempt to qualify a response will be perceived poorly.

Premises Liability Case

- **A corporate defendant can be asked:** "Do you agree it is important to provide a safe work place for those who come to your property as workers?" If the defendant says "no," then the defendant will not be well received by the jury.

The "Duty" Questions

"Duty" questions are similar to "No Lose" questions, but they incorporate concepts of "duty," "obligation," or "responsibility" into the question. These types of questions may trigger objections from opposing counsel, but the examining lawyer should make it clear that the question is not intended to solicit legal opinions or conclusions, but the witness's testimony based upon experience and training.

The lawyer asking these questions can replace the word "duty" with synonyms, such as "obligation" or "responsibility," or with verbs that create the inference of responsibility. Such auxiliary verbs include words such as "should," "must," "need," and "require," and may be used interchangeably with nouns to reinforce the testimony from an adverse witness. These types of questions are useful with corporate representatives and adverse experts. They can bind a corporate witness or force opposing experts into concessions of key points that cripple their opinions. Here are some examples:

- **Noun**—Do you agree that a company has an **obligation** to provide a safe workplace?

- **Noun**—Do you agree that a company has a **responsibility** to provide a safe workplace?

- **Verb**—Do you agree that a company **must** provide a safe workplace?

- **Verb**—Do you agree that a company **should** provide a safe workplace?

- **Noun**—Do you agree that a manufacturer has a **duty** to design safe products?

- **Noun**—Do you agree that a manufacturer has a **responsibility** to design products?

Combining Word Selections

Ultimately, the lawyer conducting the examination can take simple questions that incorporate notions of "duty" or "responsibility," then add dramatic words for more impact. Words can be mixed and matched and repeated for maximum effect. Implementation only requires planning and an effort to carefully craft simple messages with dramatic effect. Again, this is how a trial lawyer builds *pathos* and *ethos* into the case. Here are some examples that build on earlier "duty" type questions:

- Do you agree that a company has an (*important*) **obligation** to provide a safe workplace?

- Do you agree that a company has a (*significant*) **responsibility** to provide a safe workplace?

- Do you agree that a company **must** (*always*) provide a safe workplace?

- Do you agree that a company **should** (*always*) take steps to ensure a safe workplace?

- Do you agree that a company has a duty to design products that do not kill people?

- Do you agree that a company must warn patients that the drugs could lead to death?

The "Narrowing Path" Method

The examination of an adverse or hostile witness (whether lay or expert) can be likened, albeit loosely, to a sparring match with words. Every boxer knows that a key strategy is to force the opponent into the corner of the boxing ring. By doing so, the opposing boxer is "cornered" or "trapped," losing flexibility and options.

The same holds true for a witness in a deposition. Like boxers in the middle of the ring, an examination begins with broad, general questions, but the goal is to use the question-and-answer process to push the witness into a corner through a series of follow-up questions. This is done by systematically narrowing the witness's field of options until the witness is "pinned down."

This examination technique can be described as the "Narrowing Path" method, where the questions begin with broad concepts, but narrow with successive questions to progressively (and systematically) limit the witness's flexibility. The witness's pathway of available options narrows, and there are no more forks in the road. The following illustration reflects the method:

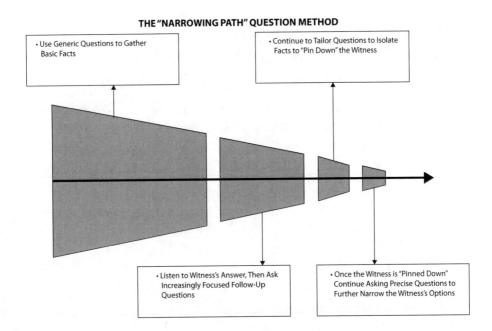

THE "NARROWING PATH" QUESTION METHOD

- Use Generic Questions to Gather Basic Facts

- Continue to Tailor Questions to Isolate Facts to "Pin Down" the Witness

- Listen to Witness's Answer, Then Ask Increasingly Focused Follow-Up Questions

- Once the Witness is "Pinned Down" Continue Asking Precise Questions to Further Narrow the Witness's Options

Illustrations of the "Narrowing Path" Method

Here are some simple illustrations of the "Narrowing Path" method:

Q: How were you hurt in the accident?

A: I hurt my back and neck.

Q: Did you hurt any other part of your body?

A: Yes, I also hurt my head.

Q: Besides your back, neck and head, did you suffer any other type of injury?

A: No.

Q: Ok. So the record is clear, you agree, that the only injuries that you are complaining of were to your body, head, and neck?

A: Yes.

Q: Have you ever received medical attention for any of your injuries?

A: Yes.

Q: For which injuries have you received medical treatment?

A: My head and my neck.

Q: Ok. So the record is clear you agree that you have received medical treatment for your head and your neck?

A: Yes.

Q: So the record is clear, it is my understanding you have not received any type of medical treatment or medical care for your back. Is that correct?

A: That is correct.

* * * * * * * *

Q: What misrepresentations are you claiming in this case?

A: They misstated how much I would receive in profits from my investment.

Q: Who are they?

A: John Doe and Jane Doe.

Q: Are you claiming any other misrepresentation by any other person?

A: No.

Q: Ok. To make sure the record is clear, do you agree that the only people who you claim made any type of misstatement were Jane Doe and John Doe?

A: Yes.

Q: And isn't it correct the only misrepresentation that you claim deals with how much profit you would receive from your investment?

A: Yes.

Q: Were these statements in writing or oral?

A: Both.

Q: Did you meet with John Doe in person?

A: Yes.

Q: Did you ever meet with Jane Doe in person?

A: No.

Q: So the only verbal representation you are claiming in this case was from John Doe? Is that correct?

A: Yes.

Q: Isn't it correct you are making no claim against Jane Doe for any verbal misrepresentation?

A: Correct.

"Bump and Run"

Another useful strategy when deposing a third-party witness is utilizing aggressive leading questions, but alternating with open-ended, non-leading questions. This "Bump and Run" strategy is particularly helpful when the lawyer is not sure about the witness's testimony, or the witness's bias or leanings in the case. In such instances, the examining lawyer can push aggressively with leading questions to determine whether the witness is favorable or unfavorable. These leading questions may inspire objections because the witness may be independent. If the answers are favorable, then the examining lawyer can resort to more open-ended questions seeking the same information in a nonleading format. In essence, the leading questions are the first step used to test the waters—that is, the witness's orientation and bias. Once the examining lawyer feels comfortable with the answers and the witness's leanings, the examination can proceed with more direct questions that do not trigger objections. Here is an example:

Q: Isn't it true you saw the light turn red when you approached the intersection?

Opposing Counsel: Objection, leading.

A: Yes.

Q: Isn't it true you saw the car run the red light and crash into my client's car?

Opposing Counsel: Objection, leading.

A: Yes.

Q: Isn't it correct you did not see my client do anything wrong?

Opposing Counsel: Objection, leading.

A: That is correct.

Q: Now sir, to address the objections that have been made, please explain to the ladies and gentlemen of the jury precisely what you saw when you arrived at the intersection.

A: I saw the car run the red light and crash into your client's car.

Knowing When to Stop, When to Follow Up, and When to Run

An old axiom is that trial lawyers should never ask questions when the answers are not known. A similar adage is that lawyers should refrain from asking "one too many" questions. This is a hard lesson to teach and, in fact, is most often learned from the school of hard knocks. Every trial lawyer has been burned by an "extra" question that unravels an otherwise successful examination, and some of these moments become etched in the lawyer's memory. Indeed, these are the moments when the examiner wishes he or she could retract the question and put it back in the bottle.

The ultimate lesson here is that lawyers do not need to win every battle, and they do not need to "win" every question and answer exchange. It is sometimes enough for a jury to draw inferences concerning questions not asked. They can fill in the blanks, and that last question may not be necessary. Sometimes a juror's imagination is more helpful than the question itself. Asking the last question gives the witness the opportunity to undo the harm already done. The witness can qualify or explain prior answers or even change his or her mind.

Simply put, lawyers need to know when to quit. Every question creates the risk of a potentially unwanted answer. No lawyer should ask a question in a trial deposition where the answer is not reasonably predictable. If the witness has been effectively examined, the jury will infer the answers to questions not asked. Juries typically understand a witness's testimony, and whether the witness is credible or not credible, without hearing the last question and answer. The good trial lawyer wants to end on a high note. The good trial lawyer never wants to end on a low note. These are rules to live by.

Listen, Listen, and Listen

Many lawyers fail to listen. They ask questions, then tune out in the middle of the answer because they are too preoccupied with scripted outlines or they are thinking about (or reading) the next question. In fact, some lawyers arrive at a deposition with pre-planned questions, and they show little interest to improvise on the fly. The result is that valuable opportunities are lost.

Sometimes witnesses provide compelling concessions that beg for follow-up, but the testimony is never fully developed. Being too dependent upon a written script or outline deprives the lawyer of spontaneity and the ability to follow up. Witnesses often say the most amazing things—even incriminating admissions—that are never developed because the lawyer is not listening. The failure to follow up may cost the lawyer opportunities to mine valuable testimony that can win the case. The failure to pursue follow-up questions may also leave the jury wondering.

Witnesses should be evaluated during the early stages of a deposition, when their personalities and unique tics become evident. It should become quickly evident if the witness is properly prepared, since an improperly prepared witness frequently provides "volunteer" testimony or long narrative responses. These extended narratives frequently contain morsels of information than can be pursued by later questions. The key here is to listen to the answers of a rambling witness because these witnesses invariably ramble into problems. In fact, some skilled lawyers actually encourage narrative responses and, once on the record, then decide what aspects of the long-winded answer to pursue. The key is to listen.

Strategic Timing

Another technique involves the timing of breaks, and what questions should be asked immediately before or following a break. An examining lawyer should assume that an adverse witness will confer with his or her lawyer during breaks and will be "schooled" or "coached" on how to better respond to any recently asked questions. Thus, it is often a tactical mistake for the examining lawyer to plow back into the same topics immediately after a break, because the witness may be primed to correct or modify prior answers with a rehearsed statement.

One tactic for the examiner is to abruptly change the subject matter of the questions upon returning from a break. The original topic matter of the questions can be addressed later in the deposition or not at all. Sometimes it is better not to disturb prior testimony that is clearly helpful. Plowing old ground may unravel what has been achieved. Sometimes the best strategy is to move on and not put the last nail in the coffin.

Changing Tempo

Tempo is important. Every trial lawyer should consider changing the tempo of an examination to maximize effectiveness. Changing voice inflection adds drama to the questions. Changing the speed of questions augments the intensity of the moment and also adds drama. The bottom line is that the trial lawyer is not just the director of the drama that is unfolding: he or she is an active participant, who can accentuate and add to the drama by changing the nature, tone, and intensity of the questions. The lawyer can inject a tone of righteous indignation into the questions, or the lawyer can inject a tone of incredulousness into the questions. These techniques send messages to a jury when they see and hear the final video product.

Lawyers need to be flexible in their style and prepared to change tempo quickly if needed. Sometimes witnesses get too comfortable with the tempo of an examination and, with this newly acquired confidence, may become less responsive or more difficult to examine. The trial lawyer can change the tempo of the questions without notice. The goal is to pierce through rehearsed responses and get to the truth. By changing tempo, the witness may be forced to provide more candid responses without all the bells and whistles that reflect a witness's rehearsed answers.

Handling Unresponsive Witnesses

Every trial lawyer encounters witnesses who provide long-winded answers that never answer the questions. This is an avoidance mechanism used by the witness to side-step the question. Unfortunately, many witnesses will continue to be unresponsive unless they fear the consequences.

The standard (and predictable) reaction to an unresponsive witness is to formally object to the answer as "nonresponsive." This is certainly an appropriate step to preserve the objection for the record. However, formal objections are frequently lost on a jury and may have little effect on the witness. In fact, some witnesses may feel encouraged when they hear these objections because they assume they are "winning" the war of the words. It is therefore more effective to attack the witness's lack of cooperation in a more direct fashion by letting the jury know that the witness is uncooperative and unreasonable.

The examining lawyer should make clear that an answer is not responsive and politely insist that the witness answer the question on the record. If the witness continues to be nonresponsive, the examining lawyer should again make it clear the answer is inappropriate and restate the question yet again, but modifying some words within the question to confirm that the witness understood the question. If the witness still persists with the same behavior, the witness should be politely reprimanded in the next question. The jury will begin to see a pattern and that the witness is acting in bad faith. The jury may even sympathize with the lawyer who is trying to elicit responsive answers to fair questions. The examining lawyer also can express righteous indignation at the witness's behavior, but should do so without becoming angry or impolite. Here are some examples:

Q: With all due respect, sir, you have not answered my question, so I am forced to re-ask the question. Here is the question: _____?

Q: Perhaps you misunderstood me, so I am restating the question again. Here is the question: _____.

Q: Is there a reason why you are not responding to my question, which was _____?

Q: Did you understand my question? If not, please explain what you did not understand.

Using Video to Control Witness Behavior

If an opposing expert (or other hostile witness) is generally evasive, the examining lawyer should object to the nonresponsive testimony and advise the witness that continued unresponsiveness may result in court action. This will typically get either the attention of the witness or opposing counsel. Certainly, no expert wants to risk having his or her testimony limited or excluded because of evasiveness.

Using a videotape is one way to control an evasive witness. As with lay witnesses, expert witnesses tend to be more cooperative if a video record is created. A video reveals far more about a witness than a written transcript because it memorializes combativeness, body language, voice inflections, and any inappropriate behaviors. An experienced witness is less likely to abuse the deposition process if a video is made.

Therefore, as a general matter, the examining lawyer should strongly consider video recordation of all depositions of adverse or hostile witnesses; this includes both lay and expert witnesses. The video record often chills inappropriate behaviors.

9

Deposing Individual Plaintiffs

Taking the deposition of an individual plaintiff is similar to other witness depositions, but there are some added twists and turns. The unique facts, claims, and defenses in each case will certainly dictate what is ultimately asked during the deposition. However, there are certain questions and strategies common to most individual plaintiffs in most cases.

Timing of the Deposition

Timing is always an important consideration. There are substantive considerations that dictate when to proceed. Any deposition in the early stages of discovery is useful to help frame the issues. That is why defense lawyers typically seek to depose the plaintiff before presenting their own client or corporate witnesses for deposition. This helps the defense lawyers better prepare their own witnesses because they can better define the issues and relevant defenses. They are also in a better position to evaluate the equitable posturing of the parties. If the plaintiff's claims and supporting facts are well defined, the defense lawyer is in a better position to define the defenses and defensive trial themes, then use those themes when preparing the defendant for deposition. However, there is always a risk of deposing a plaintiff *too* early. A balance needs to be struck that weighs the benefits and drawbacks of an early deposition.

Typically speaking, deposing individual plaintiffs should be done *only after* initial written discovery is completed. Basic document discovery is always recommended. If allowed, simple interrogatories seeking to establish the plaintiff's legal and factual contentions are helpful. Basic personal information about the plaintiff should also be obtained.

If the plaintiff's deposition is taken too early, the defense lawyer will not have the benefit of acquiring and researching background information to conduct preliminary investigations. A defense lawyer should do homework, including pre-deposition investigations, before moving forward with depositions. Otherwise, important issues may be overlooked.

Examples of basic information appropriately gathered before a plaintiff's deposition might include the following:

Personal Information

- Plaintiff's name (and all prior names or aliases)

- Age

- Current address

- Telephone contact information

- Prior employment positions (last 10 years)

- Prior addresses (last 10 years)

- Driver's license number

- Social Security number

- Marital status and children

Contention Discovery

- Contention interrogatories seeking identification of specific facts in support of the claims

- All prior witness statements

- Core document discovery supporting the claims

Common Questions

Once the lawyer decides to proceed with the plaintiff's deposition, and obtains general background information, the lawyer should start drafting a deposition outline, which incorporates the information obtained. The lawyer should then fine-tune questions to expand on that information. The following list reflects general areas for examination:

- Personal background

- Family background

- Job background

- Educational background

- Prior claims and litigation background

- Prior sworn testimony

- Unique experiences/expertise

- Prior criminal history

Educational Background and Experiences

A plaintiff's education and past experiences are always important. This information can be used as a basis for possible impeachment to the extent that a witness's education or past experiences indicates special knowledge relevant to the allegations or defenses in the case. It also helps the examining lawyer know how to treat the plaintiff in the presence of the jury. A jury may be more sympathetic to a witness who has no significant education. Conversely, the jury may be less sympathetic to a plaintiff who has a substantial education. This is particularly true if jurors are less educated. A jury may be more protective of a plaintiff who has not achieved significant levels of education because they may see the plaintiff as an underdog. Again, these are subtleties that turn on the specific facts in each case.

Clearly, however, education is important for other reasons. A witness does not have to be a college graduate to have unique experiences or expertise relevant to a case. An experienced "shade tree mechanic" may have technical know-how that may allow the witness to serve as an expert on mechanical issues. A journeyman bookkeeper who has no college education may still have expertise concerning accounting issues relevant to the case. A welder may have expertise concerning the physical properties of metals even though the welder never graduated from high school. The possible examples are endless. Thus, all levels of education and background should be explored. The goal is to find out whether the plaintiff is a "closet" expert who may offer opinions at trial. As a closet expert, the plaintiff's past experiences can potentially help undermine the claims in the case.

Questioning Regarding Witness Deposition Preparation

Every plaintiff should be questioned concerning what he or she did to prepare for deposition, and this examination should focus on identifying all materials that were considered. The examination should also include specific questions concerning whether the plaintiff met with other witnesses and the substance of those meetings, as well as identifying any pleadings or discovery the witness reviewed. Although opposing counsel may object to these questions on privilege grounds, many courts will allow this discovery because the plaintiff is using materials to refresh his or her memory. The following chart summarizes some key areas to cover:

Prior depositions	Identify all depositions the witness reviewed to prepare for deposition.
Witness statements	Identify all witness statements the witness reviewed to prepare for deposition.
Own witness statement	Determine if the plaintiff provided a witness statement and, if so, confirm that it was produced.
Pleadings	Confirm whether the plaintiff reviewed and authorized the petition or other key pleadings.
Sworn discovery	Identify all sworn declarations or discovery responses the plaintiff may have signed under oath.
Key documents	Identify key documents reviewed.

Pleadings and Prior Declarations

Every plaintiff should be questioned concerning the pleadings, discovery responses to which they have sworn, affidavits or declarations they have signed, and any other witness statements they may have provided. An examination based upon the pleadings should be used to force the plaintiff to identify specific evidence to support specific allegations or, alternatively, force the plaintiff to concede that he or she does not have that evidence. Affidavits and prior sworn discovery responses serve a similar purpose, but should also be used as a source of impeachment. All of these materials should be used to "lock in" the plaintiff's testimony. As in other witness depositions, the goal is to complete a thorough deposition to isolate plaintiff's claims, address details concerning those claims, and identify the facts known (or not known) to the plaintiff that support those claims.

The pleadings in a case are akin to topic categories in a notice of corporate representative deposition. The pleadings should be used to frame the examination concerning the plaintiff's allegations, as well as to identify the supporting evidence known to the plaintiff. The lawyer conducting the deposition should seek to pin the plaintiff down on all factual recitations in the pleadings. The following are specific examples concerning this type of examination:

- Your answers to interrogatories state that my client failed to exercise reasonable care in the following respects: [_____]. Does this list represent the entirety of your claims against my client?

- Your petition states you are suing my client for fraud based upon misrepresentations. Please identify all the misrepresentations you allege my client made, identify the specific individual who allegedly made them, and state when they were made.

- Your affidavit states you met with my client on five occasions. Isn't it correct that your affidavit represents your best memory of all occasions where you had a personal meeting with any of my client's representatives?

In sum, the pleadings (and sworn statements) should be used as a template to force the plaintiff to provide details of the plaintiff's case. This helps the defense lawyer prepare the defendant. It also prevents surprise by making it more difficult for the plaintiff to add or change claims in the future.

Litigation Background

Every plaintiff should be questioned on his or her involvement as a party in other lawsuits or instances where the plaintiff gave sworn testimony as a witness. It is important to know if a plaintiff has filed prior claims to gauge if the plaintiff is a seasoned testifier, an abusive litigant, or both. The jury will certainly want to know if the plaintiff has brought prior lawsuits, and whether any of those suits involved similar claims, injuries, or fact patterns. It is also important to track down any prior depositions or trial testimony that may better illuminate the plaintiff's current testimony or claims.

A plaintiff who has a history of suing people or companies may be perceived differently than a plaintiff who has never been in a courtroom. Veteran plaintiffs are potentially characterized as professional litigants, and evidence of prior suits may actually alienate the jury. A classic example of this involves plaintiffs who pursue multiple claims for work related injuries. Another such example arises when a plaintiff allegedly suffers a physical condition, but files different lawsuits against different defendants asserting inconsistent causation theories.

A review of prior testimony will shed light on a plaintiff's litigation history. Prior work-related injuries are potentially used to impeach current injury claims. Prior claims of disability may be relevant to current claims. Thus, multiple reasons exist for why a witness's litigation history should be discovered and closely examined.

Research regarding the history of a litigious plaintiff should specifically include identifying the names of all parties to prior lawsuits, the names of counsel, the venues of the suits, and when each suit was litigated and/or resolved. The following list summarizes topics relating to prior litigation involvements:

- Prior involvement in litigation: identify type of suit, jurisdiction, and attorneys who represented the parties.

- Prior claims: identify the type of claim—whether a personal injury claim or property damage claim.

- Prior worker's compensation action claims: identify the employer, the date of the underlying injury, the nature of the injury, and whether the witness received permanent or temporary disability.

- Prior deposition testimony: identify the case, date, and jurisdiction.

- Prior trial testimony: identify the case, date, and jurisdiction.

Employment Background

Every plaintiff should be questioned concerning his or her employment background. Again, some of this information is properly obtained through written discovery preceding the deposition. The deposition is then used to delve more deeply into that background to ferret out what may be relevant to the case. The following list outlines areas to address in a deposition regarding employment:

- Current employment: identify the witness's current place of employment, level of compensation, title, and job responsibilities.

- Prior disciplinary action: identify whether the witness has received prior disciplinary action (such as terminations, suspensions, reprimands, or warnings) in connection with the witness's current or past employment.

- Prior employment: identify a comprehensive history of prior jobs, including the identification of former supervisors and reasons for departure from previous jobs. These reasons could involve terminations for cause. The witness's personnel files from prior jobs may be relevant.

- Periods of unemployment: identify whether the witness sustained extended periods of unemployment and, if so, the reasons for that unemployment. This type of history may help the examining lawyer better understand the witness, his or her motivations, and his or her employability.

- Immediate and prior supervisors: the names of supervisors may become important if job performance becomes an issue.

Deposing a Personal Injury Plaintiff

There are basic damage and injury questions included in every outline involving a personal injury plaintiff. Such questions should typically include the following items:

- Identify the specific injuries claimed and describe in detail.

- Identify hospitals where the injuries were treated.

- Identify doctors who treated the injuries.

- Specify duration of hospitalization.

- Identify medications initially prescribed.

- Identify current medications.

- Identify pharmacies where prescriptions were filled.

- Identify work disabilities identified by physicians.

- Identify period out of work due to injury.

- Identify rehabilitation progress.

- Identify return to work—when this occurred or is projected to occur.

- Identify changes in scope of work or work limitations.

- Identify impact on hobbies and interests.

- Identify impact on daily activities.

An injured plaintiff should be examined regarding *all* his or her prior injuries and illnesses because this history may reveal other claims, pre-existing injuries, or health conditions relevant to the current claims. The examining lawyer should always seek to determine if the plaintiff is seeking damages for pre-existing injuries, then use this discovery to conduct third-party discovery through depositions or depositions on written questions, including discovery sent to prior employers, prior facilities where the plaintiff was hospitalized, and prior treating physicians. Specific questions might include the following:

- Identify all prior hospitalizations for the last 10 years and specify the location, date, and hospital name.

- Identify all treating physicians for the last 10 years, and specify the location, date, and name of the treating physician.

- Identify all prior injuries for which insurance claims have been filed at any time.

- Identify all prior injuries that resulted in lawsuits.

- Identify all prior periods of unemployment due to injuries.

- Identify any disabilities claimed due to prior existing injuries.

- Identify all prior workers' compensation claims.

Claims of Special Expertise

An examining lawyer should specifically question the plaintiff as to whether he or she claims a special expertise or unique background. This background should then be explored to determine potential relevance to the case. What follows is an example based upon a plaintiff's expertise acquired from a prior job:

A man and his wife were riding a motorcycle with a home-built trailer made from readily available supplies but with no shock absorbers. Traveling down the road at highway speeds, the trailer hit a pothole and swerved outward from the bike. The husband lost control of the motorcycle and crashed, and his wife was thrown and suffered a head injury. Both husband and wife filed a lawsuit against the motorcycle manufacturer, alleging stability and handling defects. During the deposition of the husband, it was discovered that he had an earlier career as a cross-country truck driver where he acquired significant knowledge about trailers and hauling trailers. He knew that improperly loaded trailers could jackknife, and that it was important to have a well-built trailer with directional stability. This background then became a basis for a claim of comparative fault. In effect, the plaintiff's past experiences were used to demonstrate misuse of the product (the home-built trailer), which could bar the husband's claims and significantly offset any liability exposure for the wife's claims.

General to Specific Examination Techniques

This examination technique is relevant in all cases where the goal is to isolate the witness's knowledge. The technique involves a so-called "Narrowing Path" method, which was discussed in detail in Chapter 8. It involves a sequencing of questions where broad questions are first presented, then followed with a series of increasingly narrower questions. The purpose is to isolate the facts as well as the factual evidence relied upon by the plaintiff in order to attack or limit those claims. Examples of this method are also given in Chapter 8. An illustration of the "Narrowing Path" method is again given below:

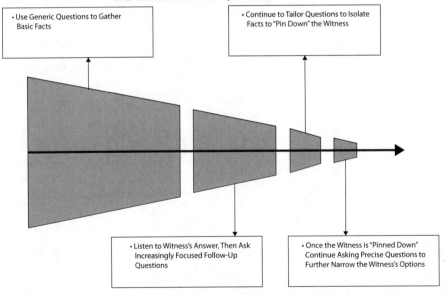

THE "NARROWING PATH" QUESTION METHOD

• Use Generic Questions to Gather Basic Facts

• Continue to Tailor Questions to Isolate Facts to "Pin Down" the Witness

• Listen to Witness's Answer, Then Ask Increasingly Focused Follow-Up Questions

• Once the Witness is "Pinned Down" Continue Asking Precise Questions to Further Narrow the Witness's Options

10

Deposing Third-Party Lay Witnesses

As with any other deposition, the trial lawyer should take the time to research and be well informed about the background of third-party witnesses before the depositions of such witnesses begin. The lawyer's goals should be clearly identified beforehand. Is the goal to neutralize the witness? Is the goal to package the witness's testimony for trial? Preparing a written outline of specific topics is always recommended, and this will help achieve the case-specific goals. A generic outline with general topics for a deposition of a third-party lay witness is also provided at the end of this chapter.

The deposition of a third-party witness should be approached as if the deposition is a trial deposition, even if the witness is within the subpoena range of the court. The trial lawyer should recognize that if the witness is located outside the jurisdictional reach of the court, then the deposition is undoubtedly a trial deposition, and the lawyer should approach the deposition as if the jury were present. There is a good chance that this witness will never come to trial, and what is accomplished (or not accomplished) will ultimately be for jury consumption.

Meetings with the Witness

A third-party lay witness is like any other witness, except the lawyer has no control over the witness and may not have an opportunity to engage in substantial (or any) discussions with the witness before the deposition. If the opportunity exists for a pre-deposition meeting or interview, then an important strategic decision must be made whether to participate in such a meeting.

In some instances, the better strategy is to forego any meeting and maintain a distance from the witness until the deposition. This is certainly the case if the witness is expected to be hostile. If a hostile witness agrees voluntarily to meet with the lawyer, the witness may seem less hostile in the eyes of the jury and the court, even if the testimony is harmful. If the lawyer meets with the witness, the fact of this voluntary meeting could impact the lawyer's ability to argue the right to use leading questions during the examination. In addition, if the witness is hostile, the witness may take advantage of any meeting by distorting what was said at the meeting, and may attribute negative or inflammatory statements to the lawyer. It should be assumed the opposing lawyer will find out about any such meeting and will seek to exploit what was said and what was not said. Therefore, in some instances, the best strategic course may be to avoid the meeting altogether.

Because a meeting with a third-party witness and the substance of any conversations are discoverable, the trial lawyer should weigh the potential benefits of a meeting against the risk that the substance of any interview will be discovered. During the deposition, the witness will be asked (and should be asked) whether the witness met with counsel; if so, the witness will be questioned regarding the frequency of the meetings, the duration of the meetings, whether the meetings were taped or recorded, whether other persons were present, the location of the meetings, and the substance of the meetings.

If the other side has already met with the witness, and the witness is antagonistic and biased against your case, then this prior meeting with opposing counsel should be used to demonstrate bias and unfairness against your client. If both sides have met with the witness, this opportunity is largely lost. Thus, under these circumstances, the best strategy may be to show favoritism to the other side.

When meeting with independent witnesses, caution should be exercised if a witness statement is obtained during the meeting. Obviously, any witness statement is discoverable. However, equally important, the method of securing the witness statement may become relevant. The lawyer should avoid any conduct that might be considered inappropriate or untoward. This is because opposing counsel will seek an opportunity to exploit any suggestion to the contrary. Here is an example:

> An oil field worker had been laid off from his job due to a recession in the oil patch. He, along with several others, had been contacted by plaintiff's counsel concerning their work on several oil and gas wells at issue in a pending case. The witness was unemployed at the time he was interviewed and he had no success finding a new job. The plaintiffs hired an investigator to conduct the in-person interview, along with interviews of several other former employees. The investigator showed up with a six-pack of beer and spent the afternoon drinking with the witness before turning on the tape recorder. Of course, the witness was both disarmed by this "friendliness" and mildly

intoxicated. The series of questions that followed were rehearsed before the recording commenced. When this behavior was discovered, the witness statement lost credibility and trustworthiness.

Obtain Witness Statements

The examining lawyer should try to obtain any witness statements that the independent witness may have provided before deciding to meet the witness. This helps the lawyer decide whether to move forward with a meeting because the statement will likely reveal if the witness will provide favorable or unfavorable testimony. In many jurisdictions, preliminary discovery can be used to obtain such statements as a matter of course. If the witness observed an accident, witness statements may have been taken by investigating authorities or law enforcement agencies. Witness statements are also frequently taken by insurance adjusters. If not already produced, the lawyer should require that the witness produce the statement at or before the deposition. This can be achieved by serving the witness with a subpoena *duces tecum*.

Pre-Deposition Investigation

In addition to obtaining witness statements, the witness's background should be investigated through online research or other noninvasive investigation. A search for criminal history can be undertaken in the county where the witness resides or offices. If the witness's prior addresses can be obtained, then the breadth of this research can be expanded for each county where the witness previously resided or worked.

Social media is a fruitful source of published information. A treasure trove of relevant information is available at the touch of a computer key. People publish a significant amount of personal information about themselves, and some of this information may be directly relevant to the case. For instance, in one case involving an intoxicated driver, the witness's social media page revealed a photograph of the witness with a beer in her hand with the typed description "Here I am with my beer, my best friend." A social media page may actually discuss an accident that the witness observed. The witness may have taken photographs and posted them online.

By way of example, an interview of a scene witness revealed that the witness had taken dozens of photographs of a tragic truck accident in front of his house, but had never disclosed the existence of these photographs to investigating authorities because "he was never specifically asked." The photographs were taken immediately after the accident, and before emergency responders arrived.

As such, these photographs contained pristine evidence that helped reconstruct the accident. The photographs showed skid marks and debris *in situ* before investigating authorities arrived.

Use of Demonstrative Exhibits

If the deposition is considered a trial deposition, which is the most prudent assumption to make, then the examining lawyer should consider enhancing the examination through the use of demonstrative exhibits. Such demonstratives might include enlargements of documents, photographs, or models that can be used to enhance or better explain the witness's testimony.

A variety of different types of demonstratives are available, and every examining lawyer should evaluate the type and need for demonstratives in each deposition. By using demonstrative exhibits, the trial lawyer accentuates important testimony for later consideration by the jury. Again, this is particularly important if the witness is not expected to be physically present at trial. The types of demonstrative exhibits are discussed in detail in Chapter 16.

Creating Exhibits During Deposition

Another useful technique is to create exhibits during deposition. This is easily done by having the witness draw pictures or diagrams of what the witness observed or that explain the witness's testimony. The witness should label and identify photographs and initial his or her references accordingly. This is particularly powerful if the deposition is on video. Here is an example:

> In one case involving a serious, high-speed automobile accident, an eyewitness was deposed. Because the witness no longer resided in the area and was not expected to be at trial, a video deposition was conducted. This was a trial deposition in all respects. The deposition became a particularly powerful weapon in the case, however, by the use of an aerial photograph of the roadway where the accident occurred. The aerial photograph was in color and showed the details of the roadway, surrounding terrain, and intersecting cross-roads. The photograph was then placed on a large magnetic board. Small model cars were created and also magnetized. The witness was then asked to demonstrate how the cars moved by placing the vehicles on the magnetic board. As the witness demonstrated the movement of these vehicles, the witness provided a step-by-step narrative of the vehicle movement and ultimate collision. The entire examination was videotaped, which created forceful images for the jury.

Developing Witness Expertise

Some lay witnesses have unique experience, education, or training that may qualify them as expert witnesses. A shade tree mechanic may be an expert on automotive maintenance because of his hobby. A member of the clergy may be an expert in grief counseling. A plumber may have expertise regarding water invasion and mold. A carpenter may have expertise on basic engineering issues. The examining lawyer should always be cognizant that a third-party lay witness may have a unique background that can be cultivated in a manner where the witness can serve as a nonretained expert.

Qualifying a lay witness as a potential expert, however, should be approached with caution. Unless the examining lawyer knows what the witness's testimony will be, the lawyer should not ask any questions about the witness's credentials until the end of the deposition. If the witness's testimony is favorable, then the witness can be qualified as an expert. If the witness's testimony is unfavorable, then the witness should not be qualified as an expert. The challenge is to then undermine the expertise. This option is lost, however, if the witness is qualified as an expert at the beginning of the deposition without knowing what the testimony will be. The lawyer should avoid putting the cart before the horse. The witness should not be qualified as an expert until after it is clear that the testimony is favorable.

Prior Testimony Background

The witness should be questioned concerning his or her experience in providing testimony, and this should be done at the beginning stages of the deposition. The witness may have been deposed on prior occasions and may exhibit comfort with the deposition process. The examining lawyer should try to ascertain this background before jumping into any aggressive cross-examination.

Sequencing the Examination

It is important to listen to all witnesses. It is particularly important to evaluate independent witnesses during the initial stages of a deposition before critical questions are asked. If the examining lawyer has never met or talked with the witness, then the best strategy is to wade into the examination slowly with basic, general questions before more critical questions. In effect, the lawyer is qualifying the witness as either "favorable" or "unfavorable." As part of this process, the examining lawyer must evaluate any bias that the witness exhibits before pressing forward with critical questions to which the answers are not known.

A sound examination strategy is to sequence important questions. There are essentially two stages—a preliminary stage and a follow-up stage. The preliminary stage is used to find out what the witness may know, without pressing into the details of that knowledge. This stage would include questions concerning basic background information about how the witness fits into the larger picture of the case. This would include whether the witness has specific memory of events or transactions, had a specific opportunity to observe relevant facts, or met with or knows the opposing counsel or party. The witness is basically "qualified" as to witness capacity and whether there is potential bias.

Once this first stage is completed, then the examining lawyer can make a more informed decision whether to proceed more aggressively with more critical questions. Keeping in mind that *every deposition is a trial deposition*, the examining lawyer must evaluate whether the questions will generate favorable or unfavorable responses. Sometimes a lawyer should not delve further if it is clear the witness intends to hurt the client's case. If that is a risk, then the remainder of the deposition should be focused on what the witness did not observe or the reasons why the witness's testimony should not be believed. Doubt should be created concerning the witness's perceptions. When the witness is passed and follow-up questions are asked by opposing lawyers, the foundation of the witness's testimony has already been undercut, if not neutralized.

Sometimes a witness does not want to be involved and essentially states that he or she does not recall specific facts. If a pattern develops, then it makes no sense to push the witness into similar answers to critical questions when the nonanswers effectively become answers. The lawyer should avoid pursuing an endless examination of a witness, even though the witness proclaimed that she did not recall basic information.

Separating Innuendo, Speculation, and Hearsay

Every deposition will likely involve occasions where the witness volunteers speculative responses or responses based upon hearsay. The examining lawyer must be prepared to cross-examine the witness to separate facts personally known to the witness and those concerning which no personal knowledge exists. This is particularly important if the testimony is unfavorable. The lawyer's goal should be to show that the testimony is not admissible because it is not based upon what the witness saw, heard, touched, felt, tasted, or smelled. In essence, if the witness did not use one of his or her basic senses to acquire the information, then the information is not based on personal knowledge and may not be admissible.

The trial lawyer should listen to the witness's answers and be prepared to challenge those answers if the witness did not have an opportunity to specifically see, hear, or otherwise use other human senses of perception.

Common Outline Questions

As an initial starting point, most third-party witness depositions should be approached with an outline that includes one or more of the following features:

- **Reminders to Witness:** Remind the witness that his or her testimony is under oath and that the penalties of perjury apply; this is more important if the witness's testimony is expected to be adverse or hostile.

- **Background:** Explore the witness's background and obtain a list of previous addresses, telephone contact information, places of employment, employment history, and relationship to the parties; this information allows further investigation.

- **Prior Testimony:** Explore prior experience in providing testimony in deposition or at trial.

- **Witness Statements:** Explore whether witness statements have been provided and to whom.

- **Preparation:** Explore whether the witness has reviewed or created any documents to prepare for the deposition.

- **Meetings with Opposing Counsel or Parties:** Explore whether the witness met with or talked (by telephone) with opposing counsel, the opposing party, or any investigators before the deposition and, if so, the location of the meetings, the frequency of the meetings, the duration of the meetings, the substantive content of the meetings, and whether any written notes of the meetings were generated or recorded.

- **Affiliations:** Explore whether the witness has any business or social affiliations with or knowledge of any of the parties in the case.

- **Other Witnesses:** Explore whether the witness has communicated with any other witnesses in the case or reviewed any other witness's testimony.

- **Connection with Case:** Ascertain a general description of the witness's connection with the case and what the witness observed or heard.

- **Availability for Trial:** Determine whether the witness resides within the subpoena range of the court and, if so, whether the witness intends to be available at the time the case is scheduled for trial.

11

Deposing a Minor Child

Taking the deposition of a minor child involves special challenges and sensitivities. The first issue is whether the deposition should be taken. If the decision is made to proceed, then due care should be given to structure the examination in a way that is not overbearing, but is still calculated to achieve the desired discovery. The best interests of the child are always first and foremost, and the deposition should proceed in a manner that respects those interests.

Competency Thresholds

All witnesses must be competent to testify, and children are no exception. In other words, if a child is not competent to testify at trial, any deposition testimony will likewise be inadmissible. A determination must be made that a child witness is capable of appreciating the importance of telling the truth and the importance of not telling a lie.

The various state jurisdictions are not uniform in how they treat child witnesses. However, most states recognize, either explicitly[1] or implicitly,[2] that age alone is not a single dispositive factor. Even in states that have rules specifically referencing child witnesses, it appears that a child of most any age may be competent.[3] In these states, all witnesses, including young children, are presumed competent and there is no *prima facie* exclusion simply because of age.

---

[1] Cal. Evid. Code § 700 (West) ("Except as otherwise provided by statute, every person, irrespective of age, is qualified to be a witness and no person is disqualified to testify to any matter.").

[2] *See* N.M. R. Evid. 11-601 ("Every person is competent to be a witness unless these rules provide otherwise."); N.J.R. Evid. 601 ("Every person is competent to be a witness unless (a) the judge finds that the proposed witness is incapable of expression concerning the matter so as to be understood by the judge and jury either directly or through interpretation, or (b) the proposed witness is incapable of understanding the duty of a witness to tell the truth, or (c) except as otherwise provided by these rules or by law.").

[3] Tex. R. Evid. Rule 601(a)(2) ("Every person is competent to be a witness unless these rules provide otherwise. The following witnesses are incompetent: ... A child—or any other person—whom the court examines and finds lacks sufficient intellect to testify concerning the matters in issue.").

In Mississippi, one case supports the right of a 6-year-old to serve as a witness.[4] In Iowa, a 4-year-old child was deemed competent.[5] In some states, such as Idaho, a court will conduct a hearing in chambers to determine whether a child under 10 is competent to testify.[6] In several states, it appears that 10 years is a threshold before the court will conduct a hearing to determine whether the child is competent. The focus here is whether a child under 10 can remember or relate truthfully the facts relating to the child's testimony.[7] Typically, a child's memory should be evaluated to confirm a clear recollection of events and to ensure that the child's recollection has not been created or molded by intervening suggestions of adults. The testimony must be a child's testimony, not the product of what others have told the child. In one state, which appears to be the exception, a child under the age of 10 who does not understand the obligation of his sworn oath is not necessarily excluded from giving testimony, but this inability is simply one factor for the jury to consider when weighing the child's testimony.[8] In some states, the child may be able to testify without taking the oath if the court determines the child understands the duty to tell the truth or the duty not to lie.[9] Thus, the trial lawyer should consult the rules in the relevant jurisdiction to determine how the child should be sworn at the beginning of the deposition.

Because the court will not rule on competency during the deposition itself, the trial lawyer should ensure that the witness's competence (or incompetence) is established in the record. Obviously, while it may not be dispositive, age is relevant. The younger the child, the more likely the child will not be competent.

---

[4] *Ryan v. State*, 525 So. 2d 799, 801 (Miss. 1988).

[5] *State v. Brotherton*, 384 N.W.2d 375, 377–78 (Iowa 1986).

[6] Idaho Code Ann. § 9-202(2) (West) ("The following persons cannot be witnesses: … Children under ten (10) years of age, who appear incapable of receiving just impressions of the facts respecting which they are examined, or of relating them truly. At the time a child under the age of ten (10) years of age is called to testify in any court proceeding, the court shall conduct a hearing in chambers to determine whether the child qualifies as a witness under this section. In conducting such hearing the court shall take every reasonable means necessary to prevent intimidation or harassment of the child by the parties or their attorneys. The judge, rather than the parties, shall examine the child but he shall do so in the presence of the parties and he shall pose to the child any reasonable questions requested by the parties and previously submitted to the court. The judge may rephrase any questions so that the child is not intimidated.").

[7] *See, e.g.,* Minn. Stat. Ann. § 595.02(n) (West) ("Every person of sufficient understanding, including a party, may testify in any action or proceeding, civil or criminal, in court or before any person who has authority to receive evidence, except as provided in this subdivision: … (n) A child under ten years of age is a competent witness unless the court finds that the child lacks the capacity to remember or to relate truthfully facts respecting which the child is examined. A child describing any act or event may use language appropriate for a child of that age."); Ohio Evid. R. 601(A) ("Every person is competent to be a witness except: (A) Those of unsound mind, and children under ten years of age, who appear incapable of receiving just impressions of the facts and transactions respecting which they are examined, or of relating them truly.").

[8] Del. Code Ann. tit. 10, § 4302 (West) ("No child under the age of 10 years may be excluded from giving testimony for the sole reason that such child does not understand the obligation of an oath. Such child's age and degree of understanding of the obligation of an oath may be considered by the trier of fact in judging the child's credibility.").

[9] Fla. Stat. Ann. § 90.605(2) (West) ("In the court's discretion, a child may testify without taking the oath if the court determines the child understands the duty to tell the truth or the duty not to lie.").

Decisions Not to Depose Children

Even though a child witness is competent and has relevant knowledge, a better practice in some cases is to forego a deposition. A child is naturally empathetic. If the child is adverse, the jury may automatically sympathize with the child and hold the examining lawyer to higher standards than usual. There are intangible sensibilities involved in the examination of a child, and any missteps by the examining lawyer could be damaging to the lawyer and his or her case.

Children are frequently identified as potential witnesses. They may be bystanders who observed an accident or an injury to a loved one. They may be plaintiffs in the case and represented by a *next friend*. They may be involved in child custody issues. In each instance, the trial lawyer is confronted with the same challenge, which is to balance the need for the child's testimony with the risks the testimony and the deposition process pose. Of course, the cost-benefit analysis of proceeding with the deposition will vary based upon the facts of each case. The importance of the child's testimony and whether the evidence offered by the child is available from other sources also vary with each case. Thus, the trial lawyer must conduct an evaluation based upon the substantive needs of each case. If the evidence can be replicated elsewhere and the child will not otherwise take the stand at trial, then the better course may be to not depose the child. An example of this involved two children who saw their mother die as a result of an explosion:

> Neither child was physically injured, but they each saw their mother's body. One child was 3 years old at the time of the incident; the other child was 7. After consulting with a child psychiatrist, it was determined that the youngest child would have no tangible memories of the event because of his very young age. However, the older child likely would have memories. When the case was approaching trial, the oldest child was almost 10 years old and competent to testify. Given the traumatic events that the oldest child observed, the defendant's trial lawyer made the decision not to depose the child and generate potentially unfavorable testimony. An agreement was reached with plaintiffs' counsel that the child would not be deposed unless the plaintiffs' counsel called the child to the witness stand. Plaintiffs' counsel agreed to provide the defendants with sufficient advance notice of this decision. Ultimately, by agreement, both children would be allowed to sit in the courtroom and be seen by the jury, but neither child would be called to the witness stand. If the deposition had been taken at the outset, it is likely the child would have been called live during trial.

Thus, restraint is often a prudent strategy. In this example, there was no doubt these children were sympathetic witnesses. Clearly, the testimony of the oldest child would have been dramatic and emotionally impactful. To minimize these risks, a sound strategic decision was made to forego the deposition.

An additional risk relating to depositions of minor children is in multi-party cases where there may be multiple lawyers in the deposition room. Further, it is likely the minor child will be entitled to be accompanied by a parent or guardian during the deposition.[10] A crowded room may intimidate a child and make the child more defensive and less forthcoming. Even further, the lawyer initially seeking this discovery cannot control the behavior or conduct of other counsel. Other counsel may be overbearing or inappropriately aggressive during the examination of the child. Everyone may be blamed.

Another consideration in a multi-party lawsuit involves the substance of the questions asked by other lawyers. Recognizing that children are vulnerable to leading questions, due consideration should be given to whether other lawyers might push the child into providing detrimental answers using questions over which the initial examining lawyer has no control. This is another factor to consider.

A lawyer representing a child may legitimately object to the deposition of the child. This may be due to the unique psychological trauma the child already experienced or because of competency. In either case, the lawyer representing the minor can (and should) seek protection. An affidavit from a consulting psychologist or psychiatrist can go a long way toward stopping an abusive or harmful deposition from proceeding. In some cases, the deposition should be prohibited because of the additional trauma that providing testimony (and re-living a traumatic experience) could cause a child by refreshing tragic memories.

Any lawyer in the case can challenge the admissibility of a child's testimony on the basis of competency. However, if the deposition already has been completed, many courts will likely allow the testimony unless it is clearly shown the child's incompetence was displayed during the examination.

Deposition Strategies

Once the decision is made to proceed with a child's deposition, the examining lawyer should pre-plan the types of questions to be asked and the tone of the questions. Clearly, the tone should be sympathetic, courteous, and solicitous and

---

[10] *E.g.*, Fla. R. Civ. P. 1.310(b)(8) ("Any minor subpoenaed for testimony shall have the right to be accompanied by a parent or guardian at all times during the taking of testimony notwithstanding the invocation of the rule of sequestration of section 90.616, Florida Statutes, except upon a showing that the presence of a parent or guardian is likely to have a material, negative impact on the credibility or accuracy of the minor's testimony, or that the interests of the parent or guardian are in actual or potential conflict with the interests of the minor.").

should *never* be antagonistic or aggressive. The jury's memory will be longstanding if the examining lawyer is overbearing.

The deposition should not be long. It should be as short as possible to achieve the needed discovery. Protracted discussions should be avoided. The examining lawyer should be disarming in his or her approach and brevity is well-advised. The lawyer should identify the specific goals and, once the witness is put at ease, seek to accomplish these goals as quickly as possible.

There have been numerous studies concerning children as trial witnesses. There appears to be a consensus that children can serve as competent witnesses and accurately relay perceived details of what they saw or heard. These studies are instructive on what children can remember and what questions are appropriately calculated to discover the truth from their memories.

One study concluded that leading questions are ill-advised. This study also determined that if a lawyer attempts to direct the child with "yes" or "no" answers, the child becomes less comfortable and less forthcoming. Stated differently, leading questions do not necessarily lead to the truth. The child witness becomes more reticent and defensive, and the child may answer questions out of fear of displeasing the adult in lieu of speaking the truth.

Interestingly, this same study concluded that a child witness was more likely to be forthcoming in response to more open-ended questions—the "how," "when," "where," and "what happened next" types of questions. A child witness may feel more comfortable providing short narrative responses. The examining lawyer then can probe more deeply once the narrative responses have been provided.

It is important to build a relationship of trust with a child witness. This requires empathy. If the child has observed a traumatic accident, then the lawyer should communicate sensitivity and understanding and reassure the child during the examination. If the child has lost a loved one, due care should be given to forming a bond with the child that encourages the child to discuss what the child saw or heard.

An important concept in any examination is to simplify questions and orient the examination so it is easily understood. As one commentator noted, "[c]hildren perceive that adults' general communication with them is to dominate, lecture or interrogate. Little wonder that every child's fear is that, when questioned, they must have done something wrong. Therefore, choose your words carefully, watch your body language, and use a neutral or matter of fact vocal delivery. Put yourself on their level."[11]

One technique is building trust by "self-disclosure." According to one study, "research shows that to do some self-disclosure helps another person become

---

[11] Roger Arnold and Renee C. Fields, *Asking the Tough Questions: How to Examine a Child Witness in Sexual Abuse Cases*, The Jury Expert, Vol. 21, Issue 3, at 32 (May 2009) *available at* http://www.thejuryexpert.com/wp-content/uploads/ChildWitnessMay2009Volume21No3.pdf.

comfortable with his and/or her own self-disclosure. Try to share some neutral issues that demonstrate things that you have in common with the child . . . that you had a pet, that you have kids, what you liked to do when you were a kid, etc."[12]

A deposition room can be intimidating even to a veteran testifier. A child witness may be understandably nervous and anxious. The early stages of the deposition should be used to explain the role of the lawyers, the role of the court reporter, and the videographer, if any. Another technique is to avoid the usual law firm conference room, and instead take the deposition at a more relaxing location. The trial lawyer should also consider having the witness use crayons or age-appropriate toys to draw or demonstrate the events at issue. The goal here is to put the child at ease.

In one example, a young boy was a trial witness in a case involving an automobile accident in which his father died. The young boy was an eyewitness. A substantial portion of the examination dealt with the boy's relationship with his father to let the young witness know that he could trust the lawyer and that the lawyer would not take advantage of him. This type of empathy is always appropriate. Only then can more difficult questions be asked because a relationship of trust has been formed.

---

[12] *Id.* at 33.

12

Depositions of Organizations

Depositions of organizations (corporations or other legal entities) are useful discovery devices that are frequently used to isolate the factual contentions of a corporate party. However, these types of depositions are frequently used with nonparties.

Typical Procedural Guidelines

Clearly, it is not possible to depose an actual corporation or other legal entity. Instead, any deposition testimony sought must be obtained from a person who is able to speak on behalf of the organization. The majority of states follow the Federal Rules of Civil Procedure regarding corporate depositions and have enacted rules substantially similar to the FED. R. CIV. P. 30(b)(6), which provides the following:

> ***Notice or Subpoena Directed to an Organization.*** In its notice or subpoena, a party may name as the deponent a public or private corporation, a partnership, an association, a governmental agency, or other entity and must describe with reasonable particularity the matters for examination. The named organization must then designate one or more officers, directors, or managing agents, or designate other persons who consent to testify on its behalf; and it may set out the matters on which each person designated will testify. A subpoena must advise a nonparty organization of its duty to make this designation. The persons designated must testify about information known or reasonably available to the organization. This paragraph (6) does not preclude a deposition by any other procedure allowed by these rules.

Under Rule 30(b)(6), a party has the right to take depositions of any public or private corporation, partnership, association, governmental agency, or other "entity."[1] This is done by issuing a notice or subpoena that "must describe with reasonable particularity the matters for examination."[2] Once noticed, the burden is then shifted to the named organization to "designate one or more officers, directors or managing agents" or "other persons" to testify on its behalf regarding the various topic categories.[3] The organization may name several representatives to testify on the stated topics, but these designations should be made prior to the deposition; there is no requirement that only one person be designated on all topics.[4]

Other state jurisdictions may have different procedures, so the trial lawyer should determine the applicable procedures in each jurisdiction. For example, at least one state, New York, allows a party seeking a corporate deposition to identify the desired witness by the person's name.[5] The responding party may then substitute alternative witnesses in place of the named witness, and the burden is shifted back to the requesting party to justify the deposition of the originally named individual.

Rule 30(b)(6) requires the named organization to present one or more witnesses to testify to "information known or reasonably available" to the organization. This means that a witness is not required to have the most personal knowledge.[6] In fact, the "most knowledgeable" witness may not be the "best witness" for a variety of reasons. The "most knowledgeable" witness may not be "jury-friendly" and may not be the best witness to personify the company. In essence, whoever appears at the deposition is the face *and* voice of the organization. Every effort should be made to make a good impression even if that means the "most knowledgeable" witness is not selected.

Purpose of Corporate Depositions

Corporate depositions are frequently used with corporate parties to isolate their factual positions in the case. They are used with a corporate plaintiff to isolate the factual underpinning of the claims; they are used with a corporate defendant to isolate a defendant's defenses, and the facts relied upon in connection with

---

[1]   *See* Fed. R. Civ. P. Rule 30(b)(6).

[2]   *Id.*

[3]   *Id.*

[4]   *Id.*

[5]   N.Y. C.P.L.R. 3106(d) (McKinney) ("A party desiring to take the deposition of a particular officer, director, member or employee of a person shall include in the notice or subpoena served upon such person the identity, description or title of such individual. Such person shall produce the individual so designated unless they shall have, no later than ten days prior to the scheduled deposition, notified the requesting party that another individual would instead be produced and the identity, description or title of such individual is specified. If timely notification has been so given, such other individual shall instead be produced.").

[6]   *See, e.g., PPM Fin., Inc. v. Norandal USA, Inc.,* 297 F. Supp. 3d 1072, 1085–86 (N.D. Ill.) *aff'd,* 392 F.3d 889 (7th Cir. 2004) (citation omitted) ("A Rule 30(b)(6) witness, however, need not have personal knowledge of the facts to which he testifies, because he testifies as to the corporation's position on the matters set forth in the Rule 30(b)(6), not his personal opinion.").

those defenses. When used to depose a corporate party, these types of depositions force the organization to marshal key evidence to support their claims or defenses; in effect, the opposing party (and its counsel) are forced to adopt formal positions and provide facts to support those positions. Thus, the timing of these depositions during the discovery process is strategically important.

From the perspective of the lawyer presenting the witness, a postponement of the corporate deposition is preferable until the lawyer knows enough about the case to appropriately prepare the witness. From the perspective of the examining lawyer, the earlier the corporate deposition is scheduled, the better. This allows the examining lawyer to force the opposing organization to commit to factual positions.

Clearly, a Rule 30(b)(6) deposition notice can be broadly worded to cover a wide spectrum of relevant issues in the case or, alternatively, the notice can focus on specific issues in great detail. This allows the examining lawyer to isolate factual disputes to determine what disputes actually exist or do not exist. A well-prepared witness can advance the client's case; whereas, an ill-prepared witness may falter, stumble, and weaken the client's case. This is particularly so because the witness's testimony will bind the corporation. If the witness has not done his or her homework and is unable to testify about a key point, the corporation may be stuck with this failure for the duration of the case.

Timing of a Corporate Representative Deposition

Significant benefits are achieved by scheduling corporate depositions during the early stages of the case, and every trial lawyer should consider this option when developing a master discovery plan. Again, an aggressive trial lawyer may seek to force the opposing side to take formal positions as early as possible. Should subsequent discovery reveal that the witness's testimony is incomplete or inaccurate, the corporation's counsel is forced to supplement the deposition and, quite possibly, provide additional depositions. This may be problematic for a variety of reasons. One practical reason is the jury may perceive that the witness (and the corporation) is equivocal or uncertain, and the original witness's credibility is adversely impacted.

Again, as a precautionary note, a corporate deposition should not be taken until all key documents are first requested, received, and reviewed. Basic written discovery should be exchanged between the parties. The trial lawyer seeking the deposition should have a good handle on the case so the examination is well informed. This means that the deposition should not be taken until the examining lawyer understands enough about the case to frame intelligent topic categories for the deposition notice. Counsel seeking the deposition should also define the key objectives for the deposition, and how the deposition advances the trial themes for his or her case.

Taking an important deposition without the benefit of prior document discovery invariably leads to inefficiencies, as well as a potentially incomplete or inaccurate record. Every trial lawyer should be fully informed and armed before taking depositions, and taking a corporate deposition is no different. This is achieved by understanding the key documents, discovery, and case themes before walking into the deposition room.

It is typically wise to complete basic written discovery before the deposition. Written discovery, including contention interrogatories, is available to help trial lawyers define key areas for future examination. A deposition notice also can require that the corporate representative be designated to testify concerning specific contentions in the pleadings and what evidence, if any, the party has to support these contentions. Furthermore, the corporate witness notice can require the witness to appear and testify about the contents of prior written discovery responses.

Duty to Reasonably Investigate and Prepare

Rule 30(b)(6) imposes a duty of due diligence on an organization to reasonably investigate the topic matters set forth in the deposition notice. As one court noted, the rule "places the burden of identifying responsive witnesses for a corporation on the corporation."[7] Another court stated that the rule "imposes a duty upon the named business entity to prepare its selected deponent to adequately testify not only on matters known by the deponent, but also on subjects that the entity should reasonably know."[8] Again, this obligation is not limited to the personal knowledge of a particular witness, but assumes there are other persons within the organization who also have knowledge of relevant facts. Thus, the organization has a duty to verify the extent and scope of knowledge for the *entire* organization, and not for any specific individual. This due diligence obligation also means the lawyer preparing the witness should be involved in the internal effort to locate important witnesses and key documents to better ensure proper preparations. At a minimum, the preparing lawyer should provide recommendations concerning who this witness should or should not be.

---

[7] *Resolution Trust Corp. v. Southern Union Co., Inc.*, 985 F.2d 196, 197 (5th Cir. 1993).

[8] *Hooker v. Norfolk Southern Ry. Co.*, 204 F.R.D. 124, 126 (S.D. Ind. 2001).

Consequences of Failing to Prepare

Because a corporate witness has a duty to prepare for a 30(b)(6) deposition, there are potentially significant consequences if a witness is unprepared or lacks the requisite knowledge to respond to questions within the scope of the notice. Some courts consider that "if a Rule 30(b)(6) witness is unable to give useful information he is no more present for the deposition than would be a deponent who physically appears for the deposition but sleeps through it."[9] Those courts may determine "producing an unprepared witness is tantamount to a failure to appear that is sanctionable under Rule 37(d)."[10] Other jurisdictions may consider that sanctions for nonappearance are only available if the deponent literally fails to appear.[11] If the court determines sanctions are available and appropriate, Rule 37 "provides a panoply of sanctions, from the imposition of costs to entry of default."[12] Thus, the obvious repercussions can include: monetary sanctions, an award of attorneys' fees, an order compelling a new deposition, or sanctions preventing the corporation from introducing evidence on the same issues at trial.

In determining whether sanctions are appropriate, the court will likely consider the corporation's efforts to prepare the witness and the extent to which the witness was able to testify concerning the subjects contained in the notice.[13] Therefore, it is imperative that the corporation, and the trial lawyer, undertake good faith efforts to designate and prepare the witness. Nevertheless, if the unanswered information is significant enough, the deposition may have to be reconvened, possibly with a new witness, at the corporation's expense.[14] Lastly, there is always the practical effect that the witness's testimony is binding upon the corporation, and any attempt to modify the testimony at a later date will be looked upon with disfavor. Thus, if a witness is not prepared and gives incomplete answers, the company may have to live with these incomplete answers for the balance of the case.

---

[9] *Black Horse Lane Assoc., L.P. v. Dow Chem. Corp.*, 228 F.3d 275, 304 (3d Cir. 2000).

[10] *Id.*

[11] *See Baker v. St. Paul Travelers Ins. Co.*, 670 F.3d 119, 122–25 (1st Cir. 2012).

[12] *United States v. Taylor*, 166 F.R.D. 356, 363 (M.D.N.C.) *aff'd*, 166 F.R.D. 367 (M.D.N.C. 1996).

[13] *Coryn Grp. II, LLC v. O.C. Seacrets, Inc.*, 265 F.R.D. 235, 239–40 (D. Md. 2010) ("On the one hand, a corporation that wholly fails to educate a corporate designee without justification is subject to mandatory monetary sanctions under Rule 37(d). On the other hand, a corporation that engages in good faith efforts to prepare and whose witness provides substantial testimony concerning the subject areas of their designation despite inadequate preparation may not be subject to sanctions.") (internal citations and quotations omitted).

[14] *Id.* at 240.

The "Preparing" Lawyer's Job

A lawyer representing a corporate deponent should play an active role to assist and guide the witness during the preparation stages. The following list identifies how lawyers can and should contribute to this effort:

1. Participate in the process of selecting the witness to make sure the "best" witness is selected.
2. Identify key documents for the witness(es) to review.
3. Identify key pleadings and discovery for the witness(es) to review.
4. Provide the witness(es) with an understanding of the client's key trial themes for the case.
5. Assist the witness in identifying what independent inquiries should be made to make sure the witness has exhausted the duty to confirm what is "reasonably available to the organization."
6. Fully preparing the witness for the deposition.

Because Rule 30(b)(6) requires that representatives "must testify about information known or reasonably available to the organization," the witness must take action and prepare for each of the topic categories for which testimony is requested. Thus, the lawyer involved in preparing the witness must be proactive to make sure the witness has taken appropriate steps to prepare.

An example of this includes helping interview other witnesses. Sometimes corporate employees with knowledge of relevant facts leave the company. Thus, the corporate witness may need to locate and interview former employees. The lawyer can facilitate this process by helping locate the former employees and preparing a script for the corporate witness to follow in the interview. In this manner, the interview is more controlled and calculated to generate helpful information. The interview can be structured beforehand to minimize the risk of a "bad" interview.

Standard Topic Categories: All Cases

The details of the topic categories in a corporate deposition notice necessarily change from case to case and will be tailored to specific issues in each case. However, there are common topics useable in a wide array of cases. These topics include such basic matters as the following:

1. **Documents reviewed and considered:** Every deposition notice should require the witness to appear at deposition prepared to discuss the

documents reviewed and considered in preparing for the deposition. By forcing the witness to identify specific steps taken as part of the witness's preparations, the examining lawyer can evaluate the reasonableness of the efforts to prepare for the deposition and determine whether court intervention is needed.

2. **Proper document production:** Every deposition should include a topic category requiring the witness to discuss how the corporate party identified and retrieved documents pursuant to prior written document requests. Document discovery is typically initiated before depositions begin. By forcing a corporate witness to address the procedures used to identify, collate, and produce responsive documents, the examining lawyer can evaluate the thoroughness of the opposing party's prior document production. This examination should include an identification of the persons involved in the document retrieval process, whether litigation holds were timely imposed to prevent destruction of evidence, whether destruction of documents has occurred, and whether all logical document production sources were identified and explored.

3. **Document retention policies:** The deposition notice should include a topic that addresses document retention policies. This examination should include a discussion of whether a retention policy exists, whether the policy is different for hard-copy documents and electronically stored information (ESI), whether documents have been destroyed or purged, and whether document retention policies were followed in connection with the documents at issue in the case. This topic should also confirm whether there are backup ESI files or whether ESI (such as emails) is automatically deleted.

4. **Contentions of the parties:** It is wise to complete some written discovery of the opposing party's factual contentions before corporate depositions begin. Interrogatories can be submitted to both the plaintiff and the defendant seeking disclosure of key factual contentions, claims, and defenses. By conducting and completing basic written discovery before the deposition, the trial lawyer is armed with specific statements as a basis to examine the corporate representative and can better flesh out factual positions and supporting evidence for each contention.

5. **Pleadings:** The deposition notice should require the corporate representative to testify as to the allegations and claims in the pleadings. A corporate plaintiff should be required to produce a representative to discuss specific factual claims in a petition or complaint. A corporate defendant should be required to designate a witness to testify as to specific defenses or affirmative defenses in the responsive pleading or answer. This provides the examining lawyer with an opportunity to pin down the

opposition, as well as to determine what evidence the opposition may have to support its offensive or defensive contentions.

6. **Personal knowledge:** The examining lawyer should question the witness to determine whether the witness has personal knowledge of the event, incident, or occurrence. The examining lawyer should specifically examine the witness to determine whether there are other employees within the company that have more knowledge than the witness concerning certain topic categories. In some jurisdictions, whether the corporate party has tendered the most knowledgeable witness may be a factor for the court in determining whether there has been a good faith effort to comply with the deposition notice.

Standard Topic Categories: Personal Injury/Death Cases

The following outline includes basic items to address in a corporate deposition involving an accident leading to either personal injury or death. Again, each case is different. However, there are some common components to every case that should be explored. Here are a few examples:

1. **Investigation of incident:** The examining lawyer should determine whether the corporation conducted an investigation of the underlying accident, who was involved in the investigation, whether a report was filed, whether witness statements were taken, whether litigation was contemplated at the time of the investigation and, if permitted, the results of the investigation. The examination should seek to determine whether the investigation was undertaken in the ordinary course of business or in contemplation of the threat of litigation and whether legal counsel was involved. If conducted in the ordinary course of business and without the involvement of legal counsel, the results of the investigation may be discoverable.

2. **Cause of incident:** Regardless of whether a formal investigation was conducted, the examination should probe the corporation's factual position concerning the cause of the accident.

3. **Witnesses:** The examination should confirm the identity of all eyewitnesses known to the corporation.

4. **Response to the incident:** The examination should determine whether subsequent remedial measures have been undertaken in response to the incident to prevent future incidents.

5. **Other incidents:** The examination should determine whether there were other substantially similar incidents that occurred prior to the incident in question. Such testimony bears on issues of notice that might support an award of punitive damages.

Standard Topic Categories: Breach of Contract Cases

There are standard topic categories common to most contract cases. Here are some examples:

1. **The contract and drafts of contracts:** The examination should confirm the terms of the contract, all persons involved in the negotiation and execution of the contract, and identification of all drafts of the contract.

2. **Negotiation of the contract:** The examination should include confirmation of all drafts exchanged by the parties to the contract and all emails or other correspondence that may bear on the intent of the parties to the contract.

3. **Alleged breaches:** The examination should include confirmation of the alleged actions or inactions that breached the contract, and whether the alleged breach was a material breach or a nominal breach.

4. **Damages:** Where appropriate, the examination should include an explanation of the measure of damages alleged, including any direct damages, expectation damages, consequential damages, or incidental damages. If the plaintiff seeks equitable remedies, such as specific performance or rescission, those topics should also be explored.

5. **Mitigation of damages:** Where appropriate, the examination should address how—and if—the plaintiff mitigated its damages.

Standard Topic Categories: Fraud/Misrepresentation Cases

The following categories are typical categories for examination in a business tort case involving misrepresentations:

1. **Due diligence:** When deposing a corporate plaintiff, the examination should include an inquiry concerning the extent of due diligence undertaken by the

plaintiff entity, all persons involved in the due diligence, and documents generated as part of the due diligence effort.

2. **Misrepresentations:** When deposing a corporate plaintiff, the examination should include an inquiry concerning the details of the alleged misrepresentation, whether the misrepresentation was verbal or written, the identity of the person or persons making the misrepresentation, and how the corporate plaintiff relied upon the misrepresentation.

3. **Damages:** When deposing a corporate plaintiff, the deposition should examine how the plaintiff claims to have been damaged and what steps were taken to mitigate those damages.

Standard Topic Categories: Product Cases

The following categories are typical categories for examination in a product liability case:

1. **Manufacturing controls, processes, and quality control:** In a manufacturing defect case, the examination should focus on what policies and procedures were in effect concerning quality control to reduce the risk of a manufacturing discrepancy.

2. **Design process:** In a design defect case, the examination should focus on each of the steps in the design process from concept idea to product realization, the evaluative steps in the design process, whether prototype or product testing was conducted, whether a failure mode analysis was undertaken to identify potential design flaws and modes of failure, and whether "safer" alternative designs were economically feasible.

3. **Preproduction testing and design validation:** The examination should include a confirmation of all prototype testing and validation of the product, all reports generated from such testing, videotapes of such testing, and flaws identified during the course of testing.

4. **Other incidents:** The examination should include a discussion of other accidents or incidents involving the same or similar products resulting in property damage, personal injury, or death. The examination should seek to identify other incidents that are substantially similar because such evidence is potentially probative of defect and also bears on the availability of punitive damages.

5. **Postmanufacturing distribution and warnings:** The examination should include any human factors and ergonomics research related to the product, how the product is subject to misuse, and the appropriateness of any warnings concerning how the product is to be used or potentially misused. This examination should also include any postmarketing product surveillance to confirm how the product is actually used in the marketplace by consumers and whether such use has resulted in incidents that are now, or should have been, foreseeable.

6. **Subsequent remedial measures:** The examination should include a discussion of whether the corporate defendant has made modifications to its product design in response to incidents, whether the manufacturing process has been modified in response to manufacturing problems, or whether the warnings and marketing materials have been changed due to incidents.

13

Preparing Corporate Witnesses

Every case is different and every witness is different. However, every deposition involving a corporate representative will require some similar strategies concerning how the witness is prepared.

First Order of Business

Upon receiving a corporate deposition notice, the first order of business is to determine whether the requested topic categories are objectionable. If the topic categories seek information that is either privileged or immaterial, then appropriate objections should be lodged. In appropriate cases, the responding lawyer may wish to file a formal motion for protection. The practitioner should consult the rules in each jurisdiction to determine whether objections (or motions) must be heard before the deposition begins. In some jurisdictions, objections may be filed and the witness may be tendered subject to the objections. The relevant rules of the appropriate jurisdiction should be consulted. Objections might be necessary because the deposition is premature, the notice seeks highly confidential information, the notice seeks privileged information, or the topic categories are vague, ambiguous, or overbroad.

Second Order of Business

The second order of business is witness selection. Some larger companies with substantial litigation experience may have witnesses pre-selected depending upon the topics outlined in the deposition notice. Most corporate clients will not. In many cases, the witness selection process may be akin to a beauty contest evaluating the demeanor, acumen, and skills of the witness candidates.

The Federal Rules do not require that an entity designate the person or persons most knowledgeable about the topic categories.[1] However, some jurisdictions may have more stringent rules. Therefore, an initial understanding of the pertinent procedural rules will impact the witness selection process. If the procedural rules require that the corporation present a witness "most knowledgeable," then the selection process should focus on employees or representatives who have the most factual knowledge concerning the individual topic categories. There may be more than one witness if the topics are broad and wide-ranging. One witness may have knowledge concerning certain topics, but is unfamiliar with others. Regardless of the requirements of the rules, it is always helpful to identify witnesses who have some knowledge because they already have a grasp of some facts. This will simplify witness preparations because the lawyer does not have to educate the witness on key facts, which can be time-consuming. It is also helpful to the witness because the witness is not forced to undergo a memory exercise.

The Lawyer's Role in Selecting the Company Witness

There are important criteria in the selection process that should be considered, and the lawyer should play a meaningful role in this process. It is not uncommon to start preparing a witness and then realize there is something in the witness's background or personality that makes the witness less than ideal as a company representative. A corporate client may not be sophisticated concerning the attributes of an effective witness; accordingly, the trial lawyer should be involved in educating the client concerning the preferred characteristics. The lawyer should also participate directly in the evaluation of potential candidates and provide candid feedback during this evaluation process. The witness or witnesses ultimately selected should be smart, knowledgeable, make a good appearance, and exhibit self-confidence.

Prior Testimony Experience

Witnesses with prior deposition experience are preferred. This prior experience helps reduce the challenge of preparing a beginner witness on the mechanics of the deposition process, how to act, how to listen, and what to expect from opposing counsel. Clearly, prior familiarity with the deposition process accelerates deposition preparations. A veteran witness is less vulnerable to aggressive

---

[1] *QBE Ins. Corp. v. Jorda Enterprises, Inc.,* 277 F.R.D. 676, 688 (S.D. Fla. 2012) ("[Rule 30(b)(6)] does not expressly or implicitly require the corporation or entity to produce the 'person most knowledgeable' for the corporate deposition.").

cross-examination and will likely exude more self-confidence when exposed to the pressures of an intense examination. On the other hand, a witness who is a complete stranger to the process may enter the deposition room with anxiety and fear, and may manifest negative emotions during the deposition. A veteran witness is typically more calm and composed under fire. All of these intangibles are important because the deposition is an important opportunity to make a good impression. A corporate witness binds the organization; therefore, it is imperative that the best witness serve as the representative.

One cautionary note, however, is necessary with regard to veteran witnesses. A company witness who has been deposed on several prior occasions may have "baggage" from prior depositions. Every effort should be made to confirm whether there is any harmful testimony given in earlier depositions in other cases. Rest assured that opposing counsel will make an effort to locate transcripts of testimony from earlier cases.

Witness Demeanor

Witness demeanor is always important. A corporate witness is the "representative" of the company and personifies the company. Such a witness will likely be the first person to provide impressions to the jury, so it is important that this first impression is favorable. The witness should be evaluated as to physical appearance, credibility, and likeability. Again, this is how the *pathos* and *ethos* of a case are developed. Because the witness is the personification of the company, he or she should be credible, likeable, and trustworthy. Jury appeal is always important.

Self-Confidence

Self-confidence is important. A jury often judges the credibility of testimony by evaluating the speaker. A witness who appears fretful or fearful is both less believable and less convincing. Thus, it is important that the witness appear self-assured. A jury will have a difficult time believing a witness who acts like a deer caught in the headlights.

Factual Knowledge

If possible, a witness should be selected who already has some foundation in the facts of the case. This is helpful during witness preparation because this familiarity reduces the challenge of educating the witness on important facts and avoids the risks of having the witness memorize facts. If a witness has no familiarity with underlying facts, deposition preparations will be more complicated and, in such cases, the burdens on the witness will be greater because the witness will be forced to learn new subject matter. Therefore, it makes good sense to identify a witness or witnesses who have some familiarity with the topic areas that the deposition notice seeks to address.

Selecting a witness who has some connection to the case also makes more sense from a jury's perspective. A jury may question why a witness designated as a company representative has no connection to the underlying facts. This lack of factual connection will certainly be exposed by opposing counsel to cast doubt on the witness's and corporation's credibility. This lack of familiarity also may serve as the basis for a discovery motion if the witness is not prepared to fully testify on the designated topic areas. These types of attacks are avoidable (or at least minimized) if the witness has a substantive connection to the factual issues and is, in fact, knowledgeable.

Seniority

Another consideration is whether the witness is *too senior* in the corporate hierarchy to present as a witness. The lawyer defending the deposition may not want to expose a senior executive (such as a member of the board, the CEO, or the corporation's president) to the deposition process. An important balancing test is required to make this decision. Depositions are time-consuming and place a burden on the company and senior executives. Also, in large companies, senior executives typically delegate tasks and responsibilities, and they may not have direct involvement in the detailed implementation of those tasks. Therefore, the learning curve for a senior executive may be significant if the factual details of job functions are an issue in the case.

As discussed in Chapter 15, many states recognize what is referred to as the "Apex Doctrine," which allows a corporation to limit, if not prohibit, depositions of senior executives unless it can be shown that the senior executive is personally involved in the underlying events or transactions. The goal is to prevent unnecessary burdens on senior executives where depositions are sought for purposes of harassment or if the testimony will have minimal relevance to the proceedings. Some of these same considerations apply to the process of selecting a corporate witness and why senior officials should not be presented.

Senior executives in large companies typically rise in their respective companies because they are skilled and effective at delegating tasks and responsibilities. However, they often do not know the details of how these various tasks are undertaken. They look to the bottom line and for end results. If they devote valuable time to knowing all of the details, they will be less effective at what they do. They may be big-picture executives. Thus, it is often ill-advised to tender a senior executive to testify because the opposing lawyer will use any lack of detailed knowledge to discredit the witness, embarrass the witness, or cast doubt on the integrity of the company.

Selecting Attorneys as Witnesses

It is rare that a corporate representative should be an in-house lawyer. Exposing corporate counsel to cross-examination invites myriad problems and potential challenges to privileged communications. Wherever possible, witness selection should *not include* lawyers or members of a corporate legal department.

Nonemployees as Witnesses

In some instances, outside consultants may be used as company representatives if they are otherwise involved in the affairs of the company in a manner relevant to the topic categories in the deposition notice. The use of outside consultants, however, should be approached cautiously because it may create suspicions in the minds of a jury. The jury may be left wondering why there is no employee in the company available to testify in the case and why an outside consultant must be paid to testify. The use of outside consultants is less effective; they should be used only when necessary and when no other suitable witness can be identified within the ranks of the organization.

General Topics for Preparing the Corporate Witness

Preparing a corporate witness is similar to preparing any other lay witness. Basic concepts related to witness technique, understanding questions, listening for unfair questions, controlling the tempo of the deposition, etc. apply to a corporate deposition. All of these preparation issues are addressed in Chapter 4. The techniques and strategies for preparing a corporate witness are no different. Additional issues that should be addressed when preparing a corporate witness typically include the following:

- A review and understanding of the specific topic categories for the deposition.

- An understanding of the unique role of the corporate witness and the binding nature of the testimony on the corporation.

- The distinction between serving as a corporate witness and a witness with personal knowledge or involvement.

- Access to and review of critical documents.

- Access to and review of operative pleadings and written discovery responses.

- Independent research by the witness.

- Understanding of the key themes in the case.

- Understanding of the key facts of the case.

Sufficient Time to Prepare

Efforts should be made to give the corporate witness sufficient time to prepare for deposition. Again, the rules of practice in many jurisdictions, including the Federal Rules of Civil Procedure, require that the witness be reasonably prepared to discuss each topic category. If there are numerous topics requiring witness testimony, the preparation period should not be rushed. Both the court and the jury will be concerned if a witness fails to prepare. If the witness does not review critical documents or is otherwise not familiar with the contentions of the parties in the case, the witness's credibility could be adversely impacted. The complexity of the topic categories, and the breadth of these categories, should dictate the amount of time devoted to preparations.

Individual Preparation Time

In many cases, a witness's preparation time is limited to meetings and privileged communications with counsel. However, both the court and jury will be more impressed with the witness's efforts if the witness undertakes individual efforts apart from meetings with the lawyer. This could include conversations with colleagues or separate time devoted to the review of documents. It is sometimes a prudent tactic to encourage the witness to contact other specific individuals or review specific documents to prepare. This will bolster the witness's credibility and the thoroughness of the deposition preparations; however, the lawyer should exercise reasonable control over who these other witnesses are and what documents should be considered.

Review of Pleadings and Key Discovery

A corporate witness should be familiar with the underlying facts of the case and the parties' contentions. A witness for a defendant corporation should be generally aware of the plaintiff's claims and the key defenses of the corporate entity. If the witness appears unfamiliar with the nature of the plaintiff's claims, he or she will be perceived as unfeeling or disinterested. This is particularly true in a personal injury or death case.

Similarly, a corporate representative for a plaintiff should be generally familiar with the plaintiff's claims. Otherwise, the witness appears to be indifferent and the legitimacy or seriousness of the plaintiff's claims may be undermined. Therefore, the witness should always review the operative pleadings and have acquired a general familiarity of the issues.

A corporate witness should be familiar with key discovery responses—particularly sworn interrogatory answers or responses to requests for admission. Otherwise, the witness is potentially exposed to impeachment if these responses relate to the topic categories for which the witness is tendered.

Using a Briefing Binder

A key document briefing binder is a valuable tool to utilize during the preparation process. This binder can include key pleadings, key discovery responses, and key documents. The binder can also include a chronology to assist the witness in preparation. However, because the binder is likely discoverable, nothing should be included in this binder unless the presenting lawyer is comfortable with its ultimate disclosure during discovery.

The presenting lawyer (and the witness) may want to use the binder in the deposition itself. This allows the witness to carry the binder into the deposition room as a reference source if the witness forgets some detailed fact or the timing of some event. It also provides the witness with enhanced comfort since it serves as a crutch if the witness needs help during the examination. Again, nothing should be placed in this binder unless it is helpful to the witness. No privileged document should be placed in this binder; otherwise, the privilege will be waived. Here are some document categories that should be considered for inclusion in this type of binder, properly tabbed for quick and easy reference by the witness:

1. A copy of the plaintiff's petition or complaint.
2. A copy of the defendant's answer or responsive pleading.
3. A short chronology of key events.

4. Answers to key contention interrogatories reflecting the position of the organization.
5. Other key discovery responses reflecting the position of the organization.
6. Selected documents that the witness has reviewed and which are critical to his or her testimony in the deposition appropriately highlighted or flagged for easy reference.

Again, this binder will likely become an exhibit to the deposition. Nothing should be contained in this binder that is privileged, harmful, confusing, or potentially embarrassing. The lawyer is creating a template for the deposition, and this template will likely become evidence.

Chronology

Using a chronology with a corporate witness is often helpful, particularly if the case involves multiple documents and other significant external and internal communications. A chronology can be prepared by counsel, but it should be reviewed by the witness, and the witness should personally confirm the accuracy of each entry by reference to underlying documents or other available evidence. The witness needs to be able to testify that he or she personally confirmed the accuracy of the chronology; otherwise, it may appear the witness is being spoon-fed attorney work product. The chronology should be neutral in tone and avoid controversial descriptions that invite cross-examination. The goal is to provide a template to organize the witness's testimony and to assist the witness if the witness becomes confused concerning the timing of events, transactions, or occurrences. Once prepared and disclosed, the chronology may become a significant exhibit in the case. Therefore, every effort should be made to ensure its accuracy before disclosure.

Trial Themes

A corporate witness is just like a lay witness concerning the importance and use of trial themes during witness preparation. The corporate witness should have an understanding of the contentions of the client and the client's thematic storyline. This understanding is important to avoid conflicts in testimony. If the witness does not understand the ultimate objectives in the case, the witness is potentially vulnerable during cross-examination. Moreover, the witness's testimony may unintentionally interfere with the client's theory of the case. If the witness understands the case objectives, the witness is better prepared to respond to challenging questions.

Review of Critical Documents

Caution should be exercised before showing a witness privileged documents during the preparation process. Key documents that have been or will be timely produced in discovery may be used.

If the witness has not reviewed critical documents that bear on the topic categories, then the adequacy of the witness's preparations will be challenged. The witness should have a working knowledge of the critical documents that a jury will likely see or consider. Anything less than this exposes the witness to unnecessary cross-examination and will create holes in the witness's preparations. A few salient examples follow:

- In a breach of contract case, the witness should review and be familiar with the contract and, where appropriate, drafts of the contract, and key correspondence exchanged during negotiations.

- In a case involving corporate policies, the witness should be familiar with the policies at issue.

- In a case involving product design, the witness for the company that designed the product should be familiar with the design process and the underlying engineering and design drawings.

- In a medical malpractice case, the representative of the hospital should be generally familiar with the patient's chart and the medical services provided to the patient.

- In an employment discrimination case, the corporate witness should be familiar with the employee's personnel file and the company's policies relating to similarly situated employees.

- In a drug liability case, the witness should be familiar with key documents relating to the new drug application and clinical trials.

The list can go on and on and there are hundreds of examples. The bottom line is that the witness should have a working knowledge of key documents, and should be comfortable in his or her understanding concerning the contents of those documents as they relate to the topic matters for the deposition. This typically requires independent homework.

Protecting Privileges

Depending upon the jurisdiction, any documents shown to a corporate witness during the preparation process may be discoverable. Therefore, the lawyer should exercise caution regarding what documents are shown to the witness.

Likewise, the presenting counsel should monitor and be involved in the witness's independent inquiries and investigation. The witness should not be given *carte blanche* to contact colleagues or co-workers without guidance from counsel. Otherwise, the witness may step into privileged areas creating the risk that privileged material becomes discoverable.

Certain discussions between counsel and the company witness are protected as privileged and are not subject to disclosure. Thus, one technique is to summarize the contents of privileged communications verbally. In that manner, the witness has not seen a specific document or documents that may be privileged. The witness should be reminded of the importance of preserving the privilege, and the witness should be instructed not to disclose any communication with counsel or any communication with co-workers investigating the case or the underlying incident. Such matters are protected as privileged or as attorney work product under the rules of practice in many, if not most, jurisdictions. Under the Federal Rules, these privileges are identified under Federal Rule of Evidence 503. This rule extends the privilege to communications between non-lawyers, if those communications were undertaken at the request or direction of counsel to facilitate the rendition of legal services.

Corporate Knowledge Versus Personal Knowledge

Corporate witnesses should understand that their testimony may involve areas concerning which they have no personal knowledge. That is why it is important for the witness to devote sufficient time to understanding the issues and the documents relating to the case. If the witness has personal knowledge, the witness may certainly rely on this knowledge in formulating answers to the questions. It is also helpful for the witness to disclose during the examination process if the answers are based upon personal knowledge as distinguished from corporate knowledge.

There is a fine line between speculation and testifying as a corporate witness where the witness has no personal knowledge. Although no witness should ever speculate, a corporate witness should go beyond personal knowledge to discuss corporate positions, contentions, and corporate conduct when called to do so by the topic categories in the Rule 30(b)(6) notice. The witness may do so with greater comfort if appropriate research has been conducted to understand this "corporate knowledge."

14

Deposing The Corporate Representative

Many of the examination techniques used in deposing lay witnesses can be used to depose a corporate representative. There are some additional considerations because of the unique posture of a corporate representative.

Review Topic Categories

Under the rules of practice in most jurisdictions, a corporate party is required to designate the name of one or more persons to testify in response to a notice that addresses specific topic categories. The notice requires identification of specific topics for the witness to address. More than one witness can be tendered to satisfy the deposition request. If that occurs, the designating party may have a procedural obligation to identify which witness will address which topic categories in the deposition notice.[1]

During the initial stages of a corporate deposition, the examining lawyer should confirm which specific categories the witness will address. This should be done on the record to avoid misunderstanding. The examining lawyer can seek a stipulation from opposing counsel concerning the designation or, as a follow-up, the examining attorney can confirm the witness's personal understanding as to which topics the witness is prepared to discuss. The bottom line is there should be no ambiguity whether the witness is appearing to testify concerning specifically enumerated topics. If possible, these topics should be read into the record and confirmed by the witness or opposing counsel. If there is more than one witness appearing on a variety of different topic categories, the examining counsel should separately confirm which witness is testifying to which topics.

---

[1] *See, e.g.,* Fed. R. Civ. P. 30(b)(6).

Under the Federal Rules, an examining lawyer may be limited to a total of 7 hours for the entire deposition, regardless of the number of topic categories and regardless of the number of witnesses who are tendered to address numerous topics. The examining lawyer should attempt to reach an agreement with opposing counsel concerning how much time should be allocated if there are multiple witnesses tendered in response to the deposition topics. This allocation should be determined in advance of the deposition, if possible. If there is significant disagreement, a court order enlarging the time allotment should be considered.

Review Efforts of Witness to Prepare for Deposition

The next order of business is to review each topic category in the deposition notice, and identify what the witness has personally done to prepare for the deposition. Again, the deposition of a corporate witness is not limited by the witness's personal knowledge. Rather, the witness is designated to testify on topics that may be beyond his or her personal knowledge, but concerning information reasonably accessible to the corporation.[2] Therefore, the witness is required to affirmatively undertake preparations that are reasonable. The witness should be prepared to address each topic category for which he or she is tendered.

The examining lawyer should confirm the details of what the witness did (or did not do) to personally prepare. Such preparations might include conversations with other colleagues or co-employees, a document review, an inspection of property or accident scene, a review of pleadings, written discovery, or other litigation-specific materials. The examining lawyer should try to determine the entire universe of what the witness did and, equally important, what the witness failed to do. If it appears the witness's preparation was superficial or rushed, the examining lawyer can reserve the right to re-depose the corporation at a later date or even seek sanctions or attorney's fees. The examining lawyer is entitled to depose a witness reasonably informed given the issues of the case.

Confirm the Witness's Understanding of a "Corporate Representative"

Another preliminary matter includes confirmation of the witness's understanding of the witness's role. The witness should confirm that he or she is appearing as a corporate representative, not in a personal capacity. The witness should

---

[2] *See, e.g.,* Fed. R. Civ. P. 30(b)(6).

also be reminded that the testimony developed during the deposition is binding upon the corporation for purposes of the case. As such, the witness should be cautioned concerning the importance of the witness's answers and that the testimony can be (or will be) used in the courtroom and before a jury at a later date. These types of reminders enhance the seriousness of the proceedings, and can be shown to the jury to underscore the importance of significant concessions or admissions.

Differences Between Corporate Knowledge and Personal Knowledge

It is important to establish whether the witness has personal knowledge of specific facts relevant to the case or the various topic categories in the notice. This personal knowledge, once confirmed during the examination, will further reinforce the importance of any admissions or concessions that may be obtained during the examination. A corporate witness who has both corporate knowledge and personal knowledge will be particularly important in the eyes of the jury.

Review of Specific Documents Considered

If possible, and appropriate in the relevant jurisdiction, a corporate deposition notice should be accompanied with a subpoena *duces tecum* or document request requiring production of documents the witness specifically reviewed or considered as part of his or her pre-deposition preparations. The examining lawyer should require that these documents be produced at or before the deposition to help define the universe of the witness's preparations. By necessary implication, this examination allows the examining lawyer to identify the universe of materials *not considered* and may reveal that important documents were not produced. If the examining lawyer subsequently demonstrates the importance of such documents and the fact the witness did not consider these documents, the credibility of the witness is undermined. The lawyer may also seek a new deposition by showing that the witness was not prepared.

Examination Techniques for Important Questions

The examining lawyer may wish to incorporate into actual questions the fact that the witness is appearing on behalf of the corporate entity for dramatic emphasis. This technique reinforces the importance of the question when the jury hears the question and answer at trial. This technique should be used when the examining lawyer expects the witness to admit or concede a particularly important factual point. Some illustrations follow:

- In your capacity as the corporate representative of ABC Corporation, is it your understanding that _____?

- In your capacity as the corporate representative of ABC Corporation, is it the position of ABC Corporation that _____?

- Because you are appearing in this deposition on behalf of ABC Corporation, please identify all evidence of which ABC Corporation is aware that supports the Corporation's allegations (or defenses that) _____.

By including the reference to the witness's capacity as a representative, an added aura of importance is added to the questions and answer. The impact of favorable responses is thereby enhanced.

Review Pertinent Pleadings and Discovery Responses

It is often strategically effective to examine the witness concerning the organization's allegations or defenses in the case. If the corporate witness failed to review basic pleadings or critical written discovery responses, the witness's credibility is undermined, and the adequacy of the witness's preparations is called into doubt. On the other hand, if the witness reviewed operative pleadings, then entire areas of examination can be explored concerning the factual support for the legal positions taken by the corporate entity. Here are some examples:

- Even though you have been designated as a corporate representative to testify on behalf of the plaintiff, is it correct you did *not* review the plaintiff's pleadings?

- Even though you have been designated as a corporate representative to testify as to the defendant's contentions, is it correct that you did not review the defendant's answer or affirmative defenses?

- Because you have been designated as a corporate representative for the plaintiff, what evidence can you identify that supports the plaintiff's specific contentions as reflected in the plaintiff's complaint that _____?

- Because you have been designated as a corporate representative for the defendant, what evidence do you have to support the defendant's specific affirmative defenses that _____?

Under Rule 30(b)(6), and by extension jurisdictions that follow similar rules, a baseline exists that stems from the topics described in the corporate notice. The corporation (and the attorney) has a duty to designate a witness who is prepared to answer on subjects outlined in the notice. "The effect of the rule is to place upon the business entity the burden of identifying witnesses who possess knowledge responsive to subjects requested in the Rule 30(b)(6) request."[3] "Consequently, it imposes a duty upon the named business entity to prepare its selected deponent to adequately testify not only on matters known by the deponent, but also on subjects that the entity should reasonably know."[4]

What is "reasonably available to the organization" may not be expressly defined in most jurisdictions. In fact, the phrase "reasonably available" is not defined in Rule 30(b)(6), and there may not be a bright-line rule applicable in any given situation.[5] What is "reasonably available to the organization" will need to be determined by analyzing the facts in the specific case.[6] Courts have noted that "[t]he 'reasonably available' language of Rule 30(b)(6) clearly contemplates information beyond the present domain of the noticed entity.'"[7] Numerous courts have "stress[ed] that a corporation must educate a 30(b)(6) designee, whether from 'documents, past employees or other sources,' in order to obtain responsive information."[8] Whether a particular piece of information is "reasonably available" will likely depend on the underlying source of information.

---

[3] *Hooker v. Norfolk S. Ry. Co.*, 204 F.R.D. 124, 126 (S.D. Ind. 2001); *see also, Resolution Trust Corp. v. S. Union Co., Inc.*, 985 F.2d 196, 197 (5th Cir. 1993) (noting Rule30(b)(6) "places the burden of identifying responsive witnesses for a corporation on the corporation.").

[4] *Hooker v. Norfolk Southern Ry. Co.*, 204 F.R.D. 124, 126 (S.D. Ind. 2001).

[5] *See Calzaturficio S.C.A.R.P.A. s.p.a. v. Fabiano Shoe Co., Inc.*, 201 F.R.D. 33, 38 (D. Mass. 2001) (noting "[n]either Rule 30(b)(6) itself nor the Advisory Notes nor reported case law addressing the rule define the terminology 'reasonably available.'").

[6] *Sanofi-Aventis v. Sandoz, Inc.*, 272 F.R.D. 391, 394 (D.N.J. 2011) ("Determining if certain information is 'known or reasonably available' to an entity requires a fact-specific analysis.").

[7] *Id.*

[8] *Id.* (quoting *Brazos River Auth. v. GE Ionics, Inc.*, 469 F.3d 416, 433 (5th Cir. 2006)).

In the context of knowledge that could have been acquired from an affiliate, subsidiary, or other related company, the issue is even more fact specific. A corporate designee does not need to acquire knowledge from an affiliate on matters in which the deposed corporation was entirely uninvolved, but the corporation may be required to designate and prepare a witness to discuss topics involving "related companies" to the extent the corporation has knowledge of those topics.[9] In fact, in some jurisdictions, "[w]here a company fails to provide sufficient evidence why it would not have access to the basic information of its affiliate(s), that information is presumed to be known or reasonably available to the corporation."[10]

The deposition notice serves as the beginning of the corporation's (and its legal counsel's) affirmative duties to conduct reasonable efforts and an investigation concerning what is "reasonably available to" and "reasonably known" by the corporation. Keeping in mind the topic matters described in the notice, an effort is required to:

- Review relevant documents on the subjects outlined in the notice.

- Speak with present and former employees with knowledge related to that specific area (so a proper witness may be designated).

- Review any prior legal materials as they relate to the corporation (i.e. admissions, pleadings, etc.).

Scope of the Examination

There is some dispute among jurisdictions concerning the scope of examination of a designated corporate representative.[11] At least one court has found "that if a party opts to employ the procedures of Rule 30(b)(6)... to depose the representative of a corporation, that party must confine the examination to the matters stated 'with reasonable particularity' which are contained in the Notice of Deposition."[12] But, "many other courts have held that the scope of the questioning at a 30(b)(6) deposition is governed not by the notice of deposition but by the relevancy under Rule 26(b)(1)."[13] Thus, the trial lawyer can likely examine the corporate designee as broadly as any deponent. However, there is no guarantee that the deponent will be able to answer such questions: "If the deponent does

---

[9] *Coryn Group II, LLC v. O.C. Seacrets, Inc.,* 265 F.R.D. 235, 239 (D. Md. 2010).

[10] *Id.*

[11] *E.E.O.C. v. Freeman,* 288 F.R.D. 92, 98–99 (D. Md. 2012).

[12] *Paparelli v. Prudential Ins. Co. of Am.,* 108 F.R.D. 727, 730 (D. Mass. 1985).

[13] *E.E.O.C. v. Freeman,* 288 F.R.D. 92, 99 n.2 (D. Md. 2012) (collecting cases).

not know the answer to questions outside the scope of the matters described in the notice, then that is the examining party's problem."[14]

Irrespective of the permissible scope of the deposition itself, "the obligation on the party being deposed to prepare the deponent extends only to the topics in the Rule 30(b)(6) notice of deposition."[15] Thus, any answers by the witness "to questions outside the scope of the notice will not bind the organization, and the organization cannot be penalized if the deponent does not know the answer."[16] In federal court, it is improper for counsel to instruct the deponent not to answer on the ground that the question is outside the scope of the deposition notice.[17] Instead, the proper course is to object to questions as being beyond the scope of the 30(b)(6) notice, and state on the record that any answers to such inquiries would not bind the corporation.[18]

---

[14] *King v. Pratt & Whitney, a Div. of United Techs. Corp.*, 161 F.R.D. 475, 476 (S.D. Fla. 1995) *aff'd sub nom. King v. Pratt & Whitney*, 213 F.3d 646 (11th Cir. 2000) and *aff'd sub nom. King v. Pratt & Whitney*, 213 F.3d 647 (11th Cir. 2000).

[15] *E.E.O.C. v. Freeman*, 288 F.R.D. 92, 99 (D. Md. 2012).

[16] *Id.*

[17] *Id.*

[18] *Id.*

15

Special Witness Doctrines

There are special doctrines and procedures that are invoked to insulate certain types of witnesses from deposition. One procedure—the so-called *Touhy* doctrine—is used by the federal government to restrict access to information and limit deposition discovery from government officials. Another doctrine—the so-called Apex Doctrine—is invoked by corporations or other business entities to insulate senior executives from the deposition process. This chapter explores both of these doctrines, when these doctrines are triggered, and how these doctrines can be addressed by the party seeking the discovery.

Deposing Governmental Officials: The Touhy Request

Numerous federal agencies are empowered to conduct official investigations as part of their legislative mandates. These investigations are as varied as the myriad agencies involved, and run the entire spectrum from consumer safety to financial integrity issues. The results of these investigations are frequently implicated in both civil and criminal proceedings, and the parties to civil litigation frequently seek discovery of the details of these investigations and the depositions of government employees who were involved.

In 1951, the United States Supreme Court decided *United States ex rel. Touhy v. Regan*, 340 U.S. 462 (1951), and that decision provides the basis for the Touhy doctrine or Touhy request. Roger Touhy, an inmate in an Illinois State prison, instituted *habeas corpus* proceedings alleging a violation of his due process rights. Touhy then issued a subpoena *duces tecum* to the Federal Bureau of Investigation (FBI), claiming that responsive documents contained evidence establishing that his conviction was allegedly brought about by fraud. The FBI refused to comply with the subpoena based on a Department of Justice order, and the agent involved was held in contempt by the trial court.

The Appellate Court reversed the contempt order, and the matter made its way to the United States Supreme Court, which upheld the reversal holding that Congress had given administrative agencies the authority to prescribe regulations for the custody, use, and preservation of their records by the adoption of 5 U.S.C. §22 (now 5 U.S.C. §301), and that the Department of Justice regulations at issue were a valid exercise of this power.

In the aftermath of *Touhy*, federal agencies enacted regulations governing the release of documents and providing depositions in response to demands or subpoenas in court cases. While each federal agency has its own set of regulations,[1] there are some common features. Care should be given to identify the pertinent regulations and then ensure full compliance with them. Depending upon the agency at issue, there may be available publications to guide the lawyer regarding discovery.[2] Otherwise, the government will likely deny the requested discovery. By way of example, these requirements might include written requests setting forth the following:

- "Identification of the parties, their counsel, and the nature of the litigation."[3]

- "The date and time on which the documents, information, or testimony sought must be produced."[4]

- "Identification of information or documents requested."[5]

- "A statement of whether factual, opinion, or expert testimony is requested."[6]

- A description of why the information is sought, including its relevance to the proceedings.[7]

- Whether the information or testimony is reasonably available from other sources.[8]

- A summary of any oral testimony sought and its relevance to the proceeding.[9]

---

[1] *E.g.,* 32 C.F.R. §§ 97.1 *et seq.* (Department of Defense); 32 C.F.R. §§ 725.1 *et seq.* (Department of the Navy); 28 C.F.R. §§ 16.21 *et seq.* (Department of Justice); 26 C.F.R. §§ 301.9000-1 *et seq.* (Department of the Treasury); 14 C.F.R. §§ 1263.100 *et seq.* (National Aeronautics and Space Administration); 22 C.F.R. §§ 172.1 *et seq.* (State Department).

[2] *See, e.g.,* Elizabeth A. O'Connell, *How to Subpoena A Government Agent: Compliance with Touhy Regulations for ICE, CBP, DEA and FBI*, Office of the Federal Public Defender Western District of Texas, (May 2011), https://txw.fd.org/how-subpoena-government-agent-compliance-touhy-regulations-ice-cbp-dea-and-fbi (follow "How to Subpoena a Government Agent: Compliance With Touhy Regulations for ICE, CBP, DEA and FBI" hyperlink).

[3] 32 C.F.R. § 725.7(a)(1).

[4] 32 C.F.R. § 725.7(a)(iii).

[5] 32 C.F.R. § 725.7(a)(2).

[6] 32 C.F.R. § 725.7(a)(2)(iii). This is often a source of contention when dealing with federal agencies, which may draw a distinction between factual matters and expert or opinion testimony. Normally the policy is to restrict federal personnel from testifying on matters of opinion, particularly when asked to respond to "matters submitted by counsel or going to the ultimate issue of causation or liability." *See, e.g.,* 32 C.F.R. § 725.4(c) (1)-(3).

[7] *See* 32 C.F.R. § 725.7(a)(3)(i), (ii).

[8] *See* 32 C.F.R. § 725.7(a)(3)(iii).

[9] 28 C.F.R. § 16.22(C).

- Whether the United States is a party to the litigation and, if not, whether it is reasonably anticipated the United States will be joined as a party.[10]

- With respect to depositions, details concerning location, reviewing and signing the transcript and payment of any fees as well as a statement regarding whether trial testimony is anticipated.[11]

The general policy of most federal agencies, with some variations, is to provide a framework for discovery. By way of example, the Department of the Navy provides that "official factual information, both testimonial and documentary, should be made reasonably available for use in federal courts, state courts, foreign courts, and other governmental proceedings unless that information is classified, privileged, or otherwise protected from public disclosure."[12] The following considerations may be addressed as part of this process:

- The ability to obtain the testimony or information from another source.

- Whether the discovery is unduly burdensome or otherwise inappropriate under applicable court rules.[13]

- Public interest.

- Whether disclosure is appropriate under procedural rules governing the case.[14]

- Whether disclosure violates or conflicts with a statute, executive order, regulation, directive, instruction, or notice.[15]

- Whether disclosure is appropriate or necessary under the relevant substantive law concerning privilege.[16]

- Whether disclosure would reveal classified information.[17]

- Whether disclosure unduly interferes with ongoing law enforcement proceedings, violates constitutional rights, reveals the identity of an intelligence source or source of confidential information, conflicts with U.S. obligations under an international agreement, or would be otherwise inappropriate under the circumstances.[18]

---

[10] *See* 32 C.F.R. § 725.7(b); *see also* 28 C.F.R. §§ 16.22-23 (providing more onerous requirements for disclosure of information with respect to those cases in which the United States is not a party).

[11] 32 C.F.R. § 725.7(b)(1)-(9).

[12] 32 C.F.R. § 725.2(a); *see also* 32 C.F.R. § 97.4 ("It is [Department of Defense] policy that official information should generally be made reasonably available for use in Federal and State courts and by other governmental bodies unless the information is classified, privileged, or otherwise protected from public disclosure.").

[13] 32 C.F.R. § 725.8(a)(2).

[14] 32 C.F.R. § 725.8(a)(3).

[15] 32 C.F.R. § 725.8(a)(4).

[16] 32 C.F.R. § 725.8(a)(6).

[17] 32 C.F.R. § 725.8(a)(7).

[18] 32 C.F.R. § 725.8(a)(8).

- The need to maintain impartiality between private litigants when a substantial government interest is not implicated.

- Whether attendance of the witness at deposition or trial will unduly interfere with the business of the agency including the need to conserve time for official business.

Practical considerations dictate that a *Touhy* request should be narrowly tailored. The lawyer seeking discovery from a government agency should avoid broad requests likely to trigger objections. "Among other purposes, *Touhy* regulations allow an agency to conserve its resources to effect the mission of the agency, rather than suffering the cumulative drain on resources that providing witnesses for private litigation can impose."[19] While practitioners often want to craft broad discovery requests to avoid missing relevant information, the more tailored a *Touhy* request, the more likely the desired discovery will be obtained.

A *Touhy* request should also include offers to reimburse the agency for the employee's time, take the deposition after normal working hours or on a weekend, or agree that the deposition will be used in lieu of trial testimony. The request also should include a statement of willingness to cooperate fully with the agency to make any necessary modifications to accommodate legitimate concerns. It is important to explain, where possible, why the particular information cannot be obtained from another source.

In *Exxon Shipping Co. v. United States Department of the Interior*, the Ninth Circuit held that federal agencies have no authority to prohibit employees from disclosing information in response to a lawful federal subpoena.[20] However, the Court noted that the federal government has a "serious and legitimate concern that its employee resources not be commandeered into service by private litigants to the detriment of the smooth functioning of government operations."[21] Approaching a federal agency with patience and respect will go a long way toward achieving the goals of obtaining the desired information or testimony.

It is a best practice to initiate a *Touhy* request early in the discovery process to permit sufficient time to cut through procedural obstacles that might arise. Otherwise, the lawyer seeking the discovery may not be successful in receiving a timely response.

---

[19] *F.T.C. v. Timeshare Mega Media & Mktg. Grp., Inc.*, No. 10-62000-CIV, 2011 WL 6102676, at *3 (S.D. Fla. Dec. 7, 2011); *see also Boron Oil Co. v. Downie*, 873 F.2d 67, 70 (4th Cir. 1989) ("The policy behind such prohibitions on the testimony of agency employees is to conserve governmental resources where the United States is not a party to a suit, and to minimize governmental involvement in controversial matters unrelated to official business.").

[20] 34 F.3d 774 (9th Cir. 1994).

[21] *Id.* at 779.

Deposing Senior Corporate Executives: The Apex Doctrine

Most lawyers will encounter the so-called Apex Doctrine, which is triggered if one party seeks the deposition of a high-ranking executive of a corporate party. This typically occurs where the defendant is a corporation and the plaintiff seeks the deposition of the CEO or other high-ranking executive of the corporate defendant. However, the doctrine is also invoked in cases where a defendant seeks the deposition of high-ranking officials of a corporate plaintiff.

The Apex Doctrine evolved from the practice of aggressive plaintiffs' counsel seeking to embarrass a corporate defendant by interrogating the highest ranking officials, harassing the corporate organization as a result, and putting pressure on the corporate party to settle to avoid presenting the official for deposition. In theory, the Apex Doctrine "presents a fair balance between the right of a plaintiff to conduct discovery in its case within the limits of the rules, and the right of someone at the apex of the hierarchy of a large corporation to avoid being subjected to undue harassment and abuse."[22] Under this doctrine, a senior executive cannot be deposed without a showing that the executive has a "unique or superior personal knowledge of discoverable information" and, absent such showing, "the court should issue the protective order and first require the plaintiff to obtain the necessary discovery through less intrusive means."[23]

In some jurisdictions, the doctrine is not meant to completely shield high-ranking officers from discovery, but is used to sequence discovery to prevent litigants from deposing high-ranking officials before engaging in less burdensome discovery methods.[24] In federal practice, the plaintiff must typically "establish that the executive has superior or unique information regarding the subject matter of the litigation and that such information cannot be obtained through a less intrusive method, such as by deposing lower-ranking executives."[25] Less intrusive methods include depositions of lower-level employees, depositions of corporate representatives under Rule 30(b)(6) and interrogatories and request for production to the corporate entity.[26]

Many other jurisdictions now frown upon an "apex" deposition, and they have established rules and procedures that must be satisfied before any such deposition is allowed. Simply put, the "apex" deposition will not be allowed unless the party seeking the deposition first establishes that the deposition is relevant, that the named

---

[22] *Monsanto Co. v. May*, 889 S.W.2d 274, 277 (Tex. 1994) (Opinion on denial of leave to file petition for writ of mandamus) (Gonzalez, J., joined by Hecht, J., dissenting).

[23] *Liberty Mut. Ins. Co. v. San Mateo Co. Superior Court*, 10 Cal.App. 4th 1282, 1289, 13 Cal.Rptr.2d 363, 367 (1992).

[24] *Alberto v. Toyota Motor Corp.*, 796 N.W.2d 490, 492 (2010).

[25] *Id.* at 493 (collecting cases).

[26] *See, e.g., Baine v. Gen. Motors Corp.*, 141 F.R.D. 332, 334-35 (M.D. Ala. 1991); *see also Crown Cent. Petroleum Corp. v. Garcia*, 904 S.W.2d 125, 127–28 (Tex. 1995).

official has relevant knowledge, and that there are no lesser intrusive means to obtaining the testimony. In some jurisdictions, the party seeking the discovery may be forced to seek discovery from lower-ranking officials if the same information can be obtained. The ultimate goal of the Apex Doctrine is to protect a highly ranked official who may have little or no knowledge concerning the factual matters at issue in the lawsuit.

Each lawyer should check the relevant jurisdiction to certify the burden of what must be shown before an "apex deposition" is allowed. However, here are some representative examples of what must be done before such discovery is allowed to go forward:

- "When a party seeks to depose a corporate president or other high level corporate official and that official (or the corporation) files a motion for protective order to prohibit the deposition accompanied by the official's affidavit denying any knowledge of relevant facts, the trial court should first determine whether the party seeking the deposition has arguably shown that the official has any unique or superior personal knowledge of discoverable information. If the party seeking the deposition cannot show that the official has any unique or superior personal knowledge of discoverable information, the trial court should grant the motion for protective order and first require the party seeking the deposition to attempt to obtain the discovery through less intrusive methods.... After making a good faith effort to obtain the discovery through less intrusive methods, the party seeking the deposition may attempt to show (1) that there is a reasonable indication that the official's deposition is calculated to lead to the discovery of admissible evidence, and (2) that the less intrusive methods of discovery are unsatisfactory, insufficient or inadequate."[27]

- "In determining whether to allow an apex deposition [i.e., the deposition of a high-level executive], courts consider (1) whether the deponent has unique first-hand, non-repetitive knowledge of facts at issue in the case and (2) whether the party seeking the deposition has exhausted other less intrusive discovery methods. However, a party seeking to prevent a deposition carries a heavy burden to show why discovery should be denied. Thus, it is very unusual for a court to prohibit the taking of a deposition altogether absent extraordinary circumstances. When a witness has personal knowledge of facts relevant to the lawsuit, even a corporate president or CEO is subject to deposition. A claimed lack of knowledge, by itself it [SIC] is insufficient to preclude a deposition."[28]

---

[27] *Crown Central Petroleum Corp. v. Garcia*, 904 S.W.2d 125, 128 (Tex. 1995).

[28] *Apple Inc. v. Samsung Elecs. Co., Ltd*, 282 F.R.D. 259, 263 (N.D. Cal. 2012) (internal citations and quotations omitted).

16

Using Demonstrative Evidence in Deposition

All lawyers should assume that all or substantially all of a deposition will be read or shown to the jury. As such, a primary objective should be to make the deposition come alive for the jury. The examining lawyer wants to grab and hold the jury's attention.

Most people are visual learners. Demonstrative exhibits can help a lawyer tell a witness's story using visuals to enhance testimony and thereby enhance the jury's understanding of the testimony. Demonstratives are used to enliven, accentuate, and dramatize key points in the testimony or provide significant context for the testimony.

Demonstrative exhibits range from the simple to the complex. Modern technology provides enhanced options for visual media. Indeed, the computer age has ushered in multiple ways to create powerful imagery to tell a story for the court, the mediator, and the jury. The possibilities are virtually endless and are limited only by the lawyer's budget and creativity.

Preliminary Strategic Considerations

The first issue that should be addressed is whether a demonstrative exhibit should be simple or elaborate. The quality and complexity of such exhibits are invariably linked to the perceived wealth of the parties in the lawsuit. If there is a significant contrast between the quality of demonstrative exhibits between a plaintiff and a defendant, a jury may perceive a disparity in the amount of funds invested in the case which, ultimately, may lead to a perception in a disparity in relative wealth. Therefore, lawyers should consider this issue before developing an arsenal of demonstratives for either deposition or trial.

If a large corporation is defending against an individual plaintiff, simplicity may be a better strategy. However, when the stakes are high, even lawyers representing individual plaintiffs typically invest significant sums in powerful visual aids. The days of the simple "blow up" or poster board in high-stakes litigation are largely gone.

Focus Groups

If the expense budget allows, a useful tool is to evaluate demonstratives with focus groups to determine visual efficacy and impact. Many lawyers in high-stakes litigation use jury consultants to help develop demonstratives based upon jury studies and feedback from focus groups. The purpose is to get guidance concerning the impact of the exhibits—what works and what does not work. Litigation budgets in routine cases may not support this type of investment. If the case is large, however, then some consideration should be given to using outside consultants to help prepare visual aids.

Hand-Drawn Diagrams

Having the witness draw diagrams or pictures is simple and effective. This is particularly true if there is a video camera making a record of the drawing exercise. The lawyer should ask questions as the drawing is prepared, then have the witness create labels and descriptive annotations. The witness should always be asked to initial the drawing to confirm that the diagram is truly the witness's product and testimony, and the drawing should be marked as an exhibit for later use. A simple handwritten drawing can be later enlarged or incorporated into a more sophisticated computer presentation, at a later date for use at trial.

Witness Charts

An effective strategy is to find opportunities for the witness to play an active role in preparing demonstrative exhibits during a videotaped deposition. When the lawyer plays the videotape during trial, the witness's active movements will capture the jury's interest because the juror's eyes will focus on and follow the witness.

One recommended method is to request the witness to stand and prepare drawings or lists on an enlarged flip chart. The chart should be prominently displayed on a nearby easel within the view of the video camera. Indelible marking pens in bold colors should be used. The video record allows the jury to actually see the witness actively drawing or writing on the chart. These drawings or lists should then be marked as exhibits for later use at trial. The charts can also be scanned and incorporated into an electronic presentation software.

If favorable points are established during the witness's testimony, these sound bites are reinforced by asking the witness to list these points in his or her handwriting on the chart. This provides a helpful summary of the witness's key testimony. The witness should then initial the chart to reinforce the authenticity of the chart when the chart is subsequently used in the presence of the jury.

Photographs

A picture speaks a thousand words. Photographs should always be used in depositions to underscore or explain a witness's testimony. Indelible marking pens can be used to color, circle, place arrows, or otherwise label the photograph in a permanent fashion. This process is akin to a handwritten drawing with the benefit of having an actual photograph as background. The witness should again initial the photograph to confirm that the markings reflect the witness's testimony and the photos should be marked as exhibits.

Aerial Photographs

Aerial photographs are extremely effective in focusing a jury's attention on specific scenes or settings. Aerial photographs literally provide a "birds-eye" view at high altitude and can help direct a jury to what is at issue in the case—whether it be a construction site, a roadway, or some other setting.

Aerials are useful in a wide variety of cases. Here are some typical examples of how aerial photographs are used for significant effect:

- **Land Use Disputes:** Aerial photographs sequenced over time can demonstrate how a particular land area evolves over time in its various stages of evolution, ranging from agricultural use, commercial use, industrial use, residential use. Aerials can depict how contiguous property is also used and how it may influence the property at issue.

- **Other Real Estate Disputes:** Aerial photographs are used to depict a particular tract or tracts at issue in litigation. They help orient a jury concerning specific real estate that may be at issue in a brokerage commission case, an appraisal case, a trespass case, a deed restriction case, a mortgage default or other similar dispute.

- **Environmental Disputes:** Aerial photographs are used to demonstrate topography and wetlands that may be at issue in an environmental case or used to pinpoint areas of particular environmental concerns.

- **Construction Disputes:** Aerial photographs are used to demonstrate the various stages of construction of a large project. Indeed, in large commercial construction projects, aerial photographs are routinely taken during the ordinary course of business to monitor building progress as an aid to contractors, engineers and architects. These aerials, when used in succession, provide a photographic timeline of the construction project. Each photograph, which is dated, will show how the construction evolved, step by step, month by month, over the course of the construction process.

- **Property Damage Generally:** Before and after aerial photographs can be used to compare and contrast the extent of property damage caused by a catastrophic event or incident, such as an explosion or fire.

- **Property Damage Due to Weather:** Before and after aerial photographs can be used to compare and contrast property damage caused by hail damage, wind damage, or flooding. This may be relevant in first-party insurance claims.

- **Accident Scenes:** Aerials of highways and roadways (whether urban or rural) help a jury focus on an accident scene, the surrounding topography and the terrain. They help orient a jury on the scene of an accident, and can be used by witnesses and accident reconstruction experts to explain changes in topography and slopes.

Magnetized Boards

Another effective device is to use a magnetized board with models or moving pieces to demonstrate the movement of people or objects, such as cars or other machinery. The witness can be directed to demonstrate the movement of people, equipment, or cars as the witness observed on an enlarged aerial photograph that has been magnetized. When this demonstration is captured on video by a videographer, a moving record is established of what the witness observed. It is akin to a movie in slow motion narrated by the witness.

Simple Demonstratives: Blow Ups

Some lawyers prefer the low key or "poor man" approach using blow-ups of photographs or documents. They shun high-tech options or other computer programs in favor of simple enlarged documents or photographs. Simplicity still remains powerful in certain cases, particularly if it is contrasted with a high-tech presentation by the opposing party. Using simple blow-ups can reinforce the notion that the lawyer (and the lawyer's client) are underdogs, and this may be particularly beneficial for a corporate defendant.

Documents: Cutaways

Many computer programs allow excerpts from documents to be lifted and magnified. These cutaways are electronically lifted from the document and highlighted by individuals who are skilled with the various software programs. The process of making the cutaway is a two-step process. First, the witness (and the jury) sees the document intact. Then, on a screen, the witness and the jury sees an image of the excerpt *magically* lifted from the document reinforcing the context of the cutaway and its underlying authenticity. The jury can see where the cutaway came from and can then see the image of the enlarged cutaway. The process is effective in capturing the jury's attention while reinforcing the authenticity of the source.

Documents: Using Overhead Projectors

Overhead projectors are frequently used in depositions. The lawyer can place a highlighted or color-coded document on the screen to highlight relevant testimony or excerpts from exhibits shown to the witness. This can be done with documentary evidence, photographs, or prior testimony. The examining attorney controls the process by directing the witness's attention to the relevant excerpts in the document. This is a simple, effective approach for examining witnesses, and it is particularly helpful when the lawyer seeks to impeach the witness. The lawyer can direct the observer to a highlighted (and enlarged) version of prior inconsistent testimony or document, thereby placing the witness on the defensive.

Using Split-Screen Videos

Split-screen videography is highly effective during depositions. A split screen allows both the document or photograph to be shown, while concurrently showing the witness responding to questions. Most frequently, the witness's head is reduced to a small corner of the screen while the document, photograph, or cutaway is shown in a larger image. The jury will focus on the exhibit, but the witness's face is still visible on the side of the monitor. This is an effective technique that allows the jury to concurrently follow the documentary evidence while watching the witness's demeanor, thereby allowing the jury to evaluate the witness's credibility. This technique is particularly useful when deposing an adverse witness or expert. The document takes "center stage" and the witness's head is "shrunk." This contrast is arguably demeaning to the witness since it places the document in a place of greater importance. As such, opposing counsel may object to this methodology.

Using Timelines

Chronologies are important in document-intensive cases, and they help witnesses and juries understand extended relationships or complicated transactions. Timelines are also useful in providing summaries of key communications or key events. These timelines can be enlarged and presented in captivating colors and graphics. Here are some simple examples:

- **Extended Contractual Negotiations:** An enlarged timeline can chronicle communications between the parties leading up to a contract, including significant email communications between the parties, meetings or other significant events, redlined drafts of contractual documents, and communications between lawyers.

- **Decision Trees and Failure Analysis Concerning Safety Issues:** A timeline can identify each step in the development of a product from concept design, prototype design, prototype manufacture, prototype testing, design revisions, manufacture, and final testing.

- **Cascading Events:** A timeline can chronical when various individuals undertook tasks that led to a product failure, accident or other catastrophic event.

Computer Simulations and Modeling

Computer simulations and modeling of dynamic events have become increasingly sophisticated. Some software programs purport to have the ability to simulate dynamic events and all relevant forces during such events. This is most readily seen in automobile crashes, truck crashes, train crashes, or plane crashes, but the technology is available to simulate other dynamic events as well. Computer simulations can be used during the course of a deposition in much the same way as documentary evidence or photographs. Split-screen technology also exists. The videographer can show a simulation on one side of the video screen while the witness's face is shown on the other. Again, this is a highly effective technique which the lawyer can package for trial.

Equipment and Machinery

Some cases may involve equipment failures or allegations of design or manufacturing defects. The actual product or device can be physically brought into the deposition room. The witness can be requested to stand and explain his or her testimony by pointing to the component parts of the machinery or the product. In essence, there is no difference between what can be done in the courtroom and the deposition room. Indeed, an entire "buck" (chassis assembly and seat of an automotive vehicle) can be brought into a deposition room for use during examination. The only limitation on what can be used is whether the facility is large enough to accommodate the equipment or product.

Internet Access

Laptops can be used during deposition. A lawyer can access the Internet via cable or wireless connection, then have the witness specifically locate documents, videos or other tangible evidence that may be accessible using the Internet. An example of this use is a prior speech that a witness may have given and then posted on some internet social medium. Another example might be a company website with which the witness is affiliated. There may be something on the website that can be used as a basis for cross-examination.

The use of such sources may trigger objections, particularly hearsay or authenticity objections. Accordingly, the offering lawyer should plan on how to address such objections beforehand.

Toys

One successful trial lawyer used a simple but effective approach that employed toy models to demonstrate car accidents. Most model shops or hobby shops will have miniature trucks and automobiles that can be purchased inexpensively. A witness can be asked to demonstrate what the witness saw or experienced by moving the toys and showing how they collided or interacted. Again, when this type of sequence is recorded as part of a video record, the witness's testimony is enhanced by providing the jury with a visual (and entertaining) record of the vehicle motions as observed by the witness. The use of toys is a simple, inexpensive way to focus the jury's attention.

Fabricated Models

Depending upon the issues in the case and the available expense budget, to-scale models can be prepared. Again, the potential for model making is only limited by a lawyer's creativity and the amount of money available in the budget. Downhole failures in oil wells can be demonstrated through modeling. Car crashes can be demonstrated through modeling. Train crashes can be demonstrated through modeling. Indeed, almost any piece of equipment, product or device can be accurately replicated in a model with extraordinary detail. These models can incorporate moving parts or removable external coverings to show interior operations.

Scene Topographical Models

Topographical models can be developed with accurate depictions of slopes and different types of terrain. Some models may be extremely large, but can be used in a deposition to explain the events leading up to an accident and how an accident occurred. There are numerous companies that specialize in large-scale model making.

Many topographical models are developed through photogrammetric analysis, which is a scientific process using photographs to ascertain precise distances to fix the orientation of objects in relation to each other as depicted in photographs. These photographs are then used to develop an accurate depiction of a scene based upon measurements that define the distances between objects. There are many consulting companies who have substantial experience and expertise in photogrammetrical analysis and modeling.

17

Motions to Quash and for Protection

This chapter addresses the procedures and strategy for asserting objections to the manner or method of the taking of a deposition, as well as motions that seek to limit testimony or protect a witness from having to provide testimony. In many cases, a party will have received a ruling on a motion for protective order prior to the start of a deposition. By doing so, all parties will be aware of what limitations are set by the court with respect to the deposition. A party's rights and obligations relating to motions for protection will differ depending on whether the deposition is sought in federal or state court and may be impacted by local rules.

Objections Before the Deposition Begins

There are several ways to protect a deponent or a party from being forced to participate in a deposition. The details of these objections and the procedures for asserting these objections are dictated by each individual jurisdiction, so practitioners should consult the rules of the jurisdiction relevant to the case. However, there are some common situations where the need to seek protection will arise.

Most jurisdictions allow parties to file motions for protection to prevent or limit the scope of a deposition. Depositions may be improper because of timing and scheduling.[1] The deposition notice may attempt to schedule a deposition in

---

[1] In this regard, the Federal Rules do not provide a specific minimum period of advanced notice before a witness is deposed, though various jurisdictions do require certain advance notice. *See, e.g., Auto-Owners Ins. Co. v. Southeast Floating Docks, Inc.*, 231 F.R.D. 426, 428 (M.D. Fla. 2005) (local rule required 10 days' advance notice). However, the Federal Rules do provide that "[a] deposition must not be used against a party who, having received less than 14 days' notice of the deposition, promptly moved for a protective order under Rule 26(c)(1)(B) requesting that it not be taken or be taken at a different time or place—and this motion was still pending when the deposition was taken." Fed. R. Civ. P. 32(a)(5)(A).

violation of a scheduling order or outside the permitted time limits for discovery, or a deposition notice may seek a deposition prematurely, before the responding party understands the nature of the claims against it. The notice may also seek testimony from a person whose testimony is exempt from discovery or where the attempt to schedule the deposition is nothing more than harassment.[2]

Some jurisdictions allow motions to quash in lieu of motions for protection. These types of motions are typically filed before a deposition commences, and they are used to completely stop the deposition from going forward. Motions to quash are different from motions for protection since motions for protection may not stop the deposition completely.

Some jurisdictions require that motions to quash and motions for protection be heard before the deposition proceeds. Other jurisdictions provide that certain types of motions to quash are deemed automatic, and the deposition is automatically halted pending further ruling of the court.

Motions in Federal Court

In federal court, motions for protections are governed by Rule 26 of the Federal Rules of Civil Procedure. Rule 26(c)(1) states:

1. **In General.** A party or any person from whom discovery is sought may move for a protective order in the court where the action is pending—or as an alternative on matters relating to a deposition, in the court for the district where the deposition will be taken. The motion must include a certification that the movant has in good faith conferred or attempted to confer with other affected parties in an effort to resolve the dispute without court action. The court may, for good cause, issue an order to protect a party or person from annoyance, embarrassment, oppression, or undue burden or expense, including one or more of the following:

    A. forbidding the disclosure or discovery;

    B. specifying terms, including time and place or the allocation of expenses, for the disclosure or discovery;

    C. prescribing a discovery method other than the one selected by the party seeking discovery;

    D. forbidding inquiry into certain matters, or limiting the scope of disclosure or discovery to certain matters;

---

[2] Under the Federal Rules, an objection to an error or irregularity in the deposition notice is waived unless promptly served in writing on the party issuing notice. *See* Fed. R. Civ. P. 32(d)(1).

E. designating the persons who may be present while the discovery is conducted;

F. requiring that a deposition be sealed and opened only on court order;

G. requiring that a trade secret or other confidential research, development, or commercial information not be revealed or be revealed only in a specified way; and

H. requiring that the parties simultaneously file specified documents or information in sealed envelopes, to be opened as the court directs.

It is important to emphasize the requirements under Rule 26 that the party (or nonparty) confer with the issuing party in a good faith attempt to resolve the dispute without the court's involvement. One particularly effective, but underutilized, way to avoid the full brunt of discovery is to negotiate limitations on the scope of the deposition or the requested document discovery. This permits the parties to avoid costly motion practice. For example, when faced with what first appears to be a relatively burdensome nonparty subpoena *duces tecum* for testimony and documents, a brief conference with opposing counsel may demonstrate their willingness to be flexible. Such discussions often lead to agreements to narrow the scope of the demanded discovery.

Practitioners should be aware of the risks associated with seeking protection. Aside from the expense associated with drafting and hearing such motions, the Federal Rules include fee-shifting provisions that allow parties to recover reasonable expenses, including attorneys' fees.[3] If the motion is denied, the court may, on such terms and conditions as are just, order that any party or other person provide or permit discovery. Thus, parties will want to carefully analyze whether striking a deal to limit, narrow, or otherwise protect against the requested deposition is a more prudent (and less expensive) alternative to motion practice.

Should a motion for protection be necessary, parties must typically show good cause for the requested relief. If possible, parties should support their motion with evidence. This is typically in the form of an affidavit or declaration. Whether the discovery requested is privileged, burdensome, irrelevant, or otherwise objectionable, the moving party should offer specific facts supported by affidavits, declarations, or other evidence to obtain the requested relief. Conclusory statements are typically not sufficient to support a claim for good cause.

Counsel need to ensure that they timely file their motions. While the Federal Rules do not provide a specific timeframe within which to seek protection, such motions should be made in advance of the scheduled deposition.[4] Parties should also check their local court rules to determine whether additional deadlines

---

[3] *See* Fed. R. Civ. P. 37(a)(5).

[4] *See Drexel Heritage Furnishings, Inc. v. Furniture USA, Inc.,* 200 F.R.D. 255, 259 (M.D.N.C. 2001); *Brittain v. Stroh Brewery Co.,* 136 F.R.D. 408, 413 (M.D.N.C. 1991).

apply. Generally, the motion should be filed far enough in advance of the deposition to permit the court sufficient time to rule, which will often force responding counsel to act immediately following service of a deposition notice or testimony subpoena. In the case of a testimony subpoena, it is a good practice to file any such motion consistent with the deadlines for objections to document discovery.[5] If more certainty is required, counsel can seek a stipulation to define the filing deadline.

Practitioners should take precautions to ensure that, after filing a motion, the requested deposition has been canceled, stayed, or suspended by the court, local rules, or other agreement. As a general proposition, the act of simply filing a motion for protection does not automatically stay a deposition under the Federal Rules. To avoid a required appearance, the receiving party must obtain a court order before the scheduled deposition begins.[6]

However, some federal court jurisdictions have instituted local rules that act to suspend a deposition once a motion for protection or a related motion is filed. By way of example, the local rules for the U.S. District Court of Kansas provide that a deposition is stayed upon the filing of either a motion to quash or modify a deposition subpoena or a motion to order appearance or production only upon special conditions within 14 days of service of the notice and no later than 48 hours prior to the deposition.[7]

If the local rules do not provide for a stay upon filing of a motion, it is not advisable that the deponent simply refuse to show up as noticed or subpoenaed. While not all jurisdictions agree,[8] parties should exercise great caution before relying on Rule 37 alone to avoid appearing at a deposition. Rule 37(d), which governs discovery sanctions, states that a failure to appear at a deposition is not excused on the ground that the discovery sought was objectionable, unless the party failing to act has a pending motion for a protective order under Rule 26(c).[9] However, several courts have concluded that "[t]he fact that conduct is not sanctionable under Rule 37 does not render it proper" and that they have "inherent authority" to sanction a party for failing to appear at a

---

[5] *See* Fed. R. Civ. P. 45(d)(2)(b) (requiring objections to document subpoenas be served by the earlier of 14 days or the date of compliance).

[6] *See* Fed. *Aviation Admin. v. Landy*, 705 F.2d 624, 634 (2d Cir. 1983)("[I]t is not the filing of such a motion [for a protective order] that stays the deposition, but rather a court order."); *see also* Fed. R. Civ. P. 37 Notes of Advisory Committee on 1993 Amendments (providing that motions for protection are "not self-executing—the relief authorized under that rule depends on obtaining the court's order to that effect.").

[7] D. Kan. Rule 26.2(b); *see also,* Fed. R. Civ. P. 32(a)(5)(A) ("A deposition must not be used against a party who, having received less than 14 days' notice of the deposition, promptly moved for a protective order under Rule 26(c)(1)(B) requesting that it not be taken or be taken at a different time or place—and this motion was still pending when the deposition was taken.").

[8] *See Ghandi v. Police Dept. of City of Detroit*, 74 F.R.D. 115, 118 n. 4 (E.D. Mich. 1977) ("witness may not disregard a subpoena he has not challenged by a motion to quash, but may refuse to comply with a subpoena until his motion to quash has been ruled upon.") (internal citations omitted).

[9] Fed. R. Civ. P. 37(d)(2).

deposition even if a motion for protection is pending.[10] Thus, any party filing a motion for protection should be diligent in not only filing the motion, but also seeking a court ruling.

Motions in State Courts

Procedures for motions for protection (or motions to quash) may vary greatly depending on the applicable state court jurisdiction. Certain jurisdictions permit a party or deponent to file a motion to quash prior to the noticed deposition, and the mere filing of such a motion instantly suspends the deposition until such time that a court can rule on the motion.[11]

However, other state court jurisdictions may require the deponent to actually secure a court ruling to excuse attendance at the deposition. In Pennsylvania and Missouri, for example, filing a motion for protection does not stay the deposition unless such relief has been ordered by the court.[12]

The deadline to file a motion for protection is jurisdiction specific. Similar to its federal counterparts, the deadline may be impacted by local rules or specific judicial requirements where the action is pending.

Protecting the Corporate Witness as to Scope

One of the most challenging depositions in litigation is that of a corporate witness. This heightened challenge is caused, in part, by the "binding" impact of the witness's testimony on the corporation. Not only does the witness's

---

[10] *See Amobi v. D.C. Dept. of Corrections*, 257 FRD 8, 10-11 (D.D.C. 2009); *see also, In re Steffen*, 433 B.R. 879, 883 (M.D. Fla. 2010) ("Sanctions for failure to appear at a deposition can be ordered in spite of a pending motion for protective order if that motion is found to be untimely, frivolous, or otherwise for the purpose of avoiding the taking of a deposition").

[11] *See, e.g.,* Tex. R. Civ. P. 199.4 ("A party or witness may object to the time and place designated for an oral deposition by motion for protective order or by motion to quash the notice of deposition. If the motion is filed by the third business day after service of the notice of deposition, an objection to the time and place of a deposition stays the oral deposition until the motion can be determined."); Cal. Civ. Proc. Code § 2025.410(c) (West) ("a party may also move for an order staying the taking of the deposition and quashing the deposition notice... [t]he taking of the deposition is stayed pending the determination of this motion").

[12] *See* Pa.R.C.P. No. 4013 ("The filing of a motion for a protective order shall not stay the deposition, production, entry on land or other discovery to which the motion is directed unless the court shall so order"); *Kingsley v. Kingsley*, 716 S.W.2d 257, 260 (Mo. 1986) (en banc) ("A bare motion to quash grants to the movant neither a continuance of the deposition nor a stay of the deposition. To hold otherwise would be to say that every party can secure to himself one stay or continuance by the filing of the bare motion to quash. If the deponent does not want to appear, then the burden is his to request and to secure from the court a stay or continuance and excuse from attendance").

testimony potentially bind the corporation in the proceeding in which the deposition is taken, but it may impact the corporation in other cases as well. Thus, before presenting a Rule 30(b)(6) corporate witness, practitioners are well advised to become familiar with the *King v. Pratt & Whitney* approach, which reflects a predominant viewpoint on handling such depositions in federal court.[13]

The prevailing view in federal court is that the corporate deposition should not be disrupted based solely on the fact that the witness is examined on facts outside the scope of the corporate notice. The *King* approach states that there is no need to stop the deposition; rather, the witness should state he or she does not know the answer or provide an answer subject to the lawyer's objections that the questions are outside the scope. Prior to *King, Paparelli v. Prudential Insurance Co. of America* held that questions outside the scope of the notice to a 30(b)(6) witness would satisfy 30(d)(4).[14] This viewpoint has been largely rejected since *King*.

Nevertheless, even with the holding in *King*, a 30(b)(6) deposition may be terminated and a party may move for a protective order for reasons of abuse, bad faith, oppression, or other harassing deposition tactics.

After the Whistle: Moving for Protection After a Deposition Begins

There are situations where a party should consider moving for protection *after* the deposition begins. A party should move to limit or terminate a deposition and seek protection if the examination is conducted in bad faith or in a manner that unreasonably annoys, embarrasses, or oppresses the party or deponent.[15] Should such tactics occur, the deposition may be stopped. Upon demand of the objecting party or deponent, the taking of the deposition must be suspended until such time that the objecting party can make a motion and obtain a court order. Thereafter, and upon a showing that the examining lawyer is conducting the deposition in bad faith or in a manner that unreasonably annoys, embarrasses, or oppresses either the deponent or a party, the court in which the action is pending or the court in the jurisdiction in which deposition is taking place may order the officer conducting the examination to stop the deposition or alternatively, may limit the scope and manner of the taking of the deposition as provided in Rule 26(c).[16]

---

[13] *King v. Pratt & Whitney*, 161 F.R.D. 475, 476 (S.D. Fla. 1996); *Am. Gen. Life Ins. Co. v. Billard*, C10-1012, 2010 WL 4367052, at *4 (N.D. Iowa Oct. 28, 2010) ("The conclusion reached in *King* has been unanimously accepted by courts addressing the issue since that time.") (collecting cases).

[14] *Paparelli v. Prudential Ins. Co. of America*, 108 F.R.D. 727, 729–30 (D. Mass. 1985).

[15] *See* Fed. R. Civ. P. 26(c)(1), 30(d)(3)(A).

[16] *See Id.; see also, e.g.*, Alaska R. C. V. P. 30(d)(3); Ariz. R. C. V. P. 30(d); Ind. R. Trial P. 30(d).

If the court orders that the deposition be terminated, it may be resumed only upon the order of the court in which the action is pending. The court may limit the scope of the deposition or prohibit specific lines of examination. The court also may award reasonable expenses, including attorneys' fees, to the prevailing party.[17]

Motions for Protection: Protecting the Named Deponent

There are a variety of reasons why a deposition of a specific individual should not proceed forward. These include situations where the witness should be protected from giving testimony because of the person's identity or a particular immunity or exemption from discovery.

Generally, the discovery rules in all jurisdictions set forth the permissible scope of discovery, and depositions that exceed the scope of these permissible limits should be prevented or quashed. Here are specific situations where a motion for protection is appropriate due to the identity of the person whose deposition testimony is sought:

- Senior executives in an organization under the so-called "Apex Doctrine"; motions for protection are used to stop the depositions because of a lack of relevance or on the basis of harassment.[18]

- Attorneys whose testimony is privileged or exempt from discovery because of the attorney-client privilege or attorney work product privilege; this frequently occurs when one party seeks to depose in-house counsel for an organization.

- Consulting experts whose work product has not been considered or relied upon by other testifying experts and, accordingly, their work-product is exempt from discovery.

- Testimony from other individuals whose testimony may be immune or exempt from discovery under established evidentiary privileges, such as the doctor-patient privilege, the marital privilege, or the clergy-penitent privilege.

- Minor children or persons not competent to testify because of medical reasons or mental competency.

---

[17] *See* Fed. R. Civ. P. 30(d)(3)(c), 37 (a)(5)(A).

[18] This Apex doctrine is discussed in detail in Chapter 15.

- Any other witness who should be protected from a deposition because of significant scheduling issues or unique hardships.

- Persons whose testimony is not remotely relevant, and the burdens of providing the testimony far outweigh the benefits of providing the testimony.

- A deposition that is accompanied by a document request or subpoena *duces tecum* that is sweeping, burdensome, or onerous.

18

Making and Responding to Objections

Making effective and appropriate objections during a deposition is more art than science. It requires both strategy and finesse. Excessive objections are never advisable, and argumentative objections or suggestive objections may be prohibited (or frowned upon) in the relevant jurisdiction. Equally important, excessive objections or argumentative objections may alienate the jury and anger the court.

It is important that the objecting lawyer not appear as an obstructionist. As such, it is important that the objecting lawyer weigh the benefits and needs of making an objection with the risks of not doing so. The same strategic analysis that a seasoned trial lawyer undergoes when making objections at trial should likewise govern objections during a deposition. There is truth in the motto "Don't sweat the small stuff." Trial lawyers should not object unless the need to do so really exists. It is never advisable to object to every *technically* objectionable question.

Jurisdictional Differences

Many jurisdictions model their discovery rules after the Federal Rules. Rule 30(c)(2) specifically states that "an objection must be stated concisely in a non-argumentative and non-suggestive manner" and that "a person may instruct a deponent not to answer only when necessary to preserve a privilege, to enforce a limitation ordered by the court, or to present a motion under Rule 30(d)(3)." The underlying principle behind Rule 30(c)(2) is to prevent the use of objections to coach witnesses. "Talking" objections are disfavored, and concise objections are preferred.

Some lawyers use verbal tirades disguised as objections. They are trying to coach the witness and are using the objection as a thinly veiled device to do so. This should not be allowed, and the lawyer taking the deposition should insist that "talking" objections cease. If the conduct persists, the examining lawyer can seek the court's involvement immediately or seek sanctions or a further deposition at a later date.

While federal courts generally agree that "talking" objections (i.e., objections that are argumentative or suggestive to the witness) are improper under Rule 30(c)(2),[1] various district courts disagree on precisely what the attorney should say to preserve an objection to the form of a question.[2] In one court, the lawyer might be limited in what he or she can say.[3] In a different court, the lawyer might have more latitude.[4] In certain districts, there may be a specific local rule that instructs counsel on the manner and substance of making objections.[5]

Given this lack of consistency, the best practice is to determine whether there is direct authority in the jurisdiction. If not, counsel should seek a stipulation or other agreement with opposing counsel regarding the proper method of making objections to the form of the question or answer.[6]

Irrespective of how an attorney should make the objections in a particular district, the Federal Rules require that objections to an irregularity relating to the "manner of taking the deposition, the form of a question or answer, the oath or affirmation, a party's conduct, or other matters that might have been corrected…" are waived if not timely made during the deposition.[7] On the other hand, an objection to competence, relevance, or materiality is not waived if a party fails to raise it during the deposition unless the ground for it might have been corrected at that time.[8]

---

[1] *See, e.g., Specht v. Google, Inc.*, 268 F.R.D. 596, 598 (N.D. Ill. 2010).

[2] *See Cohen v. Trump*, 13-CV-2519-GPC WVG, 2015 WL 2406094, at *2–3 (S.D. Cal. May 19, 2015).

[3] *Druck Corp. v. Macro Fund (U.S.) Ltd.*, 02 CIV.6164(RO)(DFE), 2005 WL 1949519, at *4 (S.D.N.Y. Aug. 12, 2005) ("Any 'objection as to form' must say *only* those four words, unless the questioner asks the objector to state a reason.").

[4] *Rakes v. Life Inv'rs Ins. Co. of Am.*, C06-0099, 2008 WL 429060, at *5 (N.D. Iowa Feb. 14, 2008) ("Plaintiffs contend that the objection should be limited to the words 'I object to the form of the question.' The Rule, however, is not so restrictive.").

[5] TX R USDCTED Rule CV-30 ("Objections to questions during the oral deposition are limited to 'Objection, leading' and 'Objection, form.' Objections to testimony during the oral deposition are limited to 'Objection, nonresponsive.' These objections are waived if not stated as phrased during the oral deposition. All other objections need not be made or recorded during the oral deposition to be later raised with the court. The objecting party must give a clear and concise explanation of an objection if requested by the party taking the oral deposition, or the objection is waived.").

[6] *Cohen*, 2015 WL 2406094, at *2 ("The Court noted that there was not consistency throughout the district courts regarding whether form objections were proper, and thus, this was not an issue that the Court needed to resolve for the parties. The Court explained that the parties should have recognized there are divergent viewpoints throughout the district courts, and resolved the issue on their own without pausing the deposition and contacting the Court for guidance.").

[7] Fed. R. Civ. P. 32(d)(3)(B).

[8] Fed. R. Civ. P. 32(d)(3)(A).

As with the Federal Rules, a state may specify the type of objections that must be made during a deposition. Some jurisdictions expressly limit the objections that can be asserted. In some states, such as Texas, all standard objections are reserved until trial *except* objections as to "responsiveness," "form," or "leading." The assertion of any other objections is frowned upon and will likely result in a discovery motion if such objections are repeated extensively. Like Texas, the civil rules in Alaska do not require any specification of the defect in the form of a question or answer unless the party asking the question requires an explanation of the basis for the objection.[9] Many other states are similar.

In New Jersey, the civil rules provide that "[n]o objection shall be made during the taking of a deposition except those addressed to the form of a question or to assert a privilege, a right to confidentiality or a limitation pursuant to a previously entered court order. The right to object on other grounds is preserved and may be asserted at the time the deposition testimony is proffered at trial."[10] The New Jersey rules do not permit an attorney to instruct a witness not to answer a question unless the basis of the objection is privilege, confidentiality, or a limitation pursuant to a prior court order.

In New York, the only objections appropriate during a deposition are those that would otherwise be waived.[11] Any objection made during a deposition "shall be stated succinctly and framed so as not to suggest an answer to the deponent and, at the request of the questioning attorney, shall include a clear statement as to any defect in form or other basis of error or irregularity."[12] Additionally, persons in attendance at a deposition shall not make statements or comments that interfere with the questioning, except as permitted by rule.[13] Thus, in New York, as in most states, it would be improper if the lawyer presenting the witness makes an objection such as "Objection, if you understand the question you can answer" or state "If you recall," in response to a question directed to the witness. Those types of statements and objections are characterized as "suggestive" or "coaching."[14]

In Connecticut, any objections raised during a deposition "shall be stated succinctly and framed so as not to suggest an answer to the deponent and, at the request of the questioning attorney, shall include a clear statement as to any

---

[9] Alaska R. Civ. P. 30(d)(1).

[10] N.J. R. Ct. 4:14-3(c).

[11] N.Y. Comp. Codes R. & Regs. tit. 22, § 221.1(a) ("No objections shall be made at a deposition except those which, pursuant to subdivision (b), (c) or (d) of Rule 3115 of the Civil Practice Law and Rules, would be waived if not interposed, and except in compliance with subdivision (e) of such rule. All objections made at a deposition shall be noted by the officer before whom the deposition is taken, and the answer shall be given and the deposition shall proceed subject to the objections and to the right of a person to apply for appropriate relief pursuant to article 31 of the CPLR.").

[12] N.Y. Comp. Codes R. & Regs. tit. 22, § 221.1(b).

[13] *Id.*

[14] *See Freidman v. Fayenson*, 41 Misc. 3d 1236(A), 983 N.Y.S.2d 203 (Sup. Ct. 2013), *aff'd sub nom. Freidman v. Yakov*, 138 A.D.3d 554, 30 N.Y.S.3d 58 (N.Y. App. Div. 2016).

defect in form or other basis of error or irregularity."[15] Similarly, in Florida, "[a]ny objection during a deposition shall be stated concisely and in a nonargumentative and nonsuggestive manner."[16] The same rule is nearly identical in Kansas as well.[17]

In Maryland, an attorney need not state the grounds for the objection unless requested by another party.[18] However, if a request is made, the objection "shall be stated specifically, concisely, and in a nonargumentative and nonsuggestive manner."[19] Moreover, "[i]f a party desires to make an objection for the record during the taking of a deposition that reasonably could have the effect of coaching or suggesting to the deponent how to answer, then the deponent, at the request of any party, shall be excused from the deposition during the making of the objection."[20] The Committee note to Rule 2-415(h) further explains that "[d]uring the taking of a deposition, it is presumptively improper for an attorney to make objections that are inconsistent with Rule 2-415(h). Objections should be stated as simply, concisely, and nonargumentatively as possible to avoid coaching or making suggestions to the deponent and to minimize interruptions in the questioning of the deponent." Examples of permitted objections under Maryland procedure include "objection, leading," "objection, asked and answered," and "objection, compound question."[21]

In some states, there may be statewide rules that govern objections during depositions, as well as local rules that affect a deposition taken in a certain judicial district or county. For example, Ohio's Rules of Civil Procedure generally govern procedural issues related to depositions.[22] However, a case filed in Cleveland, for instance, may be subject to the Cuyahoga County Common Pleas Court Local Rules. Among other things, those local rules limit objections to five permissible categories and instruct counsel how to—and how not to—make an objection during deposition.[23]

Thus, the rules for each jurisdiction should be consulted. Clearly, different states (and, sometimes venues within the same state) impose different rules concerning what objections can be made and what objections should not be made.

---

[15] Conn. Practice Book 13-30(b).

[16] Fla. R. Civ. P. 1.310(c).

[17] Kan. Stat. Ann. § 60-230(c)(2) (West).

[18] Md. Rules 2-415(h).

[19] *Id.*

[20] Md. Rules 2-415(h) Committee note.

[21] *Id.*

[22] *See* Ohio Civ. R. 30–32.

[23] Cuy. Cty. C.P. Loc. R. 13.1(B)(1)-(5) (limiting objections to those that fall in five categories); Cuy. Cty. C.P. Loc. R. 13.1(C)(3) ("Counsel may interpose an objection by stating 'objection' and the legal grounds for the objection. Speaking objections which refer to the facts of the case or suggest an answer to the deponent are improper and shall not be made in the presence of the deponent. Counsel shall not argue the reasons for the objection on the record.").

Trial Depositions

A trial lawyer should be prepared to make critical objections in all trial depositions. This would include all depositions of out-of-state witnesses or witnesses who are known to be unavailable for trial. Here, it is likely the witness will not testify at trial. The deposition testimony thus becomes the trial testimony. All appropriate objections (as allowed by the relevant jurisdiction) must be made during the deposition to preserve the objection for subsequent ruling.

Likewise, if objections are asserted, the examining lawyer should seek clarification as to why the objection has been made. In this manner, the examining lawyer can make an informed decision whether to re-fashion the question. This is well advised if the question calls for important or favorable testimony. The goal is to ensure that all important (favorable) testimony is in the record and will be admissible at trial.

Video Depositions

Every trial lawyer should be sensitive to making unnecessary objections during the course of a video deposition. The effect of the objection is re-enforced by the audio portion of the recording. Objections that tend to coach the witness should be avoided, and excessive objections should be avoided, to prevent the impression that the lawyer is obstructing the testimony. In some instances, the jury may be entitled to hear the objections at a later date, and excessive objections may send an unintended message to the jury that the lawyer appears defensive or is trying to hide facts.

Exceeding the Scope of Deposition

A presenting lawyer in a corporate deposition should be prepared to object when questions exceed the scope of the enumerated topics in the 30(b)(6) deposition notice. A witness in a 30(b)(6) deposition binds the corporation on all topics set forth in the deposition notice, but it is inappropriate for the presenting lawyer to halt the deposition unless the questions become abusive. Again, this is the prevailing view in most federal court jurisdictions.[24] The presenting lawyer should still object that the question exceeds the proper scope, and this objection will serve as a bookmark to make sure that any testimony provided in response to such questions is not binding on the organization.

---

[24] *See, e.g., King v. Pratt & Whitney*, 161 F.R.D. 475, 476 (S.D. Fla. 1996).

Privileged Matters

Rule 30(c)(2) specifically contemplates that a witness can be properly instructed not to answer questions that encroach on privileged matters. Thus, if questions call for disclosure of information that is privileged, then the lawyer should instruct the witness not to answer.

Types of Objections at Deposition

In jurisdictions where the types of objections are not limited, there are specific types of objections that should be asserted at the time of the deposition, or the objection may be waived. These objections, together with a brief explanation of each objection, are as follows:

- **Lack of Foundation:** This objection is appropriate where it has not been established that the witness has the necessary knowledge to support an answer to the question.

- **Speculation:** This objection is appropriate where the witness is asked to guess or speculate concerning matters outside the witness's personal knowledge, such as the motivations or knowledge of other persons or matters in which the witness was not personally involved.

- **Improper Hypothetical:** This objection is appropriate where a lay witness is asked to assume facts to support a lay opinion.

- **Improper Lay Opinion:** This objection is appropriate where a lay witness is asked to form an improper expert opinion.

- **Hearsay:** This objection is appropriate where the witness is asked to testify to inadmissible hearsay under Fed. R. Evid. 802 or other comparable state court rules.

- **Compound:** This objection is appropriate where the question incorporates more than one question; this frequently occurs when disjunctive or conjunctive words are used such as "and/or," "either/or," "neither/nor," etc.

- **Impermissible Scope:** This objection is appropriate where a corporate witness is presented pursuant to a Rule 30(b)(6) notice or comparable state court notice, and the questions fall outside the designated topic categories.

- **Legal Conclusion:** This objection is appropriate where the witness is asked to testify on a point of law or legal definition and not facts.

- **Privilege:** This objection (and an accompanying instruction not to answer) is appropriate where the question solicits information protected by the attorney/client privilege, attorney work product privilege, joint defense privilege or common interest privilege.

- **Mischaracterizes Earlier Testimony:** This objection is appropriate where the question attempts to misconstrue or unfairly change the witness's earlier testimony; this objection is also important to avoid any potential impeachment or credibility issues for the witness and to maintain a clear deposition record.

- **Asked and Answered:** This objection is appropriate where the question seeks to have the witness answer the same question more than one time; this objection should be made to repetitive inquiries so the witness does not give a different answer than what was provided earlier in the deposition.

19

Special Deposition Procedures

This chapter discusses unique procedures involving depositions, including procedures for securing expedited depositions, out-of-state depositions, and pre-suit depositions. These are unique proceedings that trigger special procedural requirements. This chapter also discusses important considerations when language barriers become an issue and interpreters are required in the deposition room.

Out-of-State Depositions

Cases pending in state court frequently involve instances when depositions are required outside of the state where the case is pending. A nonparty witness residing outside the forum state is not subject to the subpoena power of the court. Thus, absent an agreement where the witness appears voluntarily, the deposition will be taken pursuant to procedures involving Letters Rogatory, legal mandate, or a special commission. Again, the procedural steps for issuing commissions, mandates, or Letters Rogatory differ from state to state, but there are common features to such practices.

Typically, the state court where the case is pending has the authority to issue a request to a court in a sister state to issue a subpoena for the witness to appear for deposition in that sister state. The subpoena also may be accompanied by a subpoena *duces tecum* seeking production of documents at the time of the deposition. Once the witness is served, the deposition will proceed in the state of the witness's residence and, importantly, the witness can seek protection from or seek to quash the deposition under the procedural rules of the state of his or her residence. The rules of evidence regarding the assertion and scope of evidentiary privileges will typically be governed by the state of the witness's residence. In these circumstances, the authority to enforce the subpoena resides in the sister (or issuing) court. State court jurisdictions throughout the country typically honor the requests and commissions of a sister state, and deposition subpoenas are routinely issued and served in this manner. However, in exceptional circumstances, the public policies of different states may come into conflict, creating interesting results. One example follows:

> The case was pending in Texas state court. The Texas state court issued Letters Rogatory for the depositions of two separate banks, one located in New York, and the other in Colorado. There were two different requests for the issuance of two separate subpoenas. Both subpoenas were issued as discovery to aid a related arbitration proceeding in Texas. There was active litigation in the Texas trial court which had been filed to assist the parties in compelling discovery for their arbitration.
>
> The State of Colorado ultimately granted and enforced the subpoena, but it required a trip to the Colorado Supreme Court before the lower court was directed to issue the subpoena. The New York court, however, rejected the requested subpoena on "public policy" grounds because the State of New York frowned upon the use of depositions as a discovery device in arbitrations. The court in New York reasoned that it could not honor the Texas court's requested subpoena because to do so would prejudice the interests of one of its citizens and violate New York public policy. Thus, one state honored the request of the Texas court, the other state rejected the request, and the desired discovery was not allowed.

The bottom line is that the practitioner should be aware out-of-state discovery is routinely permitted. However, the procedural and evidentiary rules of how this discovery is accomplished may differ. It is rare such discovery will be prevented completely but, if that occurs, the issue is less procedural than it is constitutional.

In all likelihood, local counsel should be retained to help process the Letters Rogatory (or commission) in the sister court. Indeed, most jurisdictions require the engagement of local counsel to file and prosecute the issuance of any subpoena or subpoena *duces tecum*. In the event that discovery disputes arise concerning the scope or substance of the subpoena, local counsel will be helpful, if not required, in addressing these issues.

Letters Rogatory are a potentially time-consuming procedure. Therefore, advance planning is recommended. The lawyer seeking an out-of-state deposition should not wait until the end of the discovery period before initiating the process. It may take weeks or even months to satisfy all procedural requirements and secure the desired deposition testimony. Prudent planning suggests that delays should be anticipated and incorporated into the schedule.

Given recent amendments to the Federal Rules of Civil Procedure, a different result will occur in federal litigation. Specifically, in 2013, Federal Rule of Civil Procedure 45 was amended to clarify how subpoenas should be handled in federal cases. Rule 45 now provides a presiding federal court with the power to issue nationwide deposition subpoenas and compel testimony so long as the deposition is taken within 100 miles of where the witness resides, is employed, or regularly transacts business in person.[1] Thereafter, a party may offer that witness's deposition testimony at trial.[2]

Out-of-State Depositions Are Trial Depositions

Because Letters Rogatory are used when third-party witnesses are located in other states or when they refuse to appear or cannot be compelled to appear in the state where the case is pending, it goes without saying that every such deposition is, by definition, a trial deposition. Therefore, the examining lawyer should assume that the deposition will be the *only* opportunity to obtain the witness's testimony. As such, all appropriate preparations should be undertaken, and the examining lawyer should become familiar with the types of objections that may (or should) be asserted in the sister venue.

Because depositions taken pursuant to Letters Rogatory may be usable at a trial (whether in whole or in part), all substantive objections should be made at the deposition if applicable rules allow. Otherwise, a failure to timely object may constitute a waiver of the objection. Furthermore, the examining lawyer may wish to rephrase critical questions in the event objections are asserted. That way, the examining lawyer knows that a "clean" question with a "clean" answer is on the record. At the end of the day, the examining lawyer needs reasonable assurance that each important question (and each corresponding answer) is not subject to a later adverse ruling on a technical objection. A detailed discussion of making and responding to objections is separately discussed in Chapter 18.

Examinations in out-of-state depositions should be crisp, focused, and jury friendly. The examining lawyer should be prepared to use demonstrative exhibits to maximize the impact of the witness's testimony. Key exhibits should be identified well in advance so the examination is efficient, dramatic, and forceful. The lawyer should clearly identify the strategic objectives before the

---

[1] Fed. R. Civ. P. 45(a)(2), 45(c)(1)(A); *see also*, Committee Notes on Rules—2013 Amendment ("The [2013] amendments recognize the court where the action is pending as the issuing court, permit nationwide service of subpoena and collect in a new subdivision (c) the previously scattered provisions regarding place of compliance."). It is important to note that a nonparty can be commanded to attend trial (not a hearing) within the state where the nonparty resides, is employed, or regularly transacts business in person as long as the nonparty would not incur substantial expense. Alternatively, if the issuing party pays the "expense," the court can condition enforcement of the subpoena on such payment. Fed. R. Civ. P. 45(c)(1)(B)(ii), 2013 Notes to Fed. R. Civ. P. 45 at ¶ 11.

[2] Fed. R. Civ. P. 32(a)(4) ("A party may use for any purpose the deposition of a witness, if the court finds the witness is more than 100 miles from the place of hearing or trial…").

deposition begins. Also, the deposition should be videotaped. Because it is unlikely the witness will appear voluntarily at trial, the video recording will be the only opportunity for the jury to see the witness's demeanor. The videotape helps the jury assess the witness's credibility and trustworthiness. This is particularly important if the deponent is a favorable witness or if significant impeachment evidence is used that undercuts the witness's testimony.

Expedited Discovery

There are many instances where expedited or accelerated discovery will be required. All trial lawyers encounter this need, and most jurisdictions contemplate this potential by providing procedures for obtaining accelerated discovery when the facts justify. The procedures will differ depending on the jurisdiction involved, but most jurisdictions will require a court order.

Many states follow the Federal Rules or a variation of those rules. As such, Rule 30, when read in context with Rule 26, provides a meaningful overview of how such discovery is accomplished and when it can be accomplished. Rule 30 provides that depositions may be expedited with leave for various circumstances, including when the witness is "expected to leave the United States and be unavailable for examination in this country after that time."[3]

Rule 26 separately regulates the timing of all discovery, including depositions, and provides that a party may not seek discovery from any source before the parties "have conferred as required by Rule 26(f)… or when authorized by these rules, by stipulation, or by court order."[4] Thus, federal courts contemplate a modification of the sequence or timing of discovery by court order. Thus, absent an agreement with opposing counsel, a party seeking expedited discovery must do so pursuant to a motion that shows good cause or some variation of "good cause."

There are a variety of circumstances that justify expedited discovery. Some of these include:

- If the witness is expected to physically depart and leave the geographic subpoena power of the court.

- If the witness is dying or the witness's physical or mental condition is rapidly deteriorating and a deposition is needed to preserve the witness's testimony.

- As part of extraordinary proceedings, such as discovery incidental to an injunction hearing.

---

[3] *See* Fed. R. Civ. P. 30(a)(2)(A)(iii).
[4] *See* Fed. R. Civ. P. 26(d)(1).

Pursuant to the 2013 amendments to Rule 45, federal courts now enjoy nationwide subpoena power. Therefore, when addressing the witness's physical presence, expedited discovery will not be justified unless it can be shown that the witness is actually leaving the country and is not expected to return.[5] In state courts, however, expedited discovery may be available if the witness intends to leave the state. The state court may grant accelerated discovery to obviate the need of undertaking the expense and burden of alternative discovery vehicles, such as Letters Rogatory or commissions.

Good cause is typically established for accelerated discovery if a witness becomes acutely ill or the witness's mental condition is rapidly deteriorating. The purpose of expedited discovery in this instance is to preserve evidence that may be lost due to the witness's deteriorating condition. In such cases, the examining lawyer should seek a video deposition to memorialize the witness's demeanor for the jury. This is particularly important if the witness is a critical fact witness or a party.

Parties seeking restraining orders frequently include requests for expedited discovery because such discovery is typically needed to prepare for a preliminary injunction hearing. Courts routinely grant these requests, and may even do so *ex parte*. Once served, opposing parties may seek protection from or limitations on this discovery. Alternatively, they also may seek their own expedited discovery to defend against the claims underlying the request for an injunction. If the court grants expedited discovery to one of the parties, it is likely that expedited discovery will be granted to the other side as well.

The use of expedited discovery is a standard tool in the discovery arsenal when preparing for a preliminary injunction hearing. The deposition notices can identify individuals or corporate representatives with specific topic categories. The deposition notices also can be accompanied by document requests to parties or subpoenas *duces tecum* to third parties seeking expedited production of documents.

The rules of each jurisdiction should be consulted regarding the procedural requirements for obtaining leave of court. The evidentiary burden on the party seeking expedited discovery may vary depending upon the relevant jurisdiction. Some jurisdictions may require verifications or sworn proof to justify the discovery. In all likelihood, some showing of good cause (or a variation thereof) is typically required.

Depositions to Perpetuate Testimony

Most jurisdictions provide mechanisms for conducting pre-suit depositions. Indeed, some jurisdictions encourage this type of proceeding as a predicate to the initiation of a lawsuit to investigate potential claims. Pre-suit depositions are also

---

[5] *See* Fed. R. Civ. P. 30(a)(2)(iii).

encouraged if it is expected that a material witness is physically ill, may become mentally indisposed, or is moving outside the subpoena power of the court.

The rules in each jurisdiction should be consulted for the specific requirements for pre-suit depositions, and the burden of what must be shown for an appropriate order allowing such depositions. In federal court, this practice is set forth in Rule 27.

Here are some examples of situations where a pre-suit deposition should be considered:

- To preserve the testimony of the witness because of severe illness, expected death, or progressive loss of cognitive function.

- To preserve the testimony of a third party due to witness unavailability due to extended departure from the jurisdiction.

- To investigate potential claims in a potential lawsuit.

A critical feature in the procedures for pre-suit depositions involves fair notice to all third parties (and potential defendants or adverse parties) who may be impacted by the testimony. Clearly, all potential defendants should be provided an opportunity to either object to the proceedings or participate in the proceedings and conduct an examination. Accordingly, most jurisdictions provide detailed requirements for providing notice. Many jurisdictions also provide that pre-suit depositions cannot be used against any party who did not have an opportunity to participate or did not receive notice. This makes good sense and ensures fairness.

Once notice is given, an interested party will likely have an opportunity to object to the proceedings as either unnecessary or inappropriate. Accordingly, most jurisdictions provide a specific timetable that allows such parties an opportunity to object or to seek protection from the pre-suit deposition notice.

Telephonic Depositions and Video Conferencing

Modern technology is such that remote depositions are easily handled by telephonic or other video or online conference applications. Even though some modes of video conferencing may not be available for particular depositions, the ability to participate in remote conferences is increasingly prevalent, and it is an excellent alternative to telephonic depositions. Attorneys can remotely connect to a deposition, see the witness via online access or, if available, other video conferencing equipment. The depositions can be videotaped as well for the jury.

There are unique challenges and drawbacks when participating in depositions from remote locations. First, the examining lawyer will lose the ability to personally interact with the witness. This may diminish the ability of the examining lawyer to control the tempo and pace of the deposition. An aggressive examination loses intensity if the examining lawyer is several hundred miles from the deposition room. The force of the lawyer's personality is obviously reduced.

Handling exhibits is also a challenge. The examining lawyer should try to identify all exhibits that he or she expects to use and provide these exhibits to the court reporter who will be present at the deposition. Sufficient copies of the deposition exhibits should be provided to all counsel. If other attorneys are participating via remote locations, then the logistics for providing exhibits to all lawyers must be addressed prior to the deposition. Thus, there are significant preparation and planning issues that must be resolved before the deposition begins.

Obviously, providing exhibits to opposing counsel before a deposition reduces the element of surprise. An advance preview of exhibits allows opposing counsel to better prepare for the examination and also prepare the witness if the witness is a party. This is a significant drawback because the witness can rehearse responses to different questions based upon such documents. The convenience of a remote deposition is frequently offset by the diminished effectiveness of the examination.

Another important consideration is whether the examining lawyer foresees the need for impeachment and the use of impeachment exhibits. In such cases, the significant downside is that impeachment evidence is telegraphed to other parties, their counsel, and the witness. Again, this may inspire pre-deposition "coaching" and the element of surprise is lost.

As a general proposition, telephonic depositions should not be conducted with important witnesses. Too much is lost by removing the personalities of the lawyers from the deposition room, and too much is lost by allowing previews of the exhibits. Instead, telephonic depositions should only be used for less important witnesses, like document custodians or other witnesses whose testimony is not expected to have a significant impact on the outcome of the case. It is also recommended that an attorney never present his or her own client for a telephonic deposition and then participate in this deposition by telephone. It sends the wrong message to the client and to other counsel in the case. Lawyers need to be physically present with their clients when presenting their clients for deposition. Most clients expect or even demand this.

The examining lawyer should consult the rules for each jurisdiction to confirm that telephonic depositions are authorized and what procedures, if any, must be satisfied before such depositions proceed. It is also important to note that most jurisdictions provide that the substantive rules that govern such depositions will be determined by the rules of the location of the deponent.[6]

---

[6] *See, e.g.,* Fed. R. Civ. P. 30(b)(4).

Using Interpreters

The need for language interpreters is frequently encountered when deposing foreign nationals; however, it is possible in any case given that roughly one in five Americans speaks a language other than English at home.[7] The trial lawyer must be prepared to integrate interpreters into the deposition process.

Typically, parties should try to reach an agreement concerning the need for and identity of an interpreter, and there are many companies that provide certified interpreters for most languages in most jurisdictions. However, if agreement cannot be reached, then the party seeking an interpreter should seek court intervention before the deposition begins.[8]

Given the serious nature of every deposition, it is advisable to involve an interpreter if there is any question concerning a witness's ability to both understand questions *and* articulate appropriate answers in English. Some witnesses may have greater capacity to understand English than to speak it. Thus, the best practice is to provide an interpreter if there is any question concerning the witness's fluency in either understanding or speaking English. A garbled answer can be just as problematic even if the witness understood the gist of the question.

Typical interpreters should have the following knowledge, skills, and abilities:

- "Highly proficient in both English and the target language.

- Impartiality.

- Able to accurately and idiomatically turn the message from the source language into the receptor language without any additions, omissions, or other misleading factors that alter the intended meaning of the message from the speaker.

- Adept at simultaneous interpretation, which is the most frequent form of interpretation used in the courtroom, and in consecutive interpretation and sight translation.

---

[7] Camille Ryan, *"Language Use in the United States: 2011,"* U.S. Census Bureau, ACS-22 at p.2 (Aug. 2013), available at http://www.census.gov/prod/2013pubs/acs-22.pdf ("Of 291.5 million people aged 5 and over, 60.6 million people (21 percent of this population) spoke a language other than English at home.").

[8] While not expressly addressed in the U.S. Constitution, the right to an interpreter in criminal proceedings is implied in the Fifth, Sixth and Fourteenth Amendments. The law is murkier with respect to whether such right extends to civil proceedings. *See, e.g., Federal Civil Rights Act of 1964, Title VI;* see also Laura K. Abel, *Language Access in the Federal Courts,* 61 Drake L. Rev. 593 (2013). Additionally, a state specific inquiry should be undertaken to determine what, if any, case law or statutory scheme might require the provision of an interpreter in civil litigation. *See, e.g., Tex.Gov. Code* § 57.001 et seq. For a more thorough treatment of this issue reference is made to Laura Abel, *Language Access in State Courts,* Brennan Ctr. for Justice (2009), available at http:// www.brennancenter.org/content/resource/language_access_in_state_courts/.

- Able to communicate orally including appropriate delivery and poise.

- Demonstrates high professional standards for courtroom demeanor and professional conduct."[9]

Interpreters may become "certified" to participate in federal judicial proceedings. The Court Interpreters Act found in 28 U.S.C. § 1827 sets forth procedures for the use of certified interpreters in judicial proceedings in United States District Courts when initiated by the United States.[10] Because the Act applies only to those "proceedings instituted by the United States," it will not be applicable to most cases.[11] However, some courts have cited the Act even in cases to which it is seemingly inapplicable.[12]

According to the Act, "[t]he Director of the Administrative Office of the United States Courts shall establish a program to facilitate the use of certified and otherwise qualified interpreters in judicial proceedings instituted by the United States."[13] The Administrative Office classifies three categories of interpreters: (1) certified interpreters, (2) professionally qualified interpreters, and (3) language skilled interpreters.

"Certified" interpreters are those interpreters who have passed the Administrative Office certification examination. Certification programs have developed for three languages to date; however, only the Spanish certification program is still offered.[14]

For other languages, interpreters are designated as either professionally qualified or language skilled.[15] The prospective interpreter contacts the local federal court to determine whether the court needs an individual to act as an interpreter for a specific language. The court will then determine on a case-by-case basis whether the prospective interpreter is either professionally qualified or

---

[9] Administrative Office of the U.S. Courts, *Interpreter Skills*, http://www.uscourts.gov/services-forms/federal-court-interpreters/interpreter-skills (last visited Jun. 23, 2016).

[10] Administrative Office of the U.S. Courts, *Federal Court Interpreters*, http://www.uscourts.gov/services-forms/federal-court-interpreters (last visited Jun. 23, 2016). 28 U.S.C. § 1827.

[11] 28 U.S.C. § 1827(b)(1); *see also Bethlehem Area Sch. Dist. v. Zhou*, CIV.A. 09-3493, 2011 WL 1584083, at *1 (E.D. Pa. Apr. 27, 2011) ("Ms. Zhou, whose primary language is Mandarin Chinese, wishes to have an interpreter on an as-needed basis, at her own expense, at her deposition. The District relies, in its motion and memorandum, on the federal Court Interpreters Act, 28 U.S.C. § 1827, to support its assertion that Ms. Zhou is not entitled to proceed with an interpreter. However, counsel for the District conceded at the hearing on this matter that the Act is not applicable, as it pertains only to "proceedings instituted *by the United States*." 28 U.S.C. § 1827(b)(1) (emphasis added).

[12] *Malpico v. Newman Mach. Co., Inc.*, 107 F. Supp. 2d 712, 713-14 (W.D. Va. 2000) ("However, under the United States Code, interpreters utilized by the court system generally just be certified. 28 U.S.C. § 1827. 'Only in a case in which no certified interpreter is reasonably available… may the services of otherwise qualified interpreters be used.' § 1827(b)(2). The court is able to get an official interpreter for this case, thus there is no need for another interpreter.").

[13] 28 U.S.C. § 1827(a).

[14] Administrative Office of the U.S. Courts, *Interpreter Categories*, http://www.uscourts.gov/services-forms/federal-court-interpreters/interpreter-categories (last visited Jun. 23, 2016).

[15] *Id.*

language skilled.[16] Professionally qualified interpreters must meet the criteria in one of the following:

1. Pass "the U.S. Department of State conference or seminar interpreter test that includes English and the target language."[17]
2. Pass "the interpreter test of the United Nations in a language pair that includes English and the target language."[18]
3. "Is a current member in good standing of:
   - the Association Internationale des Interprètes de Conférence (AIIC); or
   - the American Association of Language Specialists (TAALS)."[19]

The websites for AIIC,[20] TAALS,[21] and Registry of Interpreters for the Deaf (RID)[22] all contain search tools to assist the practitioner in locating a suitable interpreter. Some jurisdictions also provide a list of licensed court interpreters.[23]

Language-skilled/ad-hoc interpreters are interpreters who do "not qualify as a professionally qualified interpreter, but who can demonstrate to the satisfaction of the court the ability to interpret court proceedings from English to a designated language and from that language into English."[24] Several states, such as Florida,[25] have developed programs to assist judges and trial court administrators in assessing the qualifications of court interpreters. A number of states, such as Texas, use written and oral examinations developed by the Language Access Services Section which is part of the National Center for State Courts.[26]

As noted, the Court Interpreters Act only applies to certain cases, and each state jurisdiction has its own prevailing rules and procedures concerning the availability, certification, and use of interpreters in civil proceedings in general and depositions specifically. Nevertheless, there are some general rules that all

---

[16] *Id.*

[17] *Id.*

[18] *Id.*

[19] *Id.*

[20] International Association of Conference Interpreters, *AIIC Conference Interpreters Worldwide*, http://aiic. net/directories/interpreters (last visited Jun. 23, 2016).

[21] The American Association of Language Specialists, *Find an Interpreter or Translator*, http://www.taals.net/ (last visited Jun. 23, 2016).

[22] Registry of Interpreters for the Deaf, Inc., *Find an RID Member*, https://myaccount.rid.org/Public/Search/ Member.aspx (last visited Jun. 23, 2016).

[23] *See, e.g.*, Texas Judicial Branch, *Licensed Court Interpreters*, http://www.txcourts.gov/jbcc/licensed-court-interpreters.aspx (last visited Jun. 23, 2016) (providing a list of licensed court interpreters in PDF or EXCEL form that is updated monthly).

[24] Administrative Office of the U.S. Courts, *Interpreter Categories*, http://www.uscourts.gov/services-forms/ federal-court-interpreters/interpreter-categories (last visited Jun. 23, 2016).

[25] Florida Courts, *Court Interpreters*, http://www.flcourts.org/resources-and-services/court-services/court-interpreters.stml (last visited Jun. 23, 2016).

[26] Texas Judicial Branch, *Exam Information*, http://www.txcourts.gov/jbcc/licensed-court-interpreters/ exams.aspx (last visited Jun. 23, 2016).

trial lawyers should consider. In *Ivanov v. Phenix Mut. Fire Ins. Co.*, the Supreme Court of Maine set forth many practical considerations:

> As noted above, Tchestnov's lack of fluency in English is a disputed issue in this case. We therefore take this opportunity to discuss the use of interpreters in pretrial proceedings. When Tchestnov was deposed on April 5, 2005, an interpreter was used. The interpreter, although identified, was not sworn before he began his work, and was not questioned about his qualifications or any possible conflicts. Throughout the deposition, the interpreter alternated between referring to Tchestnov in the third person, and simply speaking as though he were Tchestnov, which created some ambiguities. In addition, on at least one occasion, the interpreter admitted that he had not translated what Tchestnov had actually said stating that he was "trying to explain" something Tchestnov had said.
>
> Just as judicial officers need to monitor interpreters during trials, attorneys must monitor interpreters during depositions. Each interpreter should be sworn, and the interpreter's qualifications should be placed on the record. If there are long periods when the interpreter is not interpreting, if the length of testimony is not proportionate to the interpretation, or if the interpreter appears to be coaching or encouraging the party to answer in a certain way, the attorneys involved in the deposition should address and correct the problem. The attorneys should remind the interpreter that she/he is required to interpret everything that is being said, without omitting, subtracting, editing or summarizing, and that the interpreter must always interpret in the first person when the witness or defendant is speaking. The attorneys should interject if the interpreter says, "he said," or "she said," as the third person is to be used only when the interpreter is speaking for him or herself. Careful compliance with these guidelines will result in an accurate record.[27]

In addition to these general considerations, a party seeking the deposition where an interpreter is provided by the other party may wish to provide a "check" interpreter who is used to verify that the "primary" interpreter is providing correct, verbatim translations of each question and each answer. This is particularly important in cases involving technical issues or terms. A "check" interpreter provides a backup interpretation if there is any disagreement concerning the translation at issue. It is also a good practice to provide both the primary interpreter and the "check" interpreter with a list of such technical terms before the deposition begins. This will expedite the interpretation process and ensure greater accuracy.

---

[27] *Ivanov v. Phenix Mut. Fire Ins. Co.*, 2008 ME 20, ¶¶ 12–13, 939 A.2d 683, 686–87 (footnotes omitted).

In addition to depositions involving technical terms, a check interpreter is frequently used in situations where the meaning of a particular word substantively changes depending upon the context of how the word is used. There are several languages where definitions change depending upon how a word is used within the structure of a particular sentence. In such instances, a check interpreter is advisable to avoid any controversy regarding the context of how the word may be used. Nevertheless, some parties may challenge the attendance of multiple interpreters at a deposition, and ultimately some courts may preclude their use.[28] Thus, at a minimum, the trial lawyer should strive to ensure the deposition is videotaped so a "check" interpreter can be employed after the fact to confirm the accuracy of the testimony.

There is a substantive difference between a translator and an interpreter, and different skill sets are involved. A translator focuses on the translation of written documents, and an interpreter focuses on the spoken word. While a translator has the luxury of time to translate a document, an interpreter is forced to interpret and translate in a more compressed timeframe and must better understand the context of the spoken word. Accordingly, special care should be taken to ensure that a qualified interpreter is selected for the deposition. Exhibits used during the deposition may require translation as well; accordingly, an interpreter with both skill sets is preferred.

The use of an interpreter substantially slows the tempo of a deposition. Each question must be translated into the witness's native language. The witness then answers in his or her native tongue. The interpreter then translates the witness's answer into English. In essence, the added time required to process each question and each answer is effectively doubled. This reduced time efficiency should be considered if there are any time limitations imposed by the relevant jurisdiction (e.g., 7 hours under the Federal Rules).

As a general rule, the use of an interpreter reduces the efficiency of a deposition by at least 50%. This inefficiency is further exacerbated if there are disagreements between the interpreter and a "check" interpreter. If time limitations become a problem, then the examining lawyer should seek an agreement to enlarge the time limits or obtain an appropriate court order to do so. It is good practice to try to anticipate these types of problems in advance of the deposition.

If there are disagreements between a primary interpreter and a "check" interpreter, then these differences should be noted on the record. The deposition should not be stopped unless it is evident that there is a consistent pattern of disagreement between the two interpreters. If this occurs, there may be a question concerning the competence or bias of one or both of the interpreters. This is particularly important if there is a disagreement involving the interpretation of key questions and answers. If this becomes an issue, it may be strategically wise to abate the deposition, seek protection, and/or locate a third interpreter to resolve

---

[28] *See Malpico v. Newman Mach. Co., Inc.*, 107 F. Supp. 2d 712, 713-14 (W.D. Va. 2000).

the controversy. If significant controversies arise, then the lawyers should ask the interpreters to preserve their notes since these notes may become evidence at a later hearing before the court.

Some witnesses hide behind interpreters. They use the reduced tempo as a way of stalling for time so they can better frame their answers. Although a witness may actually have practical command of the English language, the witness may exploit the delays naturally created by the interpretation process to better formulate responses. Accordingly, the examining lawyer should question the witness thoroughly to confirm the witness's exposure to and fluency in English. If significant doubts exist concerning the need for an interpreter, the examining lawyer may wish to abate the deposition and seek a court order requiring the witness to appear without an interpreter. This is because the interpreter gives the witness significant advantages in the examination process. At a minimum, the examining lawyer can create doubts in the minds of the jury whether an interpreter was truly needed.

20

Depositions in Arbitration

Arbitrations as a means of dispute resolution are increasingly prevalent and, in many jurisdictions, preferred. Many state jurisdictions have declared that public policy interests favor arbitration. This same preference is shared in the federal system. Many companies include arbitration clauses in their contracts and/or employment agreements as a matter of course. Arbitration is here to stay, and the practitioner should become familiar with the procedural rules and discovery devices available in arbitration proceedings.

This chapter explores the availability of depositions in arbitration proceedings. Not all arbitration proceedings allow depositions as a discovery tool and, in fact, many limit discovery generally. Some jurisdictions allow depositions only to preserve evidence where the witness may not be available at the time of the final arbitration hearing. Others allow depositions only for parties but not for nonparties.

This chapter explores the availability of depositions in arbitrations conducted under various statutes and under various regimes of established arbitral tribunals. Trial lawyers should know what discovery options are available. Equally important, transactional lawyers should fully evaluate the wisdom of including arbitration clauses in their drafted contracts due to the limitations on discovery that may result.

The Nature of Arbitration

Because arbitration is a matter of contract, "the power and authority of arbitrators in an arbitration proceeding is dependent on the provisions under which the arbitrators were appointed."[1] Thus, "[w]hen contracting parties stipulate that disputes will be submitted to arbitration, they relinquish the right to certain procedural niceties

---

[1] *BNSF R. Co. v. Alstom Transp., Inc.*, 777 F.3d 785, 787–88 (5th Cir. 2015).

which are normally associated with a formal trial."[2] "One of these accoutrements is the right to pre-trial discovery."[3]

While there may not be a "right" to pre-hearing discovery, a party may still be able to take depositions in relation to an arbitration proceeding. This will depend on the terms of the arbitration agreement and the governing authority under which the arbitration is proceeding. Thus, the terms of the arbitration agreement are vital. In this regard, case law demonstrates "that procedural requirements—such as adopting the rules of an arbitration association, choice of law provisions, confidentiality requirements, and rules governing discovery— can be part of an arbitration clause."[4] Ultimately, determining whether a party in an arbitration proceeding is permitted to take depositions will likely depend on several factors, including (1) the agreement, (2) the applicable rules, (3) the arbitrator, and (4) the other party.[5]

Depositions under the Federal Arbitration Act

The Federal Arbitration Act (FAA) was enacted in 1925, more than a decade prior to the adoption of the Federal Rules of Civil Procedure. At that time, little discovery was permitted in federal courts, much less in arbitration proceedings. It has been stated that "it was a time when 'to require the disclosure to an adversary of the evidence that is to be produced would be repugnant to all sportsmanlike instincts.'"[6] Rather, "the common law's 'sporting theory of justice' permitted the litigant to reserve evidential resources (documents and witnesses) until the final moment, marshaling them at the trial before his surprised and dismayed antagonist."[7]

Given this historical backdrop, it is easy to understand why Congress, when drafting the FAA, likely contemplated the testimony of a witness at an arbitration proceeding as opposed to pre-hearing depositions. The lack of emphasis on discovery (or related procedures) is highlighted by the plain language of the FAA

---

[2] *Burton v. Bush*, 614 F.2d 389, 390 (4th Cir. 1980).

[3] *Id.*

[4] *ITT Educ. Services, Inc. v. Arce*, 533 F.3d 342, 346 (5th Cir. 2008).

[5] *See also,* Richard J. Tyler, *Discovery in Arbitration*, Constr. Law. 5 (2015) (noting that "[a]s was the case before the adoption of the Federal Rules of Civil Procedure, the discovery that may be obtained by a party in arbitration depends largely on the applicable law, the applicable arbitration rules, and the arbitrator(s) before whom the case is pending.").

[6] *Matria Healthcare, LLC v. Duthie*, 584 F. Supp. 2d 1078, 1080 (N.D. Ill. 2008) (*quoting* 6 Wigmore, Discovery § 1845 at 490 (3rd Ed. 1940)).

[7] *Id.*

and, specifically, Section 7, which has been used as a basis to allow discovery in contemporary arbitration proceedings.

Section 7, which is the only FAA provision addressing discovery, provides the following:

> The arbitrators selected either as prescribed in this title or otherwise, or a majority of them, may summon in writing any person to attend before them or any of them as a witness and in a proper case to bring with him or them any book, record, document, or paper which may be deemed material as evidence in the case... Said summons shall issue in the name of the arbitrator or arbitrators, or a majority of them, and shall be signed by the arbitrators, or a majority of them, and shall be directed to the said person and shall be served in the same manner as subpoenas to appear and testify before the court; if any person or persons so summoned to testify shall refuse or neglect to obey said summons, upon petition the United States district court for the district in which such arbitrators, or a majority of them, are sitting may compel the attendance of such person or persons before said arbitrator or arbitrators, or punish said person or persons for contempt in the same manner provided by law for securing the attendance of witnesses or their punishment for neglect or refusal to attend in the courts of the United States.[8]

Section 7 has been the source of disagreement between courts, with much of the dispute focusing on an arbitrator's ability (or lack thereof) to compel *nonparty* discovery. In fact, if the arbitration is governed solely by the FAA, the ability to take a deposition likely will be determined by whether the deponent is a party or a nonparty.

Generally, an arbitrator's power over the parties stems from the arbitration agreement.[9] "Where agreements so provide, that authority includes the power to order discovery from the parties in arbitration since 'the FAA lets parties tailor some, even many features of arbitration by contract, including... procedure.'"[10] On the other hand, the terms of an arbitration agreement likely will be immaterial in determining whether a party can take the deposition of a *nonparty*. "An arbitrator's authority over parties that are not contractually bound by the arbitration agreement is strictly limited to that granted by the Federal Arbitration Act."[11]

---

[8] 9 U.S.C.A. § 7 (West).

[9] *Life Receivables Trust v. Syndicate 102 at Lloyd's of London*, 549 F.3d 210, 217 (2d Cir. 2008).

[10] *Life Receivables Trust v. Syndicate 102 at Lloyd's of London*, 549 F.3d 210, 217 (2d Cir. 2008) (*quoting Hall Street Assocs., L.L.C. v. Mattel, Inc.*, 552 U.S. 576, 128 S.Ct. 1396, 1404, 170 L.Ed.2d 254 (2008)).

[11] *Hay Group, Inc. v. E.B.S. Acquisition Corp.*, 360 F.3d 404, 406 (3rd. Cir. 2004).

In some jurisdictions, there seems to be no dispute concerning pre-hearing depositions of nonparties.[12] Such depositions simply are not permitted. However, other jurisdictions recognize that pre-hearing nonparty depositions may be proper when the parties seeking such discovery are able to demonstrate a "special need or hardship," such as where the information sought is otherwise unavailable.[13]

Additionally, in most cases, where nonparty depositions are precluded under the FAA, it may be possible to obtain discovery from a nonparty before the final hearing; however, such testimony would necessarily be in front of an arbitrator at a "preliminary hearing"[14] as opposed to an actual deposition.

There has been considerable consternation concerning prehearing production of documents from nonparties under Section 7 of the FAA, and several circuit courts have issued conflicting opinions concerning the availability of such discovery.[15] Several circuits have held that the power to compel nonparty document productions is "implicit" in the authority of an arbitrator, while others have concluded that no such power exists.

It should be noted that courts have found that "[t]he absence of statutory provision for discovery techniques in arbitration proceedings obviously does not negate the affirmative duty of arbitrators to insure that relevant documentary

---

[12] See *Kennedy v. American Express Travel Related Services Co., Inc.*, 646 F. Supp. 2d 1342, 1344 (S.D. Fla. 2009) ("Thus, the operative clause in Section 7 is exclusive as to whom the power to summon non-parties is vested, exhaustive in prescribing the limits of that power, and explicit in the manner in which nonparties may be summoned. Therefore, based on the plain meaning of the statute, the Court finds that an arbitrator is not statutorily authorized under the FAA to issue summonses for pre-hearing depositions and document discovery from non-parties.").

[13] See *COMSAT Corp. v. Nat'l Sci. Found.*, 190 F.3d 269, 278 (4th Cir. 1999) (holding "that a federal court may not compel a third party to comply with an arbitrator's subpoena for prehearing discovery, absent a showing of special need or hardship."); see also *ImClone Sys. Inc. v. Waksal*, 22 A.D.3d 387, 388, 802 N.Y.S.2d 653, 654 (2005) ("While it is an open question in the Second Circuit whether pre-hearing nonparty depositions are authorized under the FAA, and there is substantial federal authority that they are not, in the absence of a decision of the United States Supreme Court or unanimity among the lower federal courts, we are not precluded from exercising our own judgment in this matter. We subscribe to the view that depositions of nonparties may be directed in FAA arbitration where there is a showing of "special need or hardship," such as where the information sought is otherwise unavailable. This view properly takes into consideration the realities and complexities of modern arbitration.

[14] *Stolt-Nielsen SA v. Celanese AG*, 430 F.3d 567, 578 (2d Cir. 2005) (The Court agreed that permitting an arbitrator to hold a preliminary hearing that is not a hearing on the merits "does not transform [the preliminary hearing] into a [prohibited] discovery device" and concluded that [n]othing in the language of the FAA limits the point in time in the arbitration process when [the subpoena] power can be invoked or says that the arbitrators may only invoke this power under Section 7 at the time of the final hearing.").

[15] See *All. Healthcare Services, Inc. v. Argonaut Private Equity, LLC*, 804 F. Supp. 2d 808, 810–11 (N.D. Ill. 2011) ("The Sixth and Eighth Circuits have held that the power to compel pre-hearing discovery from a third party is implicit in the power of an arbitrator to compel production of documents from a third party for a hearing. See *In re Sec. Life Ins. Co. of Am.*, 228 F.3d 865, 870–71 (8th Cir. 2000); *Am. Fed'n. of Television and Radio Artists, AFL–CIO v. WJBK–TV (New World Communications of Detroit, Inc.)*, 164 F.3d 1004, 1009 (6th Cir. 1999). The Second and Third Circuits have ruled to the contrary. *Life Receivables Trust v. Syndicate 102 at Lloyd's of London*, 549 F.3d 210, 212 (2d Cir. 2008); *Hay Group., Inc. v. E.B.S. Acquisition Corp.*, 360 F.3d 404, 408–09 (3d Cir. 2004). The Fourth Circuit has read section 7 of the FAA in more or less the same way as the Third, though it has suggested that an arbitration panel may subpoena a non-party for prehearing discovery upon a showing of a "special need." See *COMSAT Corp. v. Nat'l. Sci. Found.*, 190 F.3d 269, 275–76 (4th Cir. 1999). There is no Seventh Circuit authority directly on point.").

evidence in the hands of one party is fully and timely made available to the other side before the hearing is closed."[16] The failure to discharge that duty may constitute a violation of FAA Section 10(a)(3), where a party can show prejudice as a result. Nevertheless, there appear to be no guarantees for obtaining non-party depositions under the FAA.

Depositions under State Law

The FAA does not preempt all state law related to arbitration agreements. In fact, an arbitration agreement may be covered by both state and federal law. Therefore, in Texas, as an example, "[t]he TAA and the FAA may both be applicable to an agreement, absent the parties' choice of one or the other."[17] In such circumstances, state law is preempted "to the extent that it actually conflicts with federal law—that is, to the extent that it 'stands as an obstacle to the accomplishment and execution of the full purposes and objectives of Congress.'"[18]

The U.S. Supreme Court has explained that "[t]here is no federal policy favoring arbitration under a certain set of procedural rules; the federal policy is simply to ensure the enforceability, according to their terms, of private agreements to arbitrate."[19] Specifically, the Court stated:

> In recognition of Congress' principal purpose of ensuring that private arbitration agreements are enforced according to their terms, we have held that the FAA pre-empts state laws which require a judicial forum for the resolution of claims which the contracting parties agreed to resolve by arbitration. But it does not follow that the FAA prevents the enforcement of agreements to arbitrate under different rules than those set forth in the Act itself. Indeed, such a result would be quite inimical to the FAA's primary purpose of ensuring that private agreements to arbitrate are enforced according to their terms. Arbitration under the Act is a matter of consent, not coercion, and parties are generally free to structure their arbitration agreements as they see fit. Just as they may limit by contract the issues which they will arbitrate, so too may they specify by contract the rules under which that arbitration will be conducted. Where, as here, the parties have agreed to abide by state rules of arbitration, enforcing those rules according to the terms of the agreement is fully consistent with the goals of the FAA, even if the result is that arbitration is

---

[16] *Chevron Transp. Corp. v. Astro Vencedor Compania Naviera S.A.*, 300 F. Supp. 179, 181 (S.D.N.Y. 1969), *order confirmed sub nom. ARBITRATION BETWEEN CHEVRON TRANSPORT CORPORATION, Petitioner, AND ASTRO VENCEDOR COMPANIA NAVIERA, S.A., Respondent.*, 69 CIVIL 572, 1969 WL 173716 (S.D.N.Y. July 24, 1969).

[17] *Nafta Traders, Inc. v. Quinn*, 339 S.W.3d 84, 97 n.64 (Tex. 2011).

[18] *Id.* at 97–98 (quoting *Volt Info. Scis., Inc. v. Bd. of Trs. of Leland Stanford Junior Univ.*, 489 U.S. 468, 477 (1989)).

[19] *Volt Info. Scis., Inc. v. Bd. of Trustees of Leland Stanford Junior Univ.*, 489 U.S. 468, 476, (1989).

stayed where the Act would otherwise permit it to go forward. By permitting the courts to "rigorously enforce" such agreements according to their terms, we give effect to the contractual rights and expectations of the parties, without doing violence to the policies behind by the FAA.[20]

Given the latitude provided by the U.S. Supreme Court, parties may specify by contract those rules pursuant to which arbitration will be conducted, including an agreement to arbitrate under state rules instead of their federal counterpart. In sum, an arbitration agreement that specifies a discrete set of arbitral rules will be enforced. At the drafting stage of the arbitration agreement, one can specify a particular set of arbitral rules—or even include provisions in the arbitration agreement itself—to intentionally limit or expand the amount of discovery.

In contrast to the FAA, and as discussed below, depositions may be explicitly authorized by a state's arbitration act. For example, in Texas, arbitrators have almost "unbridled discretion regarding discovery."[21] Under the Texas General Arbitration Act (the TAA), the arbitrator, not the court, controls discovery during the arbitration. An arbitrator also has the authority, under the TAA, to issue a subpoena for: (1) attendance of a witness; or (2) production of books, records, documents, or other evidence.[22] Depositions are specifically allowed, and the TAA states that "the arbitrators may authorize a deposition: (1) for use as evidence to be taken of a witness who cannot be required by subpoena to appear before the arbitrators or who is unable to attend the hearing; or (2) for discovery or evidentiary purposes to be taken of an adverse witness."[23] Moreover, a "[]deposition under this section shall be taken in the manner provided by law for a deposition in a civil action pending in a district court."[24]

Other states have rules that specifically allow depositions in arbitration proceedings. In Alabama, if either of the parties files an application with the arbitrator, the arbitrator *must* "issue commission to take the deposition of any witness residing out of the county, which must be taken in the same manner as depositions in the circuit court."[25] In Connecticut, any party to a written arbitration agreement may apply to the appropriate court or judge "for an order directing the taking of depositions, in the manner and for the reasons prescribed by law for taking depositions to be used in a civil action, for use as evidence in an

---

[20] *Id.* at 478–79.

[21] *Perry Homes v. Cull*, 258 S.W.3d 580, 599 (Tex. 2008).

[22] Tex. Civ. Prac. & Rem. Code Ann. § 171.051(a) (West).

[23] Tex. Civ. Prac. & Rem. Code 171.050(a)(1)-(2) (West).

[24] Tex. Civ. Prac. & Rem. Code 171.050(b) (West).

[25] Ala. Code § 6-6-7 ("The arbitrators, or either of them, have power to subpoena witnesses at the request of either of the parties and to administer all oaths which may be necessary in the progress of the case and must, on the application of either party, issue commission to take the deposition of any witness residing out of the county, which must be taken in the same manner as depositions in the circuit court.").

arbitration."[26] In California, depositions may be taken in certain arbitration proceedings, but not until leave to do so is first granted by the arbitrator(s).[27] Other states, such as Louisiana, Ohio, and Wisconsin, allow depositions in arbitration, but require the involvement of both the arbitrator and the judicial system.[28]

Depositions under the Uniform Arbitration Act

Most states have adopted the Uniform Arbitration Act (UAA).[29] There are, in fact, two iterations of the Uniform Arbitration Acts: the UAA, which was originally adopted in 1955 and was amended in 1956; and the Revised Uniform Arbitration Act (the RUAA).

Similar to the plain language of the FAA, the UAA contains a single section addressing discovery. This section closely emulates the applicable text of the FAA and provides in pertinent part:

§ 7. Witnesses, Subpoenas, Depositions

(a) The arbitrators may issue (cause to be issued) subpoenas for the attendance of witnesses and for the production of books, records, documents and other evidence, and shall have the power to administer oaths. Subpoenas so issued shall be served, and upon application to the Court by a party or the arbitrators, enforced, in the manner provided by law for the service and enforcement of subpoenas in a civil action.

---

[26] Conn. Gen. Stat. Ann. § 52-412(c) (West) ("Any party to a written agreement for arbitration may make application to the Superior Court, or, when the court is not in session, to a judge thereof, having jurisdiction as provided in subsection (b) of this section, for an order directing the taking of depositions, in the manner and for the reasons prescribed by law for taking depositions to be used in a civil action, for use as evidence in an arbitration.").

[27] Cal. Civ. Proc. Code § 1283.05(a)–(e) (West).

[28] La. Stat. Ann. § 9:4207 ("Upon petition, approved by the arbitrators or by a majority of them, any court of record in and for the parish in which the arbitrators are sitting may direct the taking of depositions to be used as evidence before the arbitrators, in the same manner and for the same reasons provided by law for the taking of depositions in suits or proceedings pending in the courts of record in this state."); Ohio Rev. Code Ann. § 2711.07 (West) ("Upon petition approved by the arbitrators, or by a majority of them, the court of common pleas in the county in which such arbitrators, or a majority of them, are sitting may direct the taking of depositions to be used as evidence before the arbitrators, in the same manner and for the same reasons as provided by law for the taking of depositions in suits or proceedings pending in such court."); Wis. Stat. Ann. § 788.07 (West) ("Upon petition, approved by the arbitrators or by a majority of them, any court of record in and for the county in which such arbitrators, or a majority of them, are sitting may direct the taking of depositions to be used as evidence before the arbitrators, in the same manner and for the same reasons as provided by law for the taking of depositions in suits or proceedings pending in the courts of record in this state.").

[29] *In re Gulf Expl., LLC*, 289 S.W.3d 836, 839 (Tex. 2009).

(b) On application of a party and for use as evidence, the arbitrators may permit a deposition to be taken, in the manner and upon the terms designated by the arbitrators, of a witness who cannot be subpoenaed or is unable to attend the hearing.

(c) All provisions of law compelling a person under subpoena to testify are applicable.

(d) Fees for attendance as a witness shall be the same as for a witness in the [applicable] Court.[30]

There are obvious limitations to the scope of depositions in states that have adopted the UAA. The first limitation concerns the purpose for which a deposition may be taken. Under the UAA, the deposition is to be used "as evidence;" not "as discovery." In fact, at least one state has modified the rule to clarify this point.[31] Another state (Kansas) has completely removed such restrictions.[32]

The second limitation under the UAA is that only those who "cannot be subpoenaed" or are "unable to attend the hearing" may be deposed. Thus, depositions taken pursuant to the UAA appear to be an alternative of last resort for live testimony, and not a discovery device to explore and develop a case.

The RUAA is a modified version of the UAA. It has been enacted in several states, including Alaska, Arizona, Arkansas, Colorado, District of Columbia, Florida, Hawaii, Michigan, Minnesota, Nevada, New Jersey, New Mexico, North Carolina, North Dakota, Oklahoma, Oregon, Utah, Washington, and West Virginia. It has also been recently introduced in Massachusetts and Pennsylvania.[33]

Unlike the UAA, the RUAA expressly provides for pre-hearing discovery. Specifically, Section 17 of the Act provides the following, in relevant part:

SECTION 17. WITNESSES; SUBPOENAS; DEPOSITIONS; DISCOVERY.

(a) An arbitrator may issue a subpoena for the attendance of a witness and for the production of records and other evidence at any hearing and may administer oaths. A subpoena must be served in the manner for service of subpoenas in a civil action and, upon [motion] to the court by a party to the arbitration proceeding or the arbitrator, enforced in the manner for enforcement of subpoenas in a civil action.

---

[30] Uniform Law Commission, The National Conference of Commissioners on Uniform State Laws, Uniform Arbitration Act (1995), 3, *available at* http://www.uniformlaws.org/shared/docs/arbitration/uaa55.pdf

[31] Ind. Code Ann. § 34-57-2-8(b) (West) ("On application of a party, the arbitrators may order the deposition of a witness to be taken for use as evidence, and not for discovery, if the witness can not be subpoenaed or is unable to attend the hearing. The deposition shall be taken in the manner prescribed by law for the taking of depositions in civil actions.").

[32] Kan. Stat. Ann. § 5-407(b) (West) ("On application of a party the arbitrators may permit a deposition to be taken, in the manner and upon the terms designated by the arbitrators").

[33] Uniform Law Commission, The National Conference of Commissioners on Uniform State Laws, *Legislative Fact Sheet—Arbitration Act (2000)*; http://www.uniformlaws.org/legislativeFACTSheet. aspx?title=Arbitration%20Act%20(2000) (last visited July 28, 2016).

(b) In order to make the proceedings fair, expeditious, and cost effective, upon request of a party to or a witness in an arbitration proceeding, an arbitrator may permit a deposition of any witness to be taken for use as evidence at the hearing, including a witness who cannot be subpoenaed for or is unable to attend a hearing. The arbitrator shall determine the conditions under which the deposition is taken.

(c) An arbitrator may permit such discovery as the arbitrator decides is appropriate in the circumstances, taking into account the needs of the parties to the arbitration proceeding and other affected persons and the desirability of making the proceeding fair, expeditious, and cost effective.

(d) If an arbitrator permits discovery under subsection (c), the arbitrator may order a party to the arbitration proceeding to comply with the arbitrator's discovery-related orders, issue subpoenas for the attendance of a witness and for the production of records and other evidence at a discovery proceeding, and take action against a noncomplying party to the extent a court could if the controversy were the subject of a civil action in this State.

(e) An arbitrator may issue a protective order to prevent the disclosure of privileged information, confidential information, trade secrets, and other information protected from disclosure to the extent a court could if the controversy were the subject of a civil action in this State.

(f) All laws compelling a person under subpoena to testify and all fees for attending a judicial proceeding, a deposition, or a discovery proceeding as a witness apply to an arbitration proceeding as if the controversy were the subject of a civil action in this State.

(g) The court may enforce a subpoena or discovery-related order for the attendance of a witness within this State and for the production of records and other evidence issued by an arbitrator in connection with an arbitration proceeding in another State upon conditions determined by the court so as to make the arbitration proceeding fair, expeditious, and cost effective. A subpoena or discovery-related order issued by an arbitrator in another State must be served in the manner provided by law for service of subpoenas in a civil action in this State and, upon [motion] to the court by a party to the arbitration proceeding or the arbitrator, enforced in the manner provided by law for enforcement of subpoenas in a civil action in this State.[34]

---

[34] Uniform Law Commission, The National Conference of Commissioners on Uniform State Laws, Uniform Arbitration Act (2000), 57-59, *available at* http://www.uniformlaws.org/shared/docs/arbitration/arbitration_final_00.pdf.

In addition to the foregoing statutory language, the comments to the RUAA clearly demonstrate that arbitrators in such proceedings have the authority to order not only discovery between the parties, but also nonparties. Specifically, comment 5 to Section 17 provides that:

> In Section 17 most of the references involve "parties to the arbitration proceeding." However, sometimes arbitrations involve outside, third parties who may be required to give testimony or produce documents. Section 17(c) provides that the arbitrator should take the interests of such "affected persons" into account in determining whether and to what extent discovery is appropriate. Section 17(b) has been broadened so that a "witness" who is not a party can request the arbitrator to allow that person's testimony to be presented at the hearing by deposition if that person is unable to attend the hearing.[35]

Thus, the RUAA clearly contemplates and, in fact, expressly permits parties to engage in pre-hearing depositions of both parties and nonparties.

Depositions Pursuant to AAA

In drafting an arbitration agreement, parties are free to agree to arbitrate according to a particular set of rules or before certain organizations. One of the most common choices is the American Arbitration Association (AAA). If the arbitration agreement at issue specifies a certain set of procedural rules, those rules will determine whether a deposition may be taken. Even then, discovery will almost certainly not be as extensive as it would be in litigation. As Judge Posner noted in 1995, "the discovery provisions of the Federal Rules of Civil Procedure are more generous than those of the American Arbitration Association."[36] Twenty years later, that remains true.

The AAA has promulgated multiple sets of rules concerning arbitration procedures. The Commercial Arbitration Rules and Mediation Procedures, effective October 1, 2013, potentially allow depositions in large complex cases at the discretion of the arbitrator.[37] In more standard cases, depositions are neither allowed nor precluded. Indeed, the rules leave open the possibility of allowing such

---

[35] *Id.* at 61.

[36] *Cabinetree of Wisconsin, Inc. v. Kraftmaid Cabinetry, Inc.*, 50 F.3d 388, 391 (7th Cir. 1995).

[37] *American Arbitration Association, Commercial Arbitration Rules and Mediation Procedures* (Oct. 1, 2013) 38, Rule L-3(f), https://www.adr.org/aaa/ShowProperty?nodeId=/UCM/ADRSTG_004103&revision=latestreleased ("In exceptional cases, at the discretion of the arbitrator, upon good cause shown and consistent with the expedited nature of arbitration, the arbitrator may order depositions to obtain the testimony of a person who may possess information determined by the arbitrator to be relevant and material to the outcome of the case. The arbitrator may allocate the cost of taking such a deposition.").

discovery. During the preliminary hearing, one of the suggested subjects that the parties and the arbitrator should always discuss is "whether to establish any additional procedures to obtain information that is relevant and material to the outcome of disputed issues."[38] Further, the parties can agree to allow depositions; however, if the arbitrator has already been appointed, the arbitrator must consent to such discovery as well.[39]

In short, the ultimate decision lies with the arbitrator. In practice, the most likely source of depositions is generally by agreement with opposing counsel and, if necessary, related approval of the arbitrator.

Enforcement Mechanism and Jurisdiction

Logically, an arbitrator can generally resolve a discovery dispute between parties. In proceedings under the FAA, "an arbitrator can enforce his or her discovery order through, among other things, drawing a negative inference from a party's refusal to produce, and, ultimately, through rendering a judgment enforceable in federal court."[40]

However, obtaining compliance from a nonparty is another matter. Except in limited circumstances, arbitrators have no power to compel discovery from third parties.[41] As a result, two key issues arise upon issuance of a nonparty subpoena in an arbitration proceeding: who has the burden to challenge the subpoena and what is the procedure to enforce the subpoena.

If the subpoena is issued pursuant to the FAA, the answer to the first question is simple. "Once subpoenaed by an arbitrator, the recipient is under no obligation to move to quash the subpoena."[42] "By failing to do so, the recipient does not waive the right to challenge the subpoena on the merits if faced with a petition to compel."[43] "The FAA imposes no requirement that a subpoenaed party file a petition to quash or otherwise challenge the subpoena; the Act's only mechanism for obtaining federal court review is the petition to compel."[44]

---

[38] *Id*. at 33, Rule P-2(viii).

[39] *Id*. at 10, Rule-1(a) ("The parties, by written agreement, may vary the procedures set forth in these rules. After appointment of the arbitrator, such modifications may be made only with the consent of the arbitrator."). "The parties, by written agreement, may vary the procedures set forth in these rules. After appointment of the arbitrator, such modifications may be made only with the consent of the arbitrator."

[40] *Life Receivables Trust v. Syndicate 102 at Lloyd's of London*, 549 F.3d 210, 217 (2d Cir. 2008) (internal citations and quotations omitted).

[41] *Id*.

[42] *COMSAT Corp. v. National Science Foundation*, 190 F.3d 269, 276 (4th Cir. 1999).

[43] *Id*.

[44] *Id*.

The enforcement mechanism is, in theory, fairly straightforward. In fact, Section 7 of the FAA requires a party seeking enforcement of a subpoena do so by filing a petition in the district court in which the arbitration is pending (or where the arbitrators are sitting), and "[n]umerous courts have recognized this requirement."[45] The court will, of course, need both subject matter and personal jurisdiction over the noncompliant individual. Whether that subpoena is enforceable may be a complicated question.

Enforcement of a subpoena issued pursuant to a state arbitration statute involves a different analysis, and largely depends on the arbitration act followed by the individual state, and may likely lead to different results. For example, in Colorado, which has enacted the RUAA, the Court determined that its enforcement authority was limited to the degree of authority it would possess in a "civil action" and, as a result, the proper court to enforce an arbitration subpoena on a nonparty was the court where that individual or entity resided.[46]

International Arbitrations

While depositions are beginning to occur more frequently in arbitration proceedings in the United States, such discovery has yet to take hold internationally. Indeed, "depositions generally are considered inappropriate in international arbitration proceedings."[47] According to the International Dispute Resolution Procedures (Including Mediation and Arbitration Rules), amended and effective June 1, 2014, which are promulgated by the International Centre for Dispute Resolution, depositions and other discovery as typically used in U.S. court proceedings are generally not appropriate for discovering information in an arbitration under these international procedures.[48]

Similarly, the Protocol on Disclosure of Documents and Presentation of Witnesses in Commercial Arbitration, published by the International Institute for Conflict Prevention & Resolution (CPR), explains that "[d]epositions should be permitted only where the testimony is expected to be material to the outcome of the case and where one or more of the following exigent circumstances apply: Witness statements are not being used, the parties agree to the taking of the deposition and/ or the witness may not be available to testify, in person or by telecommunication,

---

[45] *Matter of Arbitration between Tang Energy Group, LTD v. Catic U.S.A.*, 3:15-MC-80209-LB, 2015 WL 4692459, at *1-3 (N.D. Cal. Aug. 6, 2015) (collecting cases).

[46] *See Colorado Mills, LLC v. SunOpta Grains & Foods Inc.*, 269 P.3d 731, 733 (Colo. 2012) (the language of Colorado's RUAA statute "confines the district court's enforcement authority in the arbitration context to that degree of authority it would possess 'in a civil action.'").

[47] Claudia T. Salomon, Sandra Friedrich, *Obtaining and Submitting Evidence in International Arbitration in the United States*, 24 AM. REV. INT'L ARB 549, 575 (2013).

[48] International Centre for Dispute Resolution, *International Dispute Resolution Procedures (Including Mediation and Arbitration Rules)*, 27, Article 21(10), (June 1, 2014), https://www.icdr.org/icdr/ShowProperty?nodeId=/ UCM/ADRSTAGE2020868&revision=latestreleased.

before the tribunal."[49] Even if deposition are permitted, the tribunal is cautioned to "impose strict limits on the number and length of any depositions."[50] Finally, "[d]eposition transcripts may, as the tribunal determines, be used at hearing or otherwise be made part of the record before the tribunal."[51]

---

[49] International Institute for Conflict Prevention & Resolution, *CPR Protocol on Disclosure of Documents and Presentation of Witnesses in Commercial Arbitration*, Section 2(c), *available at* http://www.cpradr.org/Portals/0/CPR%20Protocol%20on%20Disclosure%20of%20Documents%20and%20Witnesses.pdf (last visited July 28, 2016).

[50] *Id.*

[51] *Id.*

INDEX